Millennials and the Moments That Made Us

A Cultural History of the U.S.
from 1982—Present

Millennials and the Moments That Made Us

A Cultural History of the U.S.
from 1982—Present

Shaun Scott

Winchester, UK
Washington, USA

First published by Zero Books, 2018
Zero Books is an imprint of John Hunt Publishing Ltd., Laurel House, Station Approach,
Alresford, Hants, SO24 9JH, UK
office1@jhpbooks.net
www.johnhuntpublishing.com
www.zero-books.net

For distributor details and how to order please visit the 'Ordering' section on our website.

Text copyright: Shaun Scott 2016

ISBN: 978 1 78535 583 7
978 1 78535 584 4 (ebook)
Library of Congress Control Number: 2017930561

A CIP catalogue record for this book is available from the British Library.

Design: Stuart Davies

Printed and bound by CPI Group (UK) Ltd, Croydon, CR0 4YY, UK

We operate a distinctive and ethical publishing philosophy in all
areas of our business, from our global network of authors to
production and worldwide distribution.

CONTENTS

Foreword

By Marissa Jenae Johnson

The world we inhabit seems hard to understand for many. The increasing racial tensions in America, the election of Donald Trump, and the global backlash to generations of parasitic capitalism has many of us working hard to reconcile the people we always imagined ourselves to be with the reality that becomes apparent in the light of day. Life, when engaged, seems to be a continual act of unlearning—of peeling back the layers of the stories you were told about who you were to reveal all the beautiful possibilities and harrowing inadequacies.

Nothing is as we thought it was. Or as it should be. We are not as kind as we thought we were. We are not as smart as we thought we were. We are not as far along on race; we are not as open-minded with regards to gender. Far from the enlightenment ideals we were taught about ourselves, the question demands asking: Are we better people than generations before, or worse?

The answer, it seems, is somewhere in between and somewhere altogether different. In looking at the good we imagine ourselves to be and the evil we have shown ourselves capable of, there is no absolute true self. Instead we find our realities caught between the two; reaching for that which we aspire, while falling into old patterns we thought we had left behind with our fathers and mothers.

This book, like a reflection in a mirror, captures us in that war of self and imagination. It tells the truth of the time we find ourselves in and the people we have become not by answering the question, but by adding dimension to the background. Layer after layer, Scott complicates the narratives we tell about Millennials and the world we live in, and in each chapter, he reveals a part of ourselves we never knew through the poignant analysis of the moments we all remember.

As a Black woman and Millennial, it's rare these days that I read something and feel like it helps me understand who I am. This book does. Born in 1991, I'm caught right in the crosshairs of the Millennial generation. Though I consider myself someone who stands out from the crowd, my life runs parallel to the narrative Scott weaves through his unpacking of pop culture. Like many other Millennial adults, the realities of my life contradict the ideals and aspirations I was taught as a child.

Not only was I steeped in the propaganda of meritocracy against the background of worldly circumstances that proved otherwise, but my interracial family was seen as a sign of progress despite a childhood hedged by the boiling tensions of a racial past never reckoned with. I worked hard throughout school to be the best at everything, assured that that was all it took to escape poverty.

But when the time for college came, I found myself the sole income earner for my family, trapped in the fallout of the Great Recession. Everywhere I turned, all assurances went out the window.

Somehow I did make it to college, and struggled to pay for it throughout. By the time I graduated I was working six jobs and going to school full-time. Graduation day came and went and the stable, middle-class job I was always promised was nowhere to be found. Days after receiving an education that cost over six-figures, I was hopeful to get a job that paid $15 an hour. All the promises of prosperity that were made to me felt like a lie as I struggled, fully aware that my personal failure was a failure for my family. I was supposed to move socioeconomic classes and bring them along. Far from the trope of entitled Millennial, my family depended on me to survive.

I had done all the "right" things, and yet I had failed.

Though I didn't find the conventional path promised to me, the changing political climate found me. Shortly after the

Ferguson Uprising I became a part of the #BlackLivesMatter movement, rising to national prominence in August 2015 when I helped steal the stage from presidential candidate Bernie Sanders in my and Scott's city of Seattle.

For all the visibility and media and press, this movement had not made my path in life anymore sure or my socioeconomic failure any less real. I was like any other Black Millennial: struggling to find peace in a world at war with Black bodies and under the weight of a capitalist system where we could never get ahead. Far from the progressive future I was promised I could have if I worked hard, the future now looked grim.

What kind of future could there be if you could not pay your student loans, but it didn't matter because the police might kill you before then? What kind of future is there for a Black Millennial who is told to fight for prosperity but thrust into the conditions of war?

There are no simple answers for how we forge forward. But in this book, Scott paves the way by giving the question color. Scott examines how Millennials both respond to the context we have been thrown into, and also how we create new worlds of our own. Our solutions for survival—and for the thriving of the next generation—will come out of that duality. We are and will be molded by the unimaginable moments of these times, but we will also find escape and healing in the world we create that does not yet exist.

As Scott explores, it is Millennial artistry, freedom, and rebelliousness that can manifest a world starkly different than the one we inherited. Millennials may have done away with the rules, but we are painting our freedom instead.

—Marissa Jenae Johnson,
Co-Founder of Safety Pin Box

Introduction

The History of Our Future

The central argument of *Millennials and the Moments That Made Us: A Cultural History of the U.S. from 1982–Present* is that Millennials were born alongside a particular era of American capitalism, and that the popular culture of this era serves to legitimate this social order, even as some of it suggests ways out of it.

In this book, I use popular culture as a lens to explain a generational condition that began in the 1980s. This generational condition has been defined by lengthening adolescence, changing gender norms, and new attitudes towards work and property. Millennials have seen unprecedented wealth stratification; the exacerbation of already-existing divides of race and sex; and America's continuing militaristic endeavors abroad. The product of both landmark mid-20th century social reforms like the Immigration and Naturalization Act of 1965 and the arrival of Reaganomics in the 1980s, Millennials are simultaneously the most diverse and disprivileged generation ever. Our popular culture—both the culture that we have created and the culture that has been aimed at us—cannot help but reflect the condition that this book reconstructs.

My frame-of-reference as an author is that of a Black Millennial and an unapologetic progressive. But my bias should not be confused for carelessness. I have built this book on a rich body of scholarly discourse about neoliberal capitalism. I promiscuously cite authors who have written critically about American popular culture in the last three decades. And perhaps most importantly, I engage with ideas and policies that I am in utter disagreement with.

The result is a book that delivers a comprehensive explanation of the situation of the largest[1] (and to this point most-discussed)

4

generation in American history.

WHAT IS A MILLENNIAL?

In May 2015, Pew Research Center asserted that "The Millennial Generation"[2] is the age cohort of Americans born between 1981 and 1997. In his 2014 book *The Next America*, Pew senior fellow Paul Taylor defined Millennials as "empowered by digital technology; coddled by parents; slow to adulthood; conflict-averse; at ease with racial, ethnic, and sexual diversity; confident in their economic futures despite coming of age in bad times."[3]

As we'll see in Parts III and IV of this book, the idea that Millennials are coddled is a pernicious stereotype. And the notion that we are "conflict averse" does not square well with the fact that we populated a volunteer army in the aftermath of the terrorist attacks of September 11th, 2001. However, Taylor's ideas about Millennial diversity and disprivilege are rooted in statistically verifiable fact:

A 2016 study by the Brookings Institution revealed that 45% of Millennials identify as non-white and/or mixed-race; among Baby Boomers in 1990, that number was 28%.[4] Meanwhile, Millennials are the first generation ever to have a lower standard of living than their parents. These concrete socioeconomic facts are directly attributable to where Millennials are situated in history: just after the Civil Rights Act and Immigration and Naturalization Act (both of 1965), and in the middle of the era of Reaganomics that initiated a massive transfer of wealth out of the hands of America's working poor and middle class.

But while I make use of Pew Research Center's invaluable research about Millennials, I do not rely on their dates of demarcation. Pew Research Center did not pioneer the way we name, conceptualize, and describe American generations. That distinction belongs to authors Neil Howe and William Strauss, the originators of "Howe-Strauss Generational Theory."

In their 18th century constitution, the Iroquois proclaimed that all of the nation's decisions should account for the impact they may have seven generations from the present. Japanese Americans have been naming their generations of descendants since the early 20th century, and Hungarian sociologist Karl Mannheim wrote of "The Problem of Generations" in 1923. In an American academic context, Neil Howe and William Strauss have done the most systematic and theoretically rigorous thinking about generations as a whole in the United States. They coined the term "Millennial" in the first place. In the book *Generations: The History of America's Future, 1584 to 2069*,[5] the duo dubbed Americans born in 1982 with that title, in anticipation of us reaching adulthood at the time of the new millennium.

Howe and Strauss say that Millennials were born between 1982 and 2004; Pew Research Center says the range is 1981–1997. The difference is only a handful of years. But the boundaries have to be drawn somewhere. Even as I make use of Pew's data about Millennials, I side with the Howe-Strauss range in defining Millennials.[6] Ultimately, the choice between the Howe-Strauss framework and that of the Pew Research Center is a choice between the qualitative (Howe-Strauss) and the quantitative (Pew Research): Pew Research Center's research into concrete demographic trends related to Millennials is unsurpassed, but Howe-Strauss have done more to describe the cultural determinants that define American generations.

As we'll see in Chapter 1 ("The World's Oldest Millennial"), 1982 saw a significant departure in the way that childhood was framed culturally in the United States. It was the year that "Baby on Board" signs first appeared on car windows, that Nancy Reagan first uttered "Just Say No," and that we first saw glimpses of the culture of protectionism surrounding kids that has informed attitudes towards Millennials even as we've reached adulthood. I accept 1982 as a kind of front-end cutoff date for defining Millennials. Yet while Howe and Strauss explain that the last Millennials were born in 2004, I'm not so preoccupied with the back-end cutoff: In this book, I assume that all Millennials will reach something close to adulthood by the American presidential elections of 2020 or 2024.

This book focuses on American popular culture and politics. But I do not think one has to be born in the United States to be a Millennial. Generational boundaries are informed by epochs of global capitalism: mid-century capitalism for Baby Boomers, and neoliberalism for Millennials. So people born in the 1980s and 1990s in countries such as Venezuela, Greece, South Korea, Eritrea, or Iran may all have experienced similar socioeconomic and political straits. Far too much writing about Millennials erases people of color and immigrants by using the word "Millennial" as shorthand for "Caucasian college-educated 20-something who works in a white-collar field."

In his 2012 book *Why It's Still Kicking Off Everywhere*, author Paul Mason shows that the strains of political frustration and digital activism that ignited young people in the Arab Spring in April 2011 are connected to those which spurred the #OccupyWallStreet movement in October of the same year.[7] But capitalism has impacted different Millennials differently: popular stereotypes of (White) Millennials show young people mooching off of their parents—but what about Millennial émigrés who send remittances to their mother countries, or 2nd generation Millennials in white collar professions who help their parents and extended families pay their bills?

Even as the iron cage of economics encases the Millennial condition, it is critical to not lose sight of the subjective surface that rests on top of that superstructure. As an American born in 1984, you'll frequently see me describe the Millennial condition in terms of we, me, our, and us. At times, I'll also spin a personal narrative when a point I've established with evidence can be made even clearer with an anecdote. I agree with a statement writer Kate Zambreno made in her 2012 text *Heroines*: "Taking the self out of our essays is a form of repression. It feels like obeying a gag order—pretending an objectivity where there is nothing objective about the experience of confronting and engaging with and swooning over literature."[8]

WHAT ARE THE MOMENTS THAT MADE US?

The descriptor "Millennial" is a noun that refers to an age cohort. It is also an adjective that refers to a historical situation defined by the technology, politics, and pop culture of the 21st century. One can speak of "Millennials" as a group, and also refer to a "millennial" era that previous generations are also living through. Not everybody is a Millennial, but we're all passing through a millennial moment in history.

I use the word "moments" to describe pop culture spectacles and headline-grabbing events. I also employ the word "moments" to underscore macro-transitions that begin and bookend eras of global capitalism. Each broad *historical moment*—including our own—is reflected in individual *cultural moments*.

This book is preoccupied with two historical moments: 1) the American epoch that lasted from 1945–1973, and, primarily, 2) the subsequent era that lasted from roughly 1980 until the time this book was written (2016) and beyond.

The massive influx of federal spending during World War II and the subsequent establishment of a society organized around constant preparation for war created a "golden age of capitalism"[9] that lasted from the end of World War II in 1945 to the year American wages reached their all-time peak in 1973. During that period, the United States created generous social entitlements that were funded by progressive taxes on big business. Films like *The Man in the Gray Flannel Suit* (1956) and the music of Frank Sinatra displayed the social norms, benefits, and anxieties that came with living in a society committed to robust productivity and full employment.

This moment is often referred to as "the golden age of capitalism" because America was more industrious and less

8

unequal than it had been at any other point in American history then. This period came to an end in the mid-1970s when rising oil prices, recessions, and chronic inflation resulting from the Vietnam War gave business activists and antigovernment ideologues an opportunity to rewrite the American social contract in the 1970s. Subsequently, there is considerable debate over what to call the moment that came after this period.

Borrowing from economist Ernest Mandel, some use the term "late capitalism" to contrast our particular era from the earlier "golden age of capitalism." Mandel wrote his landmark text *Late Capitalism* in 1972, and applied the label to the historical era that began after 1945. It was not yet clear to Mandel that a significant historical shift was about to occur; a shift which saw America drift away from the welfare state of mid-century capitalism, and into an era of rampant privatization and antisocial democracy that defines the years from 1980 to 2016.

Citing cultural critics Jean-François Lyotard and Fredric Jameson, others have defined our current moment as "postmodernism": a period in which there are no new creative revelations, and our culture—as well as our politics—is susceptible to endless homage and reverence for the bygone past.

In a landmark thesis published in 1984, Jameson posited that "postmodernism is the cultural logic of late capitalism."[10] He uses the term "late capitalism" to refer to the moment that came after the one lasting from 1945 to 1973. This is a helpful advent to Mandel's original theory of late capitalism. And so—in the course of this manuscript—I sometimes employ the term "late capitalism" to refer to the era of American life which began in roughly 1980.

However, I don't use the label "postmodernism" to refer to the current epoch of American life, because it refers too narrowly to arts and culture. Indeed, a central theme of this book is that popular culture exists in systemic relation to the underlying socioeconomic order of the time. As a result, I often deploy the term "late capitalism" interchangeably with "neoliberalism," which is the reigning economic philosophy undergirding the period from roughly 1980 to the present.

OUR NEOLIBERAL MOMENT

If the guiding economic philosophy of the period from 1945–1973 could be summarized as a "Keynesian consensus"[11] of organized labor, government, and big business that created a state largely committed to social welfare, then the early 1980s saw the institution of *neoliberalism*: a set of economic policies that favor minimal government encroachment on market affairs ("deregulation"), and drastically reduced public expenditure on social services ("austerity"). In a deeper sense, even the word "deregulation" is a misnomer: the whims and vicissitudes of the free market have been *regularized* by law and normalized by culture to such an extent that, until the 2016 presidential candidacy of Bernie Sanders, it was political heresy to offer an alternative in the mainstream marketplace of ideas.

Neoliberalism has introduced an ethos to American life that may have historical parallels, but that is nonetheless wholly original: namely, a marketeering logic that pervades formerly public institutions like hospitals and prisons, and that even saturates the personal relationships of American citizens. We accept that schools ought to be run on a for-profit model, and liken dating to selling ourselves on the open market of potential mates.

This state of affairs is as *un-natural* as it is *naturalized*. There is value—both intellectually and politically—in showing how the world as we know it is a built environment; not a native state of affairs, but a social order propped-up by traceable political decisions and knowable ideologies (not to mention capital-intensive schemes with available receipts). In the fight against four decades of austerity measures, political repression, the repeal of voting rights and the ongoing war against women's bodies and reproductive freedoms, knowledge of history is a weapon that is as powerful as a ballot or a bullhorn at a protest.

In his 2009 text *Capitalist Realism*, Mark Fisher summarizes the emergence of neoliberalism as such:

> *Over the past thirty years, capitalist realism has successfully installed a "business ontology" in which it is simply obvious that everything in society, including healthcare and education, should be run as a business [...] It is worth recalling that what is currently called realistic was itself once "impossible": the slew of privatizations that took place since the 1980s would have been unthinkable only a decade earlier, and the current political-economic landscape (with unions in abeyance, utilities and railways denationalized) could scarcely have been imagined in 1975.*[12]

The arrival of the neoliberal moment didn't just change America socioeconomically. It also shaped American popular culture:

Mid-century capitalism saw glamorous cultural products by jazz musicians such as Miles Davis and film directors such as John Ford. These artists emphasized the beauty of structured collaboration, and mirrored the delicate consensus between organized labor, big business, and government that underwrote the golden age of capitalism. In the subsequent neoliberal moment—the one that Millennials were born into—the coarsely individualist expressions of hip-hop and personal computing have taken the place that jazz and cinema once occupied. Where jazz scored the golden age of capitalism with romance and mood, hip-hop—writes Fisher again—"has stripped the world of sentimental illusions and seen it for what it really is: a Hobbesian war of all against all, a system of perpetual exploitation and generalized criminality."[13]

Elsewhere in popular culture, neoliberal values are performed in the celebration of competition in professional sports. Video games simulate the capitalist scramble for goods and resources.

And action films spotlight the triumph of individualist heroes over the collective struggle for social justice. In the course of this book, I tie American cultural expression in all its forms to the structures of governmental and private power that have overseen the institution of our neoliberal moment.

"Moments that made Millennials" refers to both individual cultural products as well as to historical epochs. My style as a cultural historian is to take individual cultural moments—a Drake song, an episode of *Broad City*—and introduce them to the larger cultural moment of neoliberalism.

WHAT IS CULTURAL HISTORY?

There are many kinds of historians. Economic historians make sense of a period of time by tracing the trajectories of stocks and summarizing popular ideas about how to distribute wealth. Political historians explain the defining debates and candidates of a particular period. A cultural historian is somebody who describes a period in time using the cultural artifacts of that time. A cultural historian of World War II, for example, may explain how the fight against Nazism was reflected in the jazz records of Ella Fitzgerald and Duke Ellington. Or a cultural historian of Colonial America may reference artistic depictions of Native Americans or folk songs about slavery.

Culture can be "high" and "slow": stemming from books, academic papers, and presidential speeches that describe the national mood. Culture can also be "low" and "fast": films, television shows, music, and commercials that are widely consumed. Both forms of culture fall within the scope of *Millennials and the Moments That Made Us*. Neoliberal economist Milton Friedman's ideas about how to starve government of tax revenue and institute a privatized hellscape were culture; and so is a Run-D.M.C. record.

The cultural historian inevitably has to converse with the political historian and the economic historian. As I show in

Chapter 4, *The Simpsons* were an edgy sensation in the 1990s because of the country's conservative politics; and as I show in Chapter 7, Jay Z's album *The Blueprint* celebrated the country's prevailing economic ideology just as loudly as the *Wall Street Journal*.

Writing a cultural history of "1982–Present" comes with a unique set of opportunities and challenges, both of which stem from the fact that there is a glut of material to wade through. On the one hand, because I'm not describing ancient history, there are sources everywhere: YouTube vids, presidential speeches, television shows, and a literal mountain of scholarly work reveal the kind of country America has been since 1982. On the other hand, this glut of material also makes coming up with original or useful insights difficult.

My answer to this creative challenge was to use a historicist lens that makes the present seem like the past, and that makes the familiar seem strange. To do this, I repeatedly found the most harmless, innocent-seeming cultural artifacts, and showed how they were actually instruments of capitalist domination (or countercultural subversion). The greater the dissonance between the tender surface and the raw reality, the better.

HOW IS THIS BOOK ORGANIZED?

This book is divided into 12 chapters, which I group into four parts. The foci of these chapters and parts proceed in chronological fashion. Parts I and II deal with Millennial childhood and youth in the 1980s and 1990s. Predictably, the terrorist attacks of September 11th, 2001 are a major narrative turning point, as Parts III and IV deal with Millennial adulthood in the 2000s and 2010s.

Each chapter of this book is divided into thirds. Within chapters, you will find subheadings that divide the chapters into smaller, digestible points. The thesis of each chapter is contained in a subheading that shares a name with the chapter; for example, the thesis section of "Chapter 5: American Siblings" is titled

"American Siblings."

I've organized this book so that the changing cultural settings of American history in the last 35 years can be related to each stage in the life cycle of a Millennial. Because when we talk about Millennials, we are referring to someone who was once a child, then a teenager, and later an adult. The years spanning 1982–1999 saw Millennials marketed to and spoken about by our elders. But the period from 2000 to the present saw Millennials make an active impact on our surroundings as adults.

Eighty years before this book was written, Franklin D. Roosevelt prophesied, "to some generations, much is given. Of other generations much is required. This generation," Roosevelt mused, "has a rendezvous with destiny."[14] Franklin Roosevelt was not talking about Millennials. But he may as well have been.

Whether this rendezvous is a Tinder date, an internship interview where we'll show how qualified we are to do work that doesn't pay, or a dramatic political showdown, history looms large over the fate of Millennials. Fortunately, a future that can still be shaped does as well.

PART I:

CHILDHOOD

(1982–1990)

We take our shape within and against that cage of reality bequeathed us at our birth; and yet it is precisely through our dependence on this reality that we are most endlessly betrayed.[1]
–James Baldwin.

Chapter 1

The World's Oldest Millennial

Google Ngram Viewer is a massive database of digitized books that lets you track the frequency of a given word's usage over time. When you enter the word "Millennial" into it, you see a sudden spike that begins in the mid-1980s. The usage peaks in 1998 before leveling off in 2001. A precipitous decline follows from then until 2008, when Ngram's data set ends.

As a Millennial who joined Facebook on Election Night 2004 and has not left for any significant period of time since, I can attest that the word started to come back during the presidential election cycle of 2012, when I began noticing more and more articles about Millennials in my newsfeed. The new cultural crescendo trebled in 2013 when *Time Magazine* ran a cover story about "The Me Me Me Generation"[1] in May of that year.

SNAKE PEOPLE

From 2013 to 2015, articles about Millennials were largely a joke. Cranks used the topic to complain about everything they thought was wrong with America. Business eggheads blamed us for "murdering"[2] any number of industries from home ownership to jewelry. And press outlets peppered headlines with the title "Millennial," even when the articles they advertised had little to do with the age cohort of Americans born in the 1980s or 1990s.

In 2015, a trickster named Eric Bailey had enough. Bailey created a Google Chrome extension that replaced the word "Millennials" with "Snake People."[3] With articles about Millennials routinely mocked and disregarded by Millennials themselves on Twitter and on Facebook, it was not until the 2016 presidential election cycle that serious writing about the political and historical situation of Millennials emerged.

But as much as Snake People Millennials have been discussed in the 2010s, we're still collectively mystified about what a Millennial actually is. As journalist Sarah Kendzior notes in her stellar June 2016 article on Quartz.com, "the confusion lies in the way we define generations in the US, a series of labels that are as unclear as they are inconsistent."[4]

AGED OUT?

In a March 2014 article on Slate.com, writer Amanda Hess revealed that *The New York Times* consistently ran stories about Millennials that featured no Millennials.[5] Conversely, authors of anti-Millennial diatribes are often Millennials who—in their early or mid-30s—don't realize that they are Millennials.

At a Prudential Financial-sponsored event called Millennial Week in Seattle on September 15th, 2016, businesswoman Lauren Maillian began an eloquent description of her youth with the preface "When I was a Millennial," as if the label were a synonym for "20-something."[6] That's not quite how this works. Today, the word Millennial conjures images of youth. Before we know it, it will make Gen-Z[7] youths think of nursing homes and geriatric care.

THE WORLD'S OLDEST MILLENNIAL[8]

Generational categories are broad-brush descriptors that start to lose fidelity and meaning at the extremes. In his 1951 book *Minima Moralia*, Theodor Adorno wrote "in psychoanalysis, nothing is true except the exaggerations."[9] The same could be said of the way many talk about generations as cookie-cutter stereotypes that corroborate their complaints about society.

Nonetheless, it's illustrative to begin and bookend periods in history by referring to the populations that grew up in them. If we go with Neil Howe and William Strauss—the writers who coined the term "Millennial" and did some of the first research about the topic—we'll agree that the first Millennials were born in 1982. That makes somebody born on January 1st, 1982 the world's oldest Millennial. By retracing what kind of country the United States was around this seminal date, we can learn a lot about the socioeconomic terrain that American Millennials came to occupy: a country where mid-century capitalism was fading, and neoliberalism presented society with new questions about identity, family, and children.

1982 was the year when spectator capitalism in cinema reached new heights with the family friendly blockbuster *E.T. The Extra-Terrestrial.* The movie kicked off an era of marketing tie-ins that targeted children with ads and merchandise. That same year, the musical *Annie* depicted the rags-to-riches rise of a depression-era adolescent; anticipating a pile of stereotypes that portray Millennials as a coddled generation in the midst of widespread wealth disparities, Annie is told "never stop believing you are special" by a billionaire before famously singing "it's a hard knock life; instead of treated, we get tricked."

Jay Z became an icon of hip-hop culture by quoting that line in his 1998 single "Hard Knock Life." But rap was still a largely local phenomenon in 1982 when the group Grandmaster Flash and the Furious Five broadcast the conditions that had befallen the urban poor in their single "The Message." Meanwhile—not yet accused of molesting children in 1982—Michael Jackson's smash album *Thriller* was released. It became the best-selling record of all-time with the help of a ballad about a bastard Millennial titled "Billie Jean." The song was a rare public moment of parental insouciance in a society that was growing obsessed with kids:

"For the sake of our children," Ronald Reagan announced in his rollout of the War on Drugs in October of 1982, "I ask for your support in this effort to make our streets safe again."[10] And The Missing Children Act of 1982 was passed by the 97th Congress, giving local law enforcement agencies new resources to find abducted kids. These political decisions mirrored a widespread fixation on childhood that was borne out in *Time Magazine* covers which celebrated "The New Baby Boom" of 30-somethings finally deciding to have children (February 27, 1982), and the coming "Computer Generation of Whiz Kids" (May 3, 1982).

The 2013 film *1982* features a father struggling to protect his children from the ravages of drug addiction and joblessness in deindustrialized Philadelphia. The film dramatizes the mix of squalor, social panic, and high expectations that defined Millennial childhood under neoliberalism. "You're the best little girl that anybody could ever hope to have," the desperate dad tells his distraught daughter. "And none of this is your fault."

1B

On December 31st, 1981, the Cable News Network (CNN) ran a feature about its second channel, CNN Headline News.[11] CNN formed in 1979 to feature regular programming and in-depth news features. But the goal of Headline News was to create the fastest, most condensed presentation of news ever. Shortly after announcing the public rollout of Headline News on New Year's Eve, CNN cameras cut to the ceremonial ball drop in Times Square as the world said goodbye to 1981, and rang in 1982.

ROTTING APPLE

The city that the ball dropped on in Times Square on January 1st, 1982 had become a beacon of decay and despair. Gone were the glamorous days depicted in director Martin Scorsese's musical *New York, New York* (1977). The city's mid-century stability was fading beyond recovery. It was now a petri dish for a new social order—neoliberalism—that constitutes a major part of the cultural and socioeconomic disinheritance of Millennials.

"In response to growing unrest in the 1960s," writes Jason Hackworth in *The Neoliberal City*, New York was "pressured to increase expenditures for housing, healthcare, and other social services."[12] But the city struggled to pay for these services because its tax base shrank dramatically due to deindustrial-ization. Between 1969 and 1977, the city shed more than 600,000 jobs—many of which were in ethnic neighborhoods like the one immortalized in the 1957 musical *West Side Story*.

This hemorrhage of jobs curtailed the amount of taxable income that was available to the city in the 1970s. In lower Manhattan, the recently completed World Trade Center (1974) further deprived New York of revenue by attracting commercial tenants away from buildings where they had to pay property taxes, luring them into the government-subsidized confines of the Twin Towers.[13]

DROP DEAD

The phenomenon of deindustrialization leading to decreased government revenue, chronic underemployment, and declining social services is a hallmark of neoliberalism. In a 1978 editorial in *Newsweek*, neoliberal economist Milton Friedman declared that the state needed to be starved of revenue at all costs.[14] These reforms created conditions of financial desperation and insecurity for Americans who had grown accustomed to steady employment and an accompanying social safety net.

Because of decreased tax revenues, New York City was forced to appeal to the federal government for a municipal bailout in 1975. But President Gerald Ford—whose intellect was regularly disparaged on the new television show *Saturday Night Live*, which debuted in October 1975—remained unconvinced:

"I am prepared to veto any bill that has, as its purpose, a federal bailout of New York City,"[15] sneered Ford on October 29th, 1975. The words were barely out of his mouth before the *New York Daily News* paraphrased them in an infamous headline: "FORD TO CITY: DROP DEAD."[16]

THE NEW COLOR LINE

Black, Hispanic, and poor-White sections of New York City who depended on social services were hit hard by Ford's decision to not bail out the city. With working class residents displaced into the South Bronx by the construction of the Cross Bronx Expressway, citizens already reeling from perennial unemployment were soon victims of a new form of segregation known as red-lining: the systematic denial of resources to municipal areas based on the racial and financial makeup of those areas.

Real estate developers in the South Bronx discovered that setting their vacant properties on fire and collecting an insurance payoff was more profitable than making their buildings livable. They were emboldened when the city's fire department began using a RAND Institute algorithm that advised closing fire stations in the Bronx, and reopening them in more affluent parts of the city.[17]

THE BRONX IS BURNING

As Tricia Rose writes in *Black Noise: Rap Music and Black Culture*, "the disastrous effects of these city policies went unnoticed in the media until 1977."[18] But with the New York Yankees in a high-profile World Series matchup against the Los Angeles Dodgers in October of that year, there was no longer anywhere to hide. In the 1st inning of Game Two, ABC cameras cut to a roaring inferno at an abandoned public school near Yankee Stadium.[19]

HIP-HOP IS BORN

Out of this cauldron of fire, underemployment, and neglect in the South Bronx came a new art that would dominate America's cultural landscape over the next 35 years: hip-hop. A federation of visual art (graffiti), poetry (rap), music (DJ'ing), and dance (break dancing), hip-hop was created in the poorest sections of New York City, in the housing projects of the South Bronx.

STARTED FROM THE BOTTOM

A child of neoliberalism created by disaffected Baby Boomer and Gen-X youths, everything about hip-hop represented a 'something from nothing' ethos. Graffiti artists beautified burned-out buildings and bland subway cars. Break-dancers turned their very bodies into metaphors for the skill and contortionism required to survive precarious times. And DJs made masterpieces from forgotten scraps of obscure records. Rap, meanwhile, scored its first hit with Sugar Hill Gang's 1979 record "Rapper's Delight"—a boastful party tune that paved the way for Millennial stunts like Drake's "Started from the Bottom" and "Bad and Boujee" by Migos.

But rap could never resist commenting on its own squalid origins. Released July 1st, 1982, Grandmaster Flash and the Furious Five's "The Message" anticipated the urban tales of Millennial rappers like Kendrick Lamar and Meek Mill.

THE MESSAGE

The music of "The Message" is post-disco psychedelic sonic peyote pulled from urban cacti; a synth-laden mirage inspired by the rising temperatures of a hot New York City summer. The slither of a desert rattlesnake heralds the song's fifth and final verse.

Conga drums culled from the Tom Tom Club's 1981 hit "Genius of Love" punctuate a lurching groove that sounds like a slowed down version of Zapp's 1980 banger "More Bounce to the Ounce." The creeping, observational pace of the music—just over 100 beats per minute—perfectly complements a hurried pedestrian's pace. Decades after its release, the pensiveness of "The Message" still makes it a stellar song to people-watch to on a busy city street.

If any early rap song earned—begged for—music video visuals on the new medium of MTV, "The Message" was it. In the song's video, graphics with gritty documentary realism are spliced in between the performative bravado of The Furious Five, establishing them as ghetto raconteurs.[20] In the year that CNN expanded into Headline News, the footage and edits of "The Message" seem inspired by an evening news broadcast or a PBS documentary, bringing to mind rapper Chuck D's statement that "rap is Black America's CNN."

In five stanzas, Bronx rappers Melle Mel and Duke Bootee relay the fate that has befallen the urban poor under the arrival of neoliberalism: stoppages of public transportation, debt, and lack of access to adequate healthcare. Perhaps it bears pointing out that 1982 also saw the release of Queen's record *Hot Space*, which included their David Bowie collaboration "Under Pressure." The urgent cadence with which Melle Mel enunciates "don't push me, cuz I'm close to the edge/ I'm trying not to lose my head"[21] can scarcely be done justice on paper. Mel seems on the brink of madness when—at the end of every recitation of the song's hook—he adds a manic chuckle.

When the world of beleaguered adults in "The Message" has been wrung dry of narrative material, the narrators focus on children. First, a young Gen-Xer tells his dad that he doesn't want to go to school because of a condescending teacher. Then, Melle Mel chillingly forecasts the life of a young Millennial:

A child is born with no state of mind,
Blind to the ways of mankind.
God is smiling on you, but he's frowning, too,
Because only God knows what you'll go through.

Mel's intensity in this fifth verse is unflinching, as he details the life of a doomed Millennial who "grows in the ghetto, living second rate." With no positive role models to speak of, the hypothetical child succumbs to a life of crime. Too cool for school and uninterested in acquiring a skill that might lead to legitimate employment, he drops out, gets busted, and endures sexual assaults in prison. A suicide-by-hanging follows, with Mel supplying a sublimely morbid obit in the child's wake:

It was plain to see that your life was lost,
You was cold and your body swung back and forth,
But now your eyes sing the sad, sad song,
Of how you lived so fast and died so young.

32 years before the arrival of #BlackLivesMatter (and decades before the "Trap" genre of rap), Grandmaster Flash and the Furious Five were describing the lives of countless Black, brown, and poor White American youths embroiled in a rapidly expanding criminal justice system. And well before social scientists coined the word "precariat"[22] to describe the underemployed castoffs of capitalism's new phase, they depicted the financial desperation enveloping Americans because of the neoliberal turn.

Sugar Hill Records released "The Message" on vinyl in the summer of 1982; it could not have been more durable if it were etched in stone.

1C

"The Message" was meant for Americans left out of the "greed is good,"[23] Go-Go 1980s[24] and its celebration of accumulation. After the tumultuous 70s, New York City eventually rebuilt itself along neoliberal lines by slashing funding to affordable housing, hospitals, and social services, and devoting resources to growing the finance, insurance, and real-estate sectors of its economy.

"By the end of the 1980s," writes Jason Hackworth, "New York had become one of the nation's most polarized cities."[25] The same year that Bronx rap outfit Boogie Down Productions dropped their classic album *Criminal Minded* (1987), real estate developer Donald Trump released his memoir *The Art of the Deal*.

For Americans who benefited from the upward redistribution

of wealth resulting from President Reagan's tax cuts for big businesses, 1982 also offered quite a different message than the one delivered by The Furious Five: "Billie Jean," a song about an affluent father, a vindictive woman, and a baby Millennial fathered out of wedlock.

THE IRONY OF "BILLIE JEAN"

Released as a single in January of 1983 following the November 1982 unveiling of *Thriller*, "Billie Jean" survives to this day as a dance floor favorite at weddings. This is ironic, since the song is straightforwardly the first-person narrative of a bachelor who wants nothing do with commitment. The emotional subtext of "Billie Jean" is selfishness. Cues contained in the song's verses imply that the song's narrator might in fact be father of the baby Millennial in question. But the catchy chorus asks us to side with Jackson anyway—because what Yuppie should have to pay for unprotected sex with an 18-year sentence?

NEOLIBERAL CITY (2/2)

In the words of media scholar Steven Shaviro, "music videos actively construct and perform the social relations, flows, and feelings that they are ostensibly about."[26] The music video for "Billie Jean" makes the song's greedy undercurrent clear. "Billie Jean"—which broke the color barrier on MTV when it debuted there in 1983—shows Jackson as a well-off man in the desolate cityscape of downtown Chicago, just miles from where Milton Friedman incubated the ideology of neoliberalism at the University of Chicago. The homeless appear in both the videos for "The Message" and "Billie Jean." The difference is that Jackson the benevolent benefactor is present in the latter to flip the bum a quarter. Because under late capitalism, charity is the preferred substitute for a political commitment to the fair distribution of wealth.

A NEW LOOK AT CHILDHOOD

"The Message" is a cautionary tale about how terrible life could be for Millennials under neoliberalism. But "Billie Jean" is too busy centering male paranoia to consider the consequences of a kid growing up without a father. By fretting over the fate of children in the song's final verse, Melle Mel was more in tune with society's trending ideas about childhood in 1982 than Michael:

Neil Howe and William Strauss use 1982 as the cutoff date for Millennials because that year saw a renewed focus on the importance of childhood. "In 1982," Howe says, "we saw Baby on Board signs on cars. Protective helmets, protective playground materials, and the home protection industry became a billion-dollar industry by the end of the decade."[27]

By 1983, the alarmist policy paper *A Nation at Risk* called for a "back to basics"[28] movement in schools. Then in 1984, Mothers Against Drunk Driving formed and another of Congress' Missing Child Acts passed, after the initial 1982 legislation. In one of the few nonmilitary sectors of government to expand during the Reagan years, The Deficit Reduction Act of 1984 made all children born into poverty after September 30, 1983 eligible for Medicaid benefits.[29]

As we'll see in Chapters 2 and 3, this culture of coveting childhood was actually a societal act of overcompensation rooted in anxieties about working mothers. But after years of neglecting Gen-X youths and soaring divorce rates in the 1970s (symbolized by the 1979 film *Kramer vs. Kramer*), Millennials became the center of a social panic about the country's future. The conversation about children changed from how unwanted they were with the visibility of contraception and abortion in the 1970s, to how prized they were in the 1980s. In this respect "The Message" was on message, while "Billie Jean" cut against the dominant cultural grain that was emerging in 1982.

A WHOLE NEW GENERATION

Paradoxically, the song about a discarded Millennial became the anthem of "The Next Generation" when Pepsi contracted Jackson to rewrite "Billie Jean" for their "The Choice of a New Generation" ad campaign in 1984.[30] With Jackson crooning "you're a whole new generation!" to the tune of "Billie Jean," Pepsi tried associating itself with a vaguely-defined consumer vanguard. By then, major corporations everywhere were using generational identity to drive commodity capitalism. "The Baby Boom has come of age, we'll work it out," Jackson went on to sing at the beginning of his über-spectacle album *Dangerous* in 1991.

BABY BOOMER BOON

If society in 1982 was worried about children, then it was *obsessed* with their parents—specifically, with selling them things: movies, magazines, music, and, more than anything, memories of the greater times.

PAGE TURNER

"Magazines," writes historian Carolyn Kitch in *Pages from the Past: History and Memory in American Magazines*, "do more than market to generations; they also write about generations, characterizing their places in American culture and history."[31] Stories which referenced Baby Boomers increased steadily as the 1980s progressed, until *Time Magazine* published a 1986 cover story titled "The Baby Boomers Turn 40."[32] Just as Pepsi tied its product to "a new generation," *Time* used the cover image of its Baby Boomer issue to link Boomer identity to books (*All the President's Men*, 1974), music (*Meet the Beatles*, 1964), and movies (*The Big Chill*, 1983).

FREEZE OUT

An early scene in *The Big Chill* features a couple of Baby Boomer parents teaching a young Millennial the treasured songs of their youth. But despite the Motown-laden soundtrack, the movie's affluent, all-White characters only dramatize a particularly privileged Baby Boomer experience. When movie distributor The Criterion Collection re-released *The Big Chill* in 2014, they fittingly conscripted Millennial filmmaker Lena Dunham to write an accompanying essay titled "These Are Your Parents."[33] In her career as director of the hit TV show *Girls*, Dunham has been widely criticized for excluding exactly the kinds of ethnic, working class, and poor voices from the Millennial experience that are absent in *The Big Chill* and its rendition of Baby Boomers.

POLTERGEIST

And yet the privileged world of *The Big Chill* is as much a part of the Millennial inheritance as "The Message." The transition away from regimented industrial jobs and towards white-collar professions benefitted some, just as it left out others. "Baby Boomers lived in an really different economy," explained cultural critic Nicole Aschoff in a January 24, 2017 episode of Gaby Dunn's podcast *Bad With Money*; "many people could have one parent working and support the household." This changed with the arrival of depressed take-home pay under neoliberalism.

"With wages stagnating and families struggling to sustain incomes in the 1980s," writes author David Sirota, "parents began spending longer hours on the job."[34] As society grappled with the move from male breadwinners to the standard double-income household, the Millennials that parents left behind at work became the subject of moral panics about crime, gender roles, and bad influences in media.

In its plot about a largely unattended child who is besieged by a supernatural force that is transmitted through the television, the 1982 film *Poltergeist* played on fears related to the transformation of family life under neoliberalism. A neglected child in front of the TV is the conduit of the movie's terror. A decade later in the 1992 film *Batman Returns*, the predatory character Penguin plots to kill the "unattended first born" of Gotham City's greedy adults while they were out partying.

THE LATCHKEY CONDITION

The subject of Millennial latchkey children and 1980s pop culture under neoliberalism is not an academic matter to me. I was born on November 8th, 1984—two days after Ronald Reagan was elected to his second term as president—and I spent my formative years in the LeFrak City housing projects in Queens, New York.

I was one of thousands of "latchkey children"[35] that sociologist Steven Gregory documented in his landmark study *Black Corona: Race and the Politics of Place in an Urban Community*: kids who lived in the housing development LeFrak City, walked to school in groups with minimal adult supervision, attended class during the day, sought shelter at the nearby branch of the New York City Public Library until it closed at 5PM, then went home and awaited the return of my parents later in the night.

My parents were immigrants from Jamaica who were employed in fields directly related to New York's neoliberal transformation: my mother worked as a bank window teller in the city's rapidly expanding financial sector; my father was an engineer who removed asbestos from buildings downtown, readying them to be renovated in what a *New York Times* article from 1988 described as the "opulent and luxurious"[36] interior design style that dominated the Reagan-era.

Rare was the evening when either parent returned before my appointed bedtime of 8:00PM. My earliest memory in life is of watching the cartoon *Ghostbusters* (1986–1991) at home alone in a dark room, waiting for my parents to get home from work.

JUICY RATIONALIZATIONS

My situation was not unique, because Baby Boomers wanted it all: more hours on the job, a federal government that was deputized to protect their kids, and positive pop culture pedagogues that performed the roles that parents were supposed to have time for. It did not seem to occur to anyone in power that America's young would benefit from an economic system that allowed parents to spend more time with their kids, instead of a culture of fear that led to increasingly desperate acts of parental overcompensation while touting family values.

The suddenness with which this social order had arisen—as well as the subtlety of the pop culture vectors that legitimated it—placated parents who could have been more critical. "I don't know anyone who can get through the day without two or three juicy rationalizations," Michael tells Sam in *The Big Chill*. "They're more important than sex."

Chapter 2

American Dad

Images of the 1950s and 1960s celebrate the stability of the normative nuclear family. The film *Revolutionary Road* (2008) and the television show *Mad Men* (2007–2015) depicted the sordid underbelly of family life in these years. But they are wrapped in a package of glamor that ultimately encourages nostalgia for the socioeconomic landscape of mid-century capitalism: the days when male breadwinners were installed at the head of the family with massive entitlement programs like the G.I. Bill and a federal policy of full employment, and women were incentivized to be their domesticized companions.

FAMILY TIES

In her 1992 book *The Way We Never Were*, historian Stephanie Coontz shows that mid-century family life was far more complicated than the surface indicated. Wives and husbands, for example, still depended on complex kinship networks for childcare and emotional support. And systemic racism prevented minorities from buying homes in the country's coveted suburbs. Nonetheless, the modern sitcom has for decades been based on projecting the model of the nuclear family that was born right alongside television's coincidental arrival in the 1950s. Part of the appeal of the 1980s sitcom *Family Ties* (1982–1989) was that it was a throwback to the supposedly wholesome days of 50s family values.

9-TO-5

But an upheaval was underway. For American families, the neoliberal turn of the 1980s finished what the sexual revolutions of the 1970s started. Armed with contraceptives, legalized abortions, and more favorable divorce laws, women who had played a pivotal role in the Civil Rights and Feminist movements were finally empowered to seek financial independence in the workplace. Their path was paved when the economic instability of the "stagflated"[1] 1970s led American corporations to court women as a cheap source of flexible labor.

In his 2015 book *A War for the Soul of America*, historian Andrew Hartman writes that "feminism had granted women many freedoms, but it also provided businesses the freedom to restructure the labor market in ways that universalized economic insecurity."[2] Hartman continued:

> *The happy ending of the feminist-themed 1980 film* 9 to 5 *anticipated this irony. American businesses were all too pleased to comply with the changes the film's female heroes made to their workplace: an accommodating scheduling scheme, a job-share program, and an inoffice daycare center. A more flexible labor force was cheaper than the older male breadwinner model that, for all its faults, guaranteed a family wage.*[3]

Rooted though they were in the free market celebrated by American conservatives, these reforms sent traditional American masculinity into a crisis in the 1980s. The pay of male breadwinners was depressed, and wives were now swapping the kitchen for the cubicle. Decades later, the modern Republican Party survives mostly as a bullhorn for males who resent female empowerment.

FAUSTIAN BARGAIN

Ironically, conservatives who hated these alterations to the American social fabric had nobody to blame but themselves. By electing conservatives like Ronald Reagan—whose neoliberal policies despoiled the country's social entitlement programs and weakened organized labor—the American Right was making the days of the mid-century male breadwinner an increasingly faint and distant reality.

Conservatives also accepted the notion (sold to them from on high by GOP leadership) that the country's defining debates were comparatively narrow social and cultural issues related to obscenity and guns (as opposed to, say, large questions about the distribution of wealth). In exchange for nominal representation and the appearance of enfranchisement, American conservatives in the 1980s sabotaged their actual principles.

The results of this Faustian bargain between conservatives and the neoliberal elites they empowered in the 1980s were manifest in a socioeconomic climate where the corporations that conservatives placed their faith in lured women out of the home and into the workplace. Television, movies, and video games now served as surrogate parents that raised the Gen-X and Millennial children that Baby Boomers left behind at work.

COME HERE SO I CAN IGNORE YOU

In other words, neoliberalism created a country that was antithetical to the desires of the conservatives who instituted it by voting for Ronald Reagan's promise of small government in 1980 and 1984. Frustrated by the system they established, conservatives still directed their ire at a federal government that was smaller and less effectual than it had ever been. As Mark Fisher writes in his 2009 book *Capitalist Realism*, the antigovernment sentiment of the American right resembled "the fury Thomas Hardy spat at God for not existing."[4]

AMERICAN DAD

A true commitment to making America great in the way it had been in the 1950s would have meant pushing for a higher corporate tax rate that could fund entitlement programs (like the G.I. Bill) that bolstered male breadwinners, coupled with a harsh penalty on corporations that deindustrialized and relocated for cheaper sources of labor abroad. And if the "family values" of mid-century suburban America were really a priority for conservatives, they would not allow wages to become so depressed that both women and men had to enter the workforce.

Meanwhile, if the conservative framework genuinely took America's young Millennials into account, it would have allowed for the creation of a social order where double-income households did not leave latchkey children to be raised by ersatz authorities like schools and television. But instead, the 1980s saw a culture of masculine overcompensation that emphasized "law and order"[5] to protect and discipline unattended Millennials (and members of Gen-X), and that demonized the effects that double-income households were having on society.

With its debates about obscenity and the contested definition of "family values," America's culture wars became an avenue for competing visions of the country after its postindustrial fall from grace. Conservatives used Millennials as a political cover for their anxieties about the direction society was heading in since the salad days of mid-century capitalism.

2B

In the history of social policies that have targeted Millennials, *A Nation At Risk: The Imperative for Educational Reform* (1983) looms large. Produced by President Reagan's National Commission on Excellence in Education, the document is an alarmist call for attention to the apparent ruination of America's public schools. "Children born today can expect to graduate from high school in the year 2000,"[6] proclaims the report in its concluding lines:

> *We dedicate our report not only to these children, but also to others to come. We firmly believe that a movement of America's schools in the direction called for by our recommendations will prepare these children for far more effective lives in a far stronger America.*[7]

According to *A Nation at Risk*, the situation of American schools was analogous to Sylvester Stallone's character in the 1982 film *Rocky III*: a once-vigorous juggernaut whose descent into underachievement demanded a rededication to excellence. After a mid-20th century golden era that culminated in the vigorous Space Race against the Soviet satellite Sputnik, the report declared "the educational foundations of America were being eroded by a rising tide of mediocrity."[8]

PUPIL OF THE TIGER

To combat the problem, *A Nation at Risk* recommended a series of reforms. Teachers would be paid according to performance. The homework load increased. Standardized tests evaluated the performance of students. And a series of rewards and sanctions coerced students into attending class. In the disciplinary framework of *A Nation at Risk*, punishment became the midwife of education.

FULL METAL (LETTERMAN) JACKET

As Corey Mead writes in his 2013 book *War Play: Video Games and the Future of Armed Conflict*, the recommendations of *A Nation at Risk* was part of an era where "the paradigms of military training—standardization, efficiency, functionality—were everywhere in school."[9] This paradigm was demonstrated in a new devotion to skill-and-drill ("back to basics") learning methods. And as the 1980s progressed, "many of the main proponents of the computers-in-the-schools movement had worked on military-sponsored research projects, and were influenced by the military's interest in technology and computing."[10]

This collusion between corporate power, the Pentagon, and American schools was alluded to in author Orson Scott Card's 1985 book *Ender's Game*, a sci-fi novel about child-protagonist Ender Wiggin's participation in interplanetary warfare:

And for pleasure, there was the simulator, the most perfect video game that he had ever played. Teachers trained him, step by step, in its use. It was exhilarating to have such control over the battle, to be able to see every point of it.[11]

ALL YOUR GAMES ARE PROPAGANDA

Ender's Game was fantasy. But the defense establishment's use of technology to indoctrinate Millennials was not. As Ed Halter writes in *From Sun Tzu to Xbox*, "the Department of Defense [would become] the largest underwriter of the development of computer graphics technologies [in the 1980s]."[12]

The Pentagon began a partnership with Nintendo and Atari in the 1980s. The defense establishment subsidized game-controllers, consoles, and even popular games such as *Space Invaders*, *Missile Command*, and *Contra*. These games were specifically intended to militarize kids by positioning the armed forces as a rewarding career path. Video arcades in the 1980s became a popular stalking ground for military recruiters.

"Young people have developed incredible hand, eye, and brain coordination playing these games,"[13] said President Reagan in 1983; "I want you to have the training and skills to meet the future. Even without knowing it, you're being prepared for a new age."[14] For Millennials who joined the military in the 21st century, author David Sirota writes that the "games we've been playing for thirty years have prepared [this gaming generation] for drone warfare."[15]

TOP DOLLAR FOR TOP GUN

Meanwhile, *Top Gun* (1986) was one of several films—along with *Red Dawn* (1984) and the Rambo series—that the federal defense establishment used in the 1980s to recruit young people into the military. The Pentagon provided the production of *Top Gun* with valuable access to equipment and sets in exchange for creative control over the way the film framed the military. As pop-culture flâneur Bill Simmons has written, "Top Gun influenced an entire generation of kids to join the armed forces."[16]

THE WAR ON DRUGS

At the same time that the military was indoctrinating Millennials, the 1980s were also a decade when local police departments began an unprecedented march towards militarization—often under the guise of protecting America's youth:

Richard Nixon's "War on Drugs" was dramatically expanded in the regime of Ronald Reagan, as the resurgent Republican Party was able to leverage conservative backlash against Civil Rights-era protestors and militants like the Black Panthers into a party platform that emphasized "law and order." To voters, the GOP's new get-tough approach was validated when the spread of crack cocaine in the mid-1980s resulted in a spike in violent crimes and robberies in inner cities.

By 1989, footage of SWAT team shootouts and battering rams breaking down doors to trap houses were so familiar that the Fox Network filled a new television show with them; *Cops* went on to become the network's longest-running show. It intensified a nationwide panic about child drug use that led to Nancy Reagan's "Just Say No" campaign, which started when the first Millennials were born in 1982.

KETCHUP IS A VEGETABLE

In 1983, a Los Angeles police chief helped spearhead the institution of Drug Abuse Resistance Education (D.A.R.E.) in public schools. At a time when austerity measures led to the curtailment of school lunches—leading the Food and Nutrition Service to designate ketchup as a vegetable[17]—there was somehow enough energy and resources to warn kids against ever trying marijuana. As *New York Times* reporter Benjamin Weinraub noted, opponents of austerity measures in American schools "had a field day of outrage and mockery that contrasted school children's shrinking meal subsidies with the Pentagon generals' budget increases."[18]

AMERICA'S MISSING CHILDREN

Young Gen-Xers and Millennials went hungry so that the country's defense establishment could remain satiated. They were also used to kick-start America's cultural appetite for law enforcement: The television show *America's Most Wanted* was first aired on the Fox Network in 1988, after the child of host John Walsh was abducted and murdered in 1981. Walsh's efforts to find his son resulted in the Missing Children Act of 1982, and the Assistance to Missing Children Act of 1984.

LATCHKEY KIDS

But John Walsh couldn't change the fact that declining wages and the absence of adequately funded daycare centers created a world where "children [were] unsupervised after school until their parents returned from work."[19] Summarizing data taken from the turn of the decade, Stephanie Coontz wrote in 1992 that these latchkey kids were twice as likely as their supervised counterparts to try marijuana, smoke cigarettes, or drink alcohol prematurely. Employers noticed "a surge in personal calls between 3:30PM and 5:00PM, as worried parents checked in [with their kids]."[20]

A CHILD'S BEST FRIEND

In a world full of adults who could not face the facts about what neoliberalism was doing to American families, only McGruff the Crime Dog told the truth.

Created by the National Ad Council in 1980, McGruff was a cartoon dog who walked upright and spoke flawless English. The typical McGruff commercial contained a cartoon superimposition of the dog onto footage featuring human actors. In one such ad from 1983, McGruff warns that "60 children disappear every day."[21] In another, we learn that children are most frequently victims of crime when they try to walk home alone.[22]

But McGruff did not suggest lengthening the school day to keep kids busy, as *A Nation at Risk* did. And he did not advocate a martial response to the criminals that preyed on these children, like *America's Most Wanted*. Instead, he told young Millennials and their parents that children needed to "learn how to protect themselves."[23] As a menacing Cadillac follows "young Jenny"[24] in the 1983 spot, McGruff warns that she may never be seen again if she gets into it. The cartoon canine makes no bones about the fact that it's her own job to keep herself safe.

McGruff's vision is dark: but what it lacked in optimism, it makes up for in honesty. Elsewhere in the 1980s, men with barks far bigger than their bites pretended that a deputy state could be mobilized to protect unattended Millennials, keep us busy with homework, and brainwash us with uncritical patriotism.

2C

In the mid-20th century, the American social order was held together by granting discounted education, subsidized home ownership, and the promise of full employment to men in exchange for compulsory military service. "Paternal capitalism" is an accurate descriptor for this social arrangement, because it was based on elevating male breadwinners and domesticizing women. As Nikil Saval writes in his 2014 book *Cubed: A Secret History of the Workplace*, "corporate control in mid-century America reached deep into the family."[25]

PATERNAL CAPITALISM

The ultimate vendor of paternal capitalism in the mid-20th century was International Business Machines (IBM): a military-adjacent corporation with a rigidly hierarchical structure that disproportionately hired men. In its heyday, the company was infamous for interviewing the *wives* of potential hires to determine their fitness for supporting male employees.[26]

Subsequently, the demise of paternal capitalism was a crisis for American masculinity. The tenor of 1980s popular culture reflected the decentering of the male breadwinner and the decline of American industrial might.

REIGNING MEN

It may have seemed like masculine virility was everywhere in the 1980s—the decade that gave us Rambo and Hulk Hogan; the brawn of Jose Canseco and the boxer Mike Tyson; muscle cars and the porn star Ron Jeremy; the smooth operations of Tom Cruise in *Risky Business* (1983); a rapper named Ladies Love Cool James; the Robber Baron redux of Donald Trump.

But don't be confused. This was not the self-assured masculinity of mid-century capitalism; the scotch-on-the-rocks modesty of Frank Sinatra, or the equally neat Sidney Poitier. Instead, the 1980s saw an increasingly insecure *performance* of masculinity which indicated that the material foundations of male enfranchisement were already faded. In its place was put an outsized, cartoonish rendition of the real thing. Individual men like LL Cool J or Trump were ludicrously wealthy—and that was the point: they were avatars of affluence who had cultural currency precisely inasmuch as the power they projected was not widespread or evenly distributed.

HOLLOW

The discord between the indomitable surface and the sad hollowness of this performed masculinity is summarized in the careers of athletes Jose Conseco and Lyle Alzado, who traded muscular bodies for the compromised health that came with their abuse of crude anabolic steroids. "The big massive guy that I was—that was all phony,"[27] admitted Alzado, who won a Super Bowl with the Los Angeles Raiders in 1984, then died of brain cancer at age 42 in 1992.

Conversely, nothing could more clearly indicate that

American state power was insecure in the 1980s than the spectacles of authority, militarism, and discipline that the country created. The sternness of *A Nation at Risk*; the military displays of *Top Gun*; the shows of toughness on *Cops* and *America's Most Wanted*; all these were a substitute for true leadership, true strength, true discipline.

Like a father who beats his wife and kids, America asserted its authority with violence that could not mask its underlying impotence: its inability to provide jobs for its citizens; its mounting national debt; its failure to keep pace with global competitors like Germany and Japan; or the fact that it was repeatedly cuckolded by disloyal corporations who deindustrialized and relocated promiscuously.

Adoration of Cliff Huxtable's disciplinarian ways on *The Cosby Show* (1984–1992) and celebration of Rocky's fictional boxing career indicated the "failure of the Father function, the crisis of the paternal superego in late capitalism."[28]

I'M AFRAID OF AMERICANS

But at the same time that they housed an over-the-top mode of masculinity, the 1980s also saw a trio of musicians who bucked the trend: David Bowie, Prince, and George Michael. Amazingly, all three of these men died in 2016 as Donald Trump began his ascendancy to the presidency, leaving their fans with the unfortunate feeling that Trump's hollow alpha-masculine routine had somehow triumphed over their tricky androgyny. Yet this shape-shifting triumvirate's lasting legacy is the work they did to show how fragile America's masculine superstructure really was.

RISKY BUSINESS

Bowie went on MTV in 1983 with the expressed purpose of exposing MTV for being scared to air music videos by Black musicians, while Prince's honest depiction of sexuality in the song "Darling Nikki" shocked Tipper Gore into creating the

"Parental Advisory, Explicit Lyrics"[29] label. Meanwhile, by simply selling records as an openly gay male in a society that stigmatized homosexuality and ignored AIDS until the late 1980s, Michael's proud visibility in the United States was an insurrectionary act in and of itself.

CONTROVERSY

In one respect, the provocative examples of Bowie, Prince, and Michael were weapons of the weak. Bowie's 1983 hit "Let's Dance" did not stop the militarization of America's police forces nor the expansion of the carceral state; and George Michael's flamboyance did not stop Ronald Reagan from surreptitiously trading weapons for Iranian hostages in 1986, and then lying about it through his teeth.

But if these acts of rebellion were meaningless, then why did they cause such a stir? Why did MTV cave and admit "Billie Jean" in the aftermath of the Bowie-authored humiliation, and why was Prince a symbol of *Controversy*—as he titled his 1981 album—in the culture wars?

FATHER FIGURE

Because, as all parents under duress discover, the semblance of law and order depends on enforcing authority wherever it may be undermined (and especially where it may not). This is doubly true when there are impressionable children observing how parents respond to threats to their authority.

Icons like Bowie and Prince live on for Millennials in direct proportion to the trumped-up culture of paternalism seen in the 1980s. They were a symbol of rebellion against a culture that was obsessed with rules. The "Father function of late capitalism"[30] was not—as George Michael sang in his 1987 song "Father Figure"—"something special, something sacred." It was an insidious mode of social control fronted by capital-intensive marketing schemes, television, and the make-believe world of movies where American potency was projected. With young Millennials watching, Bowie, Prince, and Michael sullied prevailing notions of what it meant to grow up and be a man. In the 1980s, there was no riskier business.

Chapter 3

American Mom

Porn creates unlikely bedmates.

In the 1980s, the American Right and feminists stood on two very distant sides of America's culture wars. Conservatives combatted obscenity in music and movies, resented *Roe v. Wade*, and demonized workingwomen who flaunted their domestic duties to enter the workforce. Feminists—meanwhile—believed in the social, political, and economic equality of the sexes. These two competing flanks found common ground in their shared antipathy for dirty pictures.

THE GOLDEN AGE OF OBSCENITY

Pornography became a billion-dollar business in the 1980s when cheap VHS tapes revolutionized the industry, allowing viewers to consume smut in the privacy of their own homes. At the start of the music video for Survivor's 1982 hit "Eye of the Tiger,"[1] lead singer Jimi Jamison pensively exits a porn theatre; but the days when viewers had to watch 16mm nudie reels in conspicuous kink shops on crowded streets were coming to a close. Instead, wildly popular porn stars like Christy Canyon, Nikki Randall, and John Holmes powered sales of take-home filth, becoming celebrities—and political lightning rods—in the process.

STRANGE BEDFELLOWS

Right-wing anti-obscenity crusaders and many feminists were both revolted. The former had their Christian sensibilities offended by such savory titles as *Porno Holocaust* (1981), *Confessions of a Nymph* (1985), and *Caught From Behind 5—Blondes and Blacks* (1986). At the same time, feminists decried the degrading nature of films that centered male pleasure at the

44

expense of female dignity.

In 1983, radical feminists Catherine MacKinnon and Andrea Dworkin teamed with the conservative mayor of Indianapolis to designate pornography as a civil rights violation.[2] While federal courts later overturned the measure, many feminists never forgave Dworkin for co-conspiring with Indianapolis's city council, which had opposed legal abortion in the past.

WAVE THE PAST GOODBYE

But Dworkin was not alone. A selection of names from the anti-pornography movement of the late 1970s and 1980s reads like a Who's Who? of second-wave feminism: Audre Lorde, Gloria Steinem, and Adrienne Rich. The battle against porn may have been—in the words of Ariel Levy—a "spectacular failure."[3] But the larger culture war for female liberation was still ablaze, with books by Dworkin, Steinem, Lorde, bell hooks, and more fanning the flames in the 1980s.

GLORIA STEINEM

Born in 1934, Gloria Steinem penned a 1963 feature story titled "A Bunny's Tale," where she posed as a Playboy model to expose the exploitative conditions that sex workers were subject to. Steinem co-founded the feminist magazine *Ms.* in 1972, and continued to work as a freelance journalist before releasing a book of essays titled *Outrageous Acts and Everyday Rebellions* in 1983. In the essay "Words and Change," Steinem wrote that "new words and phrases are [an] organic measure of change. Now, we have terms like *sexual harassment* and *battered women*. A few years ago, they were just called life."[4]

ALICE WALKER

A confidant of Gloria Steinem's, Alice Walker achieved widespread fame with her 1982 novel *The Color Purple*. As if to counter the stifling of Black women's voices in the American literary establishment, the story of *The Color Purple* is told entirely from the perspective of a Black female protagonist named Celie who lives in Georgia in the 1930s. "There is no third-person narrator to distance the reader from feelings and events," wrote Gloria Steinem of *The Color Purple*. "We are inside Celie's head, seeing through her eyes, experiencing her suffering and humor."[5]

AMY TAN

Walker's narrative focus on an underrepresented ethnic group is echoed in Amy Tan's 1989 book *The Joy Luck Club*: a novel about a Chinese-American family who wrestled with the problem of "how to recognize a country to which they were bound by heritage, but to which they had never [actually traveled]."[6] Tan's placement of her female protagonists on the precipice between history and the present brings to mind a scene in the 1988 film *Working Girl*:

A gaggle of professional women arrive to lower Manhattan via the Staten Island Ferry for the first day at a new job. An expansive shot of the Statue of Liberty marks their passage into the new world of neoliberal New York. The visual-emotional implication is that these women were in a sense immigrants who have disembarked from the land of domesticity and second-class citizenship to travel to the strange, unfamiliar territory of female enfranchisement.

Like all immigrants of the past, women faced nativist resentment: specifically, from defensive men who thought of the economy as a zero-sum game where the gains of feminists meant the demise of men.

AMERICAN MOM

Subsequently, 1980s popular culture revealed society's fears and anxieties around the upheaval of women leaving the home to enter the workforce. Even though the economic facts of life under neoliberalism were making single-income households less tenable, young Millennials were repeatedly positioned as "anchor babies"[7] who could wed women back to the domestic dead ends many wished to flee.

The fear that women would abandon their domestic responsibilities was cynically soothed by the cultural celebration of "Supermoms" who balanced work and familial responsibilities to young Millennials with graceful ease. Conversely, the stigma of the "welfare queen" was used to dissuade mothers from ever asking government entitlement programs to help the household bottom line.

More darkly, the 1980s also saw several films and movies that brandished premises about dead moms. This plot device — present in the television shows *Full House* and *Who's the Boss* and the film *The Land Before Time* — reminded audiences of the importance of a feminine presence in the home by showing how families were sent into (comedic) disarray without them.

Neoliberalism did not seem to know what to do with its 80s babies: it permitted our mothers to enter the workforce, and then gave us politicians and cultural products that bemoaned the subsequent social upheaval.

GUILT TRIP

In her 1982 book *In a Different Voice*, Carol Gilligan wrote that women still "sensed it was dangerous to say or even know what they wanted."[8] Exercising their newfound freedoms "carried with it the threat of abandonment or retaliation"[9] from fragile men. But late capitalism still required women to be laborers. So if selfish boys couldn't stop working girls from making the trip from home to office, the least they could do was try to make that trip a guilt-ridden one.

3B

A 1986 article in *The Atlantic* titled "Women in the Work Force"[10] exclaimed that "dramatic shifts in sex roles seem to be sweeping through America."[11] The article explained that "from 1972 to 1985, women's share of professional jobs increased from 44 to 49 percent, and their share of management jobs nearly doubled."[12]

In her 1989 study *The Second Shift*, sociologist Arlie Hochschild raised the stakes of these social shifts, announcing that "women's move into the economy is the basic social revolution of our time."[13] Hochschild further summarized the impact of neoliberalism, explaining that "the motor of this revolution is the decline in the purchasing power of the male wage, the decline in male blue-collar jobs, and the rise of 'female' jobs in the growing service sector."[14]

THIS GIRL IS ON FIRE

As depicted in the 2014 AMC television show *Halt and Catch Fire*, women coders and programmers in the 1980s were able to find work in new tech industries.[15] They also helped buoy a growing nonprofit sector that expanded to deliver goods and resources to communities affected by Ronald Reagan's cuts to the social safety net.[16]

POWERSUIT

The new era of women's empowerment was reflected sartorially. In 1987, *The Woman's Dress for Success Book* coached women entering white-collar fields to wear shoulder pads and power suits. This gear conveyed confidence and competence, and was "designed to ignore a woman's shape so it didn't hinder her mobility as she worked her way up the corporate ladder."[17] A few years earlier in a 1984 *Adweek* article, journalist Gay Bryant (editor of *Working Woman* magazine) coined the term "glass ceiling"[18] to call attention to the invisible but nonetheless pervasive barriers that prevented women from achieving full professional mobility.

THE PASSION OF ANITA HILL

Increased professional proximity of men and women did not magically curb bad behavior that used to go unnamed. Instead, it brought it out in the open. The sleazy boss in the 1980 film *9 to 5* anticipated a decade in which the phrase "sexual harassment" first entered media parlance.

In 1986, the Supreme Court heard *Meritor v. Vinson*—the first sexual harassment case in history; five years later, one of its own eventual judges, Clarence Thomas, became the subject of a media circus surrounding his harassment of an aide named Anita Hill in 1991.

In 1992, American Women in Radio and Television, Inc. ran an anti-sexual harassment public service announcement on television.[19] In the PSA, a creepy boss cautions a female employee into "using her assets" and "being a little more sexy" if she hoped to keep her job.

A "SICK" SOCIETY?

It may be tempting to say that sexual harassment was an "epidemic" in the 1980s. But harassment was not a disease like drug addiction, or an uncaring contagion like AIDS. It was a specific set of deliberate behaviors perpetrated mostly by men.

As Richard Beck notes in *We Believe the Children: A Moral Panic in the 1980s*, "the word epidemic became an important feature of the political and rhetorical landscape in the 1980s."[20] This was a time when crack cocaine, missing children, and child abuse scandals were framed on the evening news as dire threats that menaced American children on all sides.

At the heart of the cultural construction of these epidemics were "people's fears about the social changes that began to work their way through American society at the end of the 20th century."[21] First and foremost among these changes was "the inexorable breakdown of the country's sexual hierarchy"[22] that accompanied neoliberalism's socioeconomic enfranchisement of

American women.

THE CURIOUS CASE OF THE MISSING AND MOLESTED MILLENNIALS

As Barbara Ehrenreich noted in her 1990 book *The Worst Years of Our Lives*, stories of missing children like Adam Walsh horrified Americans in the 1980s. In the same decade, a string of scandals surrounding alleged child abuse in American daycare centers dominated the nightly news. On the surface, this was a concerned society's concerted effort to, in the words of McGruff the Crime Dog, "take a bite out of crime."

But dozens of convictions related to the daycare scare were later overturned, as the much-publicized prosecutorial focus was largely based on overreach and outright lies. In the scores of cases alleging widespread sexual abuse in the country's daycare centers in the 1980s, no child pornography, blood, semen, weapons, or other instruments of abuse were ever found.[23] What's more, prosecutors extracted fake stories of abuse from young Millennials (and Gen-Xers) using coercive interviewing techniques.[24] Over the next 20 years, the haze of false accusations and bogus news reports—even one on CNN's reputable *Larry King Live*—dissolved.

By the 1990s, widespread suspicion of Michael Jackson's purported pedophilia never resulted in a conviction or admission of guilt from the King of Pop. "Why are kids going to school with guns?" Jackson asked journalist Martin Bashir in the 2003 documentary *Living With Michael Jackson*; "the parents are busy, off on their day job, and they leave them at home on the computer and they just [end up] doing all kinds of crazy stuff."

But society kept telling itself the story of unattended children being abused because it was the story it wanted to hear.[25]

DAYS OF OUR LIES, ALL LIES

The center of this hollow social panic was not, as was alleged, the safety of young Millennials. The real intention was to exorcise economic anxieties under neoliberalism, and to guilt parents—specifically mothers—who participated in double-income households. In his 2015 book *We Believe the Children: A Moral Panic in the 1980s*, Richard Beck summarizes the fake abuse epidemic in the following terms:

> *The day care trials were a powerful instrument of the decade's resurgent sexual conservatism, serving as a warning to mothers who thought they could keep their very young children safe while simultaneously pursuing a life outside the home. As some of the country's most basic social arrangements began to shift, the trials dramatized the consequences of that shift in the manner of a gothic play.*[26]

While conservatives believed in traditional gender roles that kept women out of the workforce, the corporations they placed their faith in made male breadwinners largely extinct. As a result, popular culture in the 1980s and 1990s exhibited a duplicitous tendency: increased visibility of working women, coupled with anxieties over the families these workingwomen were "leaving behind."

THE CRUCIFIXION OF MURPHY BROWN

Consider *Murphy Brown* (1988–1998), a television sitcom about a news reporter:

The sitcom's namesake was played by Candice Bergen, whose role was so popular that the news program *60 Minutes* once offered her a job as an *actual journalist*.[27] In 1991, the character of Murphy Brown became pregnant with a young Millennial named Avery, and Brown subsequently juggled single motherhood with a blossoming career: a lifestyle choice that became increasingly normal in the United States starting in the 1980s.

This fictional portrayal was not without real world enemies. In May of 1992, Vice Presidential candidate Dan Quayle cited

Murphy Brown as a "character who supposedly epitomizes today's intelligent professional women [who] mock the importance of fathers."[28] Conservative disdain for working women who exercised their sexual freedom was so deep-seeded that prominent politicians attacked *even the representations of* these women as traducers of traditional values.

THE DEAD MOM SITCOM

America's cultural fixation with the changing gender norms of neoliberalism didn't just visit Millennials like Avery at the moment of our arrival into this world. It was also revealed in a morbid preoccupation with killing our mothers.[29]

The Dead Mom Sitcom showed how awkward family life had become with society's changing gender norms in the 1980s. But rather than depict the honest reality of these changes, many shows decided on a more exaggerated tact: removing the mom altogether, usually in an accident or illness that is part of the sitcom backstory. The amount of 1980s and early 90s sitcoms that contained a dead mom premise is too multitudinous to be a mere coincidence:

- *Diff'rent Strokes* (1978–1986)
- *Punky Brewster* (1984–1988)
- *My Two Dads* (1987–1990)
- *Gimme a Break* (1981–1987)
- *Full House* (1987–1995)
- *Who's the Boss* (1984–1992)
- *Blossom* (1990–1995)
- *Empty Nest* (1988–1995)

These shows portrayed the accelerated (and clumsy) process of emotional maturation that men were forced to undergo in order to make up for the lack of a traditional maternal presence in their families. Structures of reward and punishment were complicated by the fact that there is no paternal-maternal division of emotional labor; men like Danny Tanner (*Full House*) and Philip Drummond (*Diff'rent Strokes*) embrace a kind of emotional androgyny, offering support one minute and rebuke the next.

Maturity had to be hoisted on these men as a result of tragedy because they were never expected to start the process on their own. So when we laugh at Uncle Jesse[30] in *Full House* or Anthony Russo in *Blossom* as they fail to dispense appropriate advice and flail when providing emotional support, we're laughing at our own expectation that women are supposed to be carrying out this emotional labor.

In Dead Mom Sitcoms, the macabre joke is on the fictional families for not having a mom around to do the family's requisite emotional management—and on the audience for thinking that placating the emotions of others is "women's work." By showing men in awkward domestic arrangements, the shows implicitly highlight the unnaturalness of not having a woman in the home.

YOUNG MILLENNIALS IN A LAND BEFORE TIME
Dead Mom Sitcoms often made young White Millennials like Michelle Tanner (played by Mary-Kate Olsen and Ashley Olsen on *Full House*) seem like emotionally fragile creatures in need of constant reinforcement. The 1988 cartoon film *The Land Before Time* inverts the trend, showing how the untimely demise of a dinosaur matriarch left her offspring to develop his inner emotional reserve.

In *The Land Before Time*, it is not memory of the father figure that motivates young Littlefoot to persevere past scary Tyrannosaurus Rexes and inept teammates. Instead, it is the internalized voice of the mother that ushers him to follow the rising sun to the Great Valley. Once there, the film's narrator tells us, "generation after generation [will recall] the tale of their ancestors' journey."[31]

Just as maternal guilt animates Kate McCallister to reunite

with her son Kevin in the 1990 film *Home Alone*, the narrative of *The Land Before Time* makes the mother's connection to her child carry most of the film's emotional weight. Littlefoot's father is never heard, while the maternal voice of Littlefoot's inner-monologue guides his quest for safety.

A story like *The Land Before Time* might have been made in any era. But in the particular late capitalist context, it comforted audiences assaulted by rapid social change with the notion that the mother-child connection was a primordial and unchanging bond that could not be undone by death, divorce, or geological catastrophe.

This was not an appeal to reason. It was an invocation of saccharine sentiment that tied womanhood to childrearing at a time when that link was more suspect than ever. "Some things you see with your eyes," Littlefoot's mother tells him, "and others you see with your heart."

3C

The traditionalism of *The Land Before Time* could not change the fact that women were the change agents of neoliberal society. Their labor fueled white-collar and service industry fields that expanded rapidly past the country's industrial sector. When Apple devised its famous 1984 Super Bowl ad for its new line of desktop computers, it is no mistake that they selected a female actress to deliver the deathblow to the IBM patriarchy.[32]

Coincidentally, Apple learned to package its personal computers as teaching aides and proxy parents. Teachers buckling under the burden of austerity measures in public schools found Apple's kid-friendly terminals to be useful co-tutors, while parents employed computers as babysitters. The 2015 film *Steve Jobs* depicts the titular tech tycoon getting inspiration for Apple's accessible line of "Lisa" desktops while watching his daughter fiddle around with a computer in 1982. In his 1993 company history *Big Blues: The Unmaking of IBM*, author

Paul Carroll observes that Steve Jobs' main competitive advantage came from "figuring out how to build motherhood into the machine."[33]

But many *actual* women were still contributing a disproportionate amount of domestic labor to raise young Millennials. Arlie Hochschild's 1989 book *The Second Shift* details the phenomenon of newly employed women leaving work, only to come home and pick up the slack for aloof husbands.

SUPERMOM

When the first Millennials were born in the 1980s, capitalism did not alleviate the physical, fiscal, and emotional strain on mothers who were burning the candle at both ends. Instead, society contrived cultural stories that made women feel they were personal failures if they were not able to navigate the socioeconomic obstacle course of Reagan-era America without help. As Hochschild noted in *The Second Shift*:

The front cover of the New York Times Magazine *for September 9, 1984, features a working mother walking home with her daughter. The woman is young. She is good-looking. She is smiling. The daughter is smiling as she lugs her mother's briefcase. If images could talk, this image would say, "Women can combine career and children." There is no trace of stress, no suggestion that the mother needs help from others.*[34]

WELFARE QUEEN

The so-called "welfare queen"[35] was the corollary of the Supermom. The trope of the lazy (usually Black) mother who milked public assistance was used to legitimate ruthless cuts to public assistance spending. A favorite punching-bag in Reagan's speeches, the welfare queen "marked millions of America's poorest people as potential scoundrels, and fostered the belief that welfare fraud was a nationwide epidemic that needed to be stamped out."[36]

STUPID BABIES NEED THE LEAST ATTENTION[37]

Competing models of motherhood—the Supermom versus the Welfare Queen—therefore became the simulation of a larger debate about how to allocate resources under late capitalism. As the 1990s arrived, these debates extended into the womb.

Speaker of the House Newt Gingrich's 1994 policy proposal *Contract With America* advanced a measure to keep women on welfare from having babies, and several state legislatures across the country debated implementing mandatory insertion of Norplant as a condition of receiving aid.[38] Apparently, an unborn Millennial was better than one that might be a drain on the state.

In 1994, the controversial book *The Bell Curve* used pseudo-science to convince readers that White and Asian children belonged to a cognitive elite by virtue of being born to morally and intellectually superior parents. *The Bell Curve* became a bestseller, with its authors (Richard Herrnstein and Charles A. Murray) appearing on *The Phil Donahue Show* (1967–1996) in 1995 to casually debate the pros and cons of neoliberal racism.[39]

With large blocs of children consigned to failure, austerity hacks seized on *The Bell Curve* to continue directing resources away from public education. In a National Public Radio segment that aired weeks after *The Bell Curve* was released, a Chicago civil rights lawyer named Barack Obama denounced the book as an excuse "to push the elimination of affirmative action and welfare programs aimed at the poor."[40]

MATERNAL CAPITALISM

What we were witnessing in the 1980s was the demise—or rather the transformation—of what might be called *maternal capitalism*:

The home, schools, and hospitals were once spaces where the labor and social perspective of women was employed to enforce the norms and values of mid-century capitalism. It was widely recognized that this work had value, and it was compensated as such: by tax revenues that kept caregiving institutions afloat, and—indirectly—by the generous salary of the male bread-winner, which he was expected to share with his spouse.[41]

But the arrival of neoliberalism squeezed resources and social capital out of these sectors, subjecting them to austerity measures, and subtly making them objects of ridicule—places where dreams of feminist liberation went to die. Career-centric women like Oprah Winfrey were celebrated in the 1980s and 1990s, while first lady Hillary Clinton mocked women who "stayed home to bake cookies and have tea"[42] in 1992.

Housewives were now spoken of derisively as "just" house-wives, while female nurses and school teachers were placed on a pedestal where they were patronizingly praised for "all that they sacrificed." The declining visibility (but certainly not declining importance) of these spheres was indicated in the derisive label "Nanny State,"[43] which further feminized care labor and therefore prepared it for the financial chopping block.

On the run, maternal capitalism turned lemons into lemonade by forging its new formation in the workplace, the corporate boardroom, and in popular culture. The terms of engagement on this terrain was still overwhelmingly set by men, just as Whites largely controlled hip-hop's commercialized projection of Black empowerment. But it is undeniable that the feminization of capitalism (or is it the capitalization of feminism?) has been a source of both empowerment and frustration for American women. Millionaire CEOs such as Sheryl Sandberg and celebrities like Beyoncé lead the most recognizable guise of the modern feminist movement.

Tellingly, the phrase "Nanny State" was popularized by British Prime Minister Margaret Thatcher, therefore showing that the project of despoiling the social safety nets on which millions of families worldwide rely often utilizes the authority of "empowered" women to implement austerity measures that place an added strain on workingmen and women.

KIDS RULE

This shift could not help but be reflected in parenting and popular culture. Working parents in the 1980s looked to offshore their duties onto responsible surrogates. Pop culture therefore became a giant babysitter's club, with television, movies, and video games swooping in to do the work adults once had time for.

The Nickelodeon Network formed in 1977. But it did not blossom until the 1980s, when neoliberal attrition took full hold in American households, creating a need for a televised source of entertainment and education that kids could watch while their parents were away.

Nickelodeon promised adults child-appropriate entertainment. But it also offered young Millennials and Gen-Xers a world where their fantasies and fears were indulged. The network's founders intended green slime to be the symbol of everything children wanted: the ability to transgress, and make a mess. As the channel's slogan went, "Kids Rule."[44]

In his 2009 book *Capitalist Realism*, Mark Fisher describes the milieu of Millennials and Nickelodeon as follows:

> *When the parent sees the child very little, the tendency will often be to refuse to occupy the "oppressive" function of telling the child what to do. The parental disavowal of this role is doubled at the level of cultural production by the refusal of "gatekeepers" to do anything but give audiences what they already (appear to) want.*[45]

THE MILLENNIAL OBSTACLE COURSE

As Megan Erickson—author of the 2015 book *Class War: The Privatization of Childhood*—has written, "childhood has become a period of high-stakes preparation for life in a stratified economy."[46] The Nickelodeon show *Double Dare* (1986–2000) provided a metaphor for the world that young Millennials were born into in the 1980s: the obstacle course.

Children on *Double Dare* were split into teams and quizzed on their knowledge of popular culture: "How many pieces of meat are in a Big Mac?" and "What animal is the symbol of the Republican Party?" are two examples from one episode that aired in 1988.[47] The questions get increasingly harder, leading contestants to engage in "physical challenges" to accumulate enough points to defeat the opposing team.

At the conclusion of every episode, all contestants run through a grotesque obstacle course that includes retrieving a flag from the snotty nasal cavity of a fake nose, and crawling through a massive vat of refried beans. This hurried ritual of physical shame is endured in hopes of securing prizes provided by the show's corporate sponsors. The formula was replicated in the Nickelodeon show *Wild & Crazy Kids* (1990–1992).

1980s dance films like *Flashdance* (1983), *Wild Style* (1983), and *Footloose* (1984) made the human body a slab on which neoliberalism's ethics were inscribed. In precarious and deindustrialized landscapes, adults hustled and scraped for increasingly scant crumbs.

These films were the pop culture complement to the political portrayal of the Supermom: a rugged individualist who absorbs it all without ever asking for help. Just as team sport became an arena where the capitalist value of competition was performed, dance in the 1980s became a celebration of survivalism. As the morbid theme song of the film *Flashdance* put it, "I'm dancing for my life!"

The Nickelodeon obstacle course cast Millennials in a similar mold: by running, jumping, scampering and scurrying to avoid coming in last in a race nobody should have to run, we were prepared to embrace the "dirty, messy, crazy world"[48] in front of us. But as writer Ted Pillow has written of *Double Dare*, we should think twice about "the implications of quantifying children to the tenth of a second by their performance in a capitalistic race for goods and products."[49]

Part II: YOUTH

(1991–2000)

The message of *The Simpsons* is that your moral authorities don't always have your best interests in mind. I think that's a great message for kids.[1]
–Matt Groening.

Chapter 4

Entertain Us

Ronald Reagan ushered in an economic doctrine of austerity. But the dominant cultural tenor of the 1980s was excess.

Led by sluggers Mark McGwire and Jose Conseco, the Oakland Athletics bashed their way to the World Series title in 1989. The power ballad—exemplified by "cock rock" bands like Def Leppard and Poison—converted the guitar into a symbolic extension of the penis. Popular purveyors of female sexuality like Madonna and Cyndi Lauper were adrenal in their hyperactivity; a gust of pent-up estrogen released upon a society that required the mothers of young Millennials to be "supermoms."

If decades are drugs, then the 1980s were anabolic steroids. But a funny thing happened on the way to the 21st century: America got tired.

In his 1986 book *The Cycles of American History*, Arthur Schlesinger wrote that America is susceptible to mood shifts.[1] Periods of overdetermination and exertion (like the 1980s) give way to periods of apathy and withdrawal. With the collapse of the Berlin Wall in 1989 and the demise of the Soviet Union in 1991, the United States found itself alone atop the summit of geopolitical supremacy. With no global foe to form its identity around fighting, the country's cultural ego became feeble and self-possessed.

Political scientist Francis Fukuyama summarized the cause of America's changing national mood in his 1992 book *The End of History*:

What we may be witnessing is not just the end of the Cold War, but the end of mankind's ideological evolution, and the universalization of Western liberal democracy. There are powerful reasons for believing that it is the ideal that will govern the material world in the long run.[2]

WINNERS AND LOSERS IN LATE CAPITALISM

Sports in the 1980s simulated the bilateral battle of the Cold War: Rocky versus Ivan Drago in the 1985 film *Rocky IV*, and the U.S. Olympic hockey team versus their Soviet counterparts throughout the decade. Even John McEnroe's tennis tilts with Bjorn Borg and Magic Johnson's basketball bouts with Larry Bird quenched the public's thirst for polar foes.

But without a global rivalry to replicate in the 1990s, Americans celebrated uncontested greatness: athletics mirrored capitalism's defeat of the communist threat, as the public celebrated unimpeachable superteams like the Dallas Cowboys and the Chicago Bulls. In his reign as 6-time NBA champion and consensus greatest basketball player of all-time, Michael Jordan amassed a multi-million dollar fortune in the 1990s as a commercial spokesperson for Nike and McDonald's.

The pop culture celebration of winners in the 1990s led to a *countercultural* current that glorified the losers under late capitalism: MTV elected *Beavis and Butt-Head* as representative Generation X "slackers."[3] And Kurt Cobain and Tupac Shakur attracted droves of passionate fans that followed them all the way to the terminal end of their struggles with self-destruction. With the arrival of the 1990s, popular culture took a turn for the apathetic; for the enervated rage of alternative rock bands like Nirvana, and the embrace of irony flaunted by Alanis Morissette and *Daria*.

24 HOURS TO LIVE

Meanwhile, anxieties arising from the exhaustion of all alternatives to global capitalism were expressed in Ma$e's 1997 rap single "24 Hours To Live." The song's rappers explain how they'd spend their last days on earth seeking suicidal solutions to socioeconomic marginalization. Sheek Louch describes strapping himself with TNT to liquidate a biased criminal justice system, while DMX hopes to "turn 3 buildings on Wall Street into a fog."

These statements were made in the shadow of the 1993 World Trade Center bombing, and presaged the terrorist attacks of September 11th, 2001. According to Francis Fukuyama, all the United States had left to worry about in the 1990s was solving its own internal "class contradictions"[4] and squelching the terrorist attacks of ideologically bankrupt radicals.[5]

CAPITALISM FOR ITS OWN SAKE

When they weren't fending off right-wing radicals like David Koresh or terrorists like Osama bin Laden, Fukuyama opined that Americans could look forward to the "endless satisfaction of their increasingly sophisticated consumer demands."[6] No longer pressured to make consumption seem like a Cold War strike against Soviet authoritarians, capitalism was free to celebrate consumerism for its own sake. The Lisa Frank corporation's message for young Millennials who lusted after their stationery in the 1990s was perhaps the most direct ad slogan in American history: *"You gotta have it."*[7]

THE Y2K BUG TAKES FLIGHT

With no Soviet menace to focus their energies on, American conservatives doubled down on domestic culture wars. The culture of young Millennials became the battleground for conservatives who bemoaned the deteriorating "moral fabric" of the United States. These anxieties were heightened by the race towards the year 2000.

As James Hunter wrote in his 1991 book *Culture Wars*, the year 2000 was a futurist deadline whose "hopes for the future [were provided by] the millennial and messianic promise of the Hebrew scriptures."[8] The music video for the grunge band Soundgarden's 1994 song "Black Hole Sun" shows celestial catastrophe destroying a suburban utopia and its hedonistic inhabitants. Early in the video, a gaggle of smarmy churchgoers congregate beneath a sign that reads "The End is Nigh." While Francis Fukuyama was predicting the "end of history," some others were predicting the end of days:

As the bloody 20th century waned, fringe factions took up arms to prepare for the millenarian showdown to come. David Koresh barricaded himself inside a federal building in Texas in April of 1993. Two years later, terrorist Timothy McVeigh detonated a pickup truck filled with explosives in April of 1995 at the Oklahoma City Federal Building, killing 168 people and injuring 600 more. A 1998 Anti-Defamation League report[9] tied this rise of extremist activity to the "Y2K" panic in conservative circles. But despite director Spike Jonze's 1999 Nike commercial[10] that showed determined joggers hustling to lose weight in the midst of the apocalypse, the world did not end.

CASH-STRAPPED PARENTS

At the dawn of the 1990s, the United States had much more than "24 hours to live." Nonetheless, American culture showed signs of temporal desperation stemming from the arrival of the year 2000, and the effects of a decade of neoliberal reforms. Fear-mongering pundits predicted that a so-called "Y2K bug" would mangle computer systems that couldn't tell the difference between the year 2000 and the year 1900. Cash-strapped parents feared utility companies would mistakenly invoice them for 100 years of service.

NEW MILLENNIUM, YOUNG MILLENNIALS

On the eve of the new millennium, social anxiety was also expressed in attempts to police the images that young Millennials were exposed to. Few concluded that latchkey Millennials learned bad manners and recalcitrance because their parents — busy at work — left them to be raised by popular culture. A real commitment to the country's youth would've meant alleviating this socioeconomic pressure. Instead, cultural conservatives continued their contradictory politics: support of the unfettered free market, coupled with culture wars that complained about the effects capitalism had on the country's social fabric.

4B

In September of 1991, the Seattle-based alternative rock band Nirvana released their 13-track cry of late capitalist despair, *Nevermind*. Everything about the record—from the melancholy of the music to the social commentary of its cover—belied a critical anti-commercial awareness. A member of Generation X, the group's lead singer, Kurt Cobain, once expressed disgust with his generation's "apathy"[11] and "spinelessness."[12] Well after Cobain took his own life in 1994, *Nevermind* continued to speak (and screech) volumes about the times that produced them.

Nevermind was as much a referendum on the 1980s as it was representative of the 1990s. "In Bloom" was a radical critique of frat bros and gun nuts who assumed a countercultural pose simply by showing up to Nirvana concerts. Michael Jackson and Madonna learned to lure audiences with MTV mini-epics like "Smooth Criminal" (1987) and "Like A Prayer" (1989). But with the gritty visuals for their lead single "Smells Like Teen Spirit," Nirvana undermined the expectation of high-production values that came with the commercialization of their songs.

WORKERS OF THE WORLD, UNITE! YOU HAVE NOTHING TO LOSE BUT YOUR... ACTUALLY, NEVERMIND

If the purpose of Nirvana's tactics was to scare away fair-weather fans, it did not work. Listeners who hadn't heard of the group's 1989 debut *Bleach* helped vault *Nevermind* past Michael Jackson's *Dangerous* to the top spot of the *Billboard* 100 on January 11, 1992.[13] That very evening, the group performed the album's punkish B-side "Territorial Pissings" on *Saturday Night Live*. 26 million viewers[14] tuned in that night to watch Nirvana party like no one was watching. After a searing recital, they destroyed their instruments, resulting in dissonant feedback that complemented the chaos of the original composition.

The set-ending chaos epitomized the cultural terrain of the 1990s: antiestablishment histrionics that are commoditized and made compatible with the capitalist establishment itself. With the socialist threat officially vanquished, capitalism could afford to give more airtime to its own critics.

THE COMMERCIALIZATION OF CHILDHOOD

Nirvana made extremely loud statements every opportunity they could get. Bassist Krist Novoselic began "Territorial Pissings" with a satirical citation of The Youngbloods' Baby Boomer anthem "Get Together."[15] Kurt Cobain posed on the April 16th, 1992 cover of *Rolling Stone* wearing a T-shirt that read "Corporate Magazines Still Suck."[16] And the cover image of *Nevermind* showed a naked baby Millennial named Spencer Elden swimming in a pool, flailing after a dollar bill attached to a string.

That cover provided an immortal commentary on the commercialization of childhood—a process that escalated with young Millennials. In the words of a student blog from Stoke Newington College in London, "big business aims to hook everyone from as early an age as possible. Once the boy is hooked on the almighty dollar, we can be reeled in to readily accept capitalism."[17]

"Commercial interests invaded childhood in the 1980s and 1990s,"[18] writes Gary Cross in *An All-Consuming Century: Why Commercialism Won in Modern America*. In the 1960s, children aged 2 to 14 influenced $5 billion in the purchases their parents made; by 1997, this figure leapt to $132 billion.[19] That same year, Nickelodeon published a how-to manual for marketing to kids.

COLOR SCHEME

The 1990s are remembered as a decade when bright neon colors became popular in clothes and music videos. The open secret to this fad was the rise in child-focused marketing that appealed to the eyeballs of young Millennials with bright lights and shiny objects. Nerf foam weapons, Koosh balls, and innumerable candy products used loud colors to attract kids. As Akhil JK has written in his 2016 book *Fashion Forecasting: Economic Edition,* "in the 1990s, children developed a love for neon colors [that adults avoid]. This segmentation by color preference makes it important for marketers to carefully observe the target consumers in their natural habitat, and research their preferences."

THE PRIVATIZATION OF PUBLIC SCHOOL

"Kids are getting older younger," noted a creative consultant at The Acme Idea Company; "we've always known that kids are impressionable and brand-conscious."[20]

In the 1980s and 1990s, young Millennials became the subject of a "vast interconnected industry"[21] that encompassed their schooling, nutrition, recreation, and mental health. Neoliberal austerity measures in the 1970s and 1980s leveled the amount of public funding provided to public schools in cities across the country. Desperate for cash and pressured to behave like "small businesses," schools opened their doors to major corporations who offered discounted educational materials in exchange for the opportunity to promote their brands to young Millennials:

General Mills sent 8,000 teachers the science kit "Gushers: Wonders of the Earth,"[22] which used Fruit Gushers candy as a tool to teach about volcanoes. Apparel companies Nike and Reebok sold athletics programs gear and shoes.[23] And for students in the civics and arts who were marginalized by schools' new obsession with prized fields like the sciences and sports, Prozac distributed "depression awareness" promotion materials.[24]

DIET AUSTERITY

Soft drinks were well positioned to capitalize on the commercialization of Millennial childhood. Throughout the 1990s, Pepsi continued its "Choice of a New Generation" ad campaign by appealing to Millennials. The VHS release for the 1990 film *Home Alone* included a 30-second Pepsi spot with child actors who proclaim that "being cool is not about your haircut or the clothes you wear."[25] Their prepubescent appeal to the "inner self" was ironically undercut when it turns out that securing female attention hinges on having Pepsi—a drink that was decisively linked to childhood obesity in 1998.

In 1999, the American Beverage Association defended itself against naysayers by pointing out that beverage companies helped to narrow the funding gap in American schools by providing grants and scholarships to disprivileged schools.[26] Neoliberal austerity measures and corporate charity therefore combined to produce a Millennial childhood filled to the brim with fizzy sugar drinks.

GIRL POWER

In 1997, Pepsi partnered with the Spice Girls to create the "Generation Next" campaign. A British pop group formed as a business venture,[27] the Spice Girls belonged to the same constellation of fabricated stars as the Backstreet Boys, NSYNC, and 98 Degrees. What differentiated them from the other products on the shelf was their socially progressive packaging.

The Spice Girls introduced Millennial teenagers to the concept of "girl power": a vaguely defined but strongly expressed female-positive aesthetic that was marketed to para-pubescent teenagers.[28] Their hit record "Wannabe" was a celebration of the primacy of female friendship, while "Mama" may as well have been a love letter to the neoliberal supermom. The Spice Girls' potent brand of commercialized 3rd wave feminism made them an attractive corporate partner to Pepsi.

The Spice Girls were a sanitized version of Riot Grrrl, an Olympia, Washington-bred punk band whose lead singer Tobi Vail was close friends with Kurt Cobain. They were also anticipated by the success of the rap group Salt-N-Pepa, the first female rap act to earn a platinum plaque (for their 1987 single "Push It").[29] If Nirvana was the anarchist Generation X response to late capitalism, then the Spice Girls were their centrist counterparts: propped-up by capital-intensive marketing schemes, but just edgy enough to appeal to consumers' sense of political purpose.

MOVE OVER

In 1997, Pepsi produced a limited edition version of the Spice Girls single "Move Over (Generation Next)," an extended corporate jingle that listeners acquired after obtaining 20 ring-pull tabs from the company's canned diabetes water.[30]

Like a polished politician who speaks out of both sides of their mouth, the message behind "Move Over" was not transparent. On the one hand, the symbols and rhetoric of societal transformation were at the fore. Lyrics like "sow me the seed, every color every creed" and "teach never preach, listen up take heed" appropriated progressive symbols of protest and critical pedagogy. On the other hand, these lyrics could not speak louder than the corporate bullhorn that broadcasted them.

The Spice Girls were not pushovers. One can observe the feminist indignation when—speaking to *New York Daily News* in 1998—Emma 'Baby Spice' Bunton exclaimed, "We've always taken responsibility for everything we've done. It's very unsettling for male-dominated newspapers to realize that five women in short skirts have got a brain."[31] But while their message sold incredibly well to Millennial teens, it was not clear that the Spice Girls had more to offer than more stuff to buy.

By all indications, the "next phase, next stage" the Spice Girls sung about on "Move Over" was the capitalist future that

Millennial teens were expected to partake in when we reached adulthood after the year 2000.

4C

The Spice Girls resembled the 1980s fem-glam television series *Jem* (1985–1988).

Jem was one of scores of Hasbro-licensed cartoons—along with *My Little Pony* (1986–1987) and *The Transformers* (1984–1987)—that were created when FCC deregulation of television advertising allowed companies to target young Millennials directly. Shows like *G.I. Joe* (1985–1986) and *She-Ra* (1985–1987) were little more than ads for action figures.

In episodes of *Jem*, all five main characters were carefully posed to take up the entire frame of the screen as often as possible: marketers wanted to entice young Millennials into obtaining the five action figure dolls that the show was based on.[32]

In their adventures as female rock stars who balanced demanding careers with romance and friendship, *Jem* introduced young Millennials to a corporatized ripple of 3rd wave feminism. The Spice Girls capitalized on this resonance. In 1997, they released their own line of dolls through a Hasbro subsidiary called Galoob Toys.[33]

THE BABYSITTER CLUB

The cartoonish cross-promotion of the Spice Girls and *Jem* speaks to the way that marketers targeted young Millennials in the 1990s. Television networks did not want young Millennials to watch one cartoon and then turn the television off. In a strategy known as "strip programming," they broadcast blocks of similar programs at critical points in the day when they knew children were more likely to be unsupervised. These shows were frequently vehicles for video games and action figure tie-ins that children pestered their parents to purchase for them:

- Warner Bros. teamed with Steven Spielberg to produce *Tiny Toon Adventures* (1990–1995), and the Fox Network lumped the show with *Animaniacs* (1993–1998), *Pinky and the Brain* (1995–1998), and a groundbreaking *Batman: The Animated Series* (1992–1995).

- Disney countered Fox with a "Disney Afternoon" block that featured *DuckTales* (1987–1990), *TaleSpin* (1990–1991), *Darkwing Duck* (1991–1995), and *Gargoyles* (1994–1996).

- Meanwhile, for parents who sought respite from the travails of the workweek by going out on Saturday night, Nickelodeon rolled out "SNICK" (Saturday Night Nickelodeon) in 1992: a two-hour programming block that featured the network's first forays into animation: *The Ren & Stimpy Show* (1991–1996), *Doug* (1991–1994), and *Rugrats* (1990–2006).

The programmatic intent behind these cartoons says as much about the socioeconomic terrain of the 1990s as the cartoons themselves. Wage depression under neoliberalism created a condition where parents were forced to work longer hours for lower pay. The latchkey Millennials they left at home craved connection. Television filled this void.

Young Millennials learned valuable lessons about the world around them from these shows: *Tiny Toon Adventures* simulated and satirized the social hierarchies of American schools. *DuckTales* modeled sibling rivalry while glorifying money and power in the laughable guise of Scrooge McDuck. The anxiety-riddled main character of *Doug* was 12 years old at the time of the show's debut in 1996, making him a Millennial born in 1984. His poignant voice-overs reflected the social pressures of male puberty, which apparently included obsessing over independent women like Patti Mayonnaise who felt no obligation to requite unwanted romantic attention.

A 1992 episode of *Rugrats* titled "The Bank Trick"[34] has Tommy and Chucky running amok while the former's inattentive mother fills out papers to attain a new ATM card. Chucky subsequently sends the global financial system into disarray with the simple push of a button, as young Millennials learn that the money-grubbing world of adults under neoliberalism is predicated on chance and greed.

A 1998 *New York Times* review of *Rugrats* highlighted the show's "biting [portrayal] of career-obsessed working moms and daydreaming dads."[35] The article also noted how popular the show was among children aged 2 to 11, as well as its "appeal to families" that were drawn to its "slyly observant child's-eye-view" of the world.[36]

CARTOONS IN THE CULTURE WARS

Disney's 1989 film *The Little Mermaid* and its animated series *The Gummi Bears* (1985–1991) forecasted the massive successes the media giant enjoyed in the 1990s. *The Lion King* (1994) anthropomorphized the relationship between Baby Boomers (Mufasa) and Millennials (Simba) into a parable about responsibility and social rites of passage. In the midst of the culture wars, the movie endorsed an isolationist model of the nuclear family by showing how bad influences threaten to interrupt the "circle of life."[37]

But while Disney was using animation to advance wholesome family values, a new crop of cartoonists saw the medium as a space for subversion. While *Aladdin* (1992) was a phantasmagoria of chromatic delight, *The Ren & Stimpy Show* (1991–1996) was a demented panic dream. The show's trademark move was the profane close-up that revealed the sick substance of a seemingly benign surface.

In the 1992 episode "Big Baby Scam,"[38] the show spoofs a pair of inattentive parents who allow their kids to crawl around completely unattended. Ren and Stimpy—who are a cat and a dog—bribe the babies into disappearing so that they can take their place and live a rent-free life as infants. Preoccupied by work, the parents do not notice that a Chihuahua and an overweight cat have replaced their children. This episode is a deeply skeptical look at the price of human life under capitalism. The babies who take Ren and Stimpy's bribe—a pair of young Millennials named Shawn and Eugene—are revealed to be money-grubbing thugs who accept a quick payoff over a lasting relationship with their parents.

Because Nickelodeon and MTV both had the same parent company (Viacom), episodes of *The Ren & Stimpy Show* aired on MTV beginning in 1994. By then, animator Mike Judge's *Beavis and Butt-Head* (1993–1997) was also cementing MTV's place in pop culture as the premiere purveyor of countercultural angst.

Beavis and Butt-Head follows two imbecilic teens whose only interests appear to be scatological humor, failing miserably at having sexual intercourse, and watching music videos. While they work at the fictional fast food restaurant "Burger World," they have no desire to accrue other employable skills, and cannot be bothered to take their schooling seriously. Beavis and Butt-Head represented society's fear that America's young were growing to be good-for-nothing freeloaders.

For some,[39] the absence of global conflict like the Cold War that required civic sacrifice was the root cause of Beavis and Butt-Head's—and by extension, Generation X's—nihilism. In the pilot episode of *Beavis and Butt-Head*, the brain-dead bros learn that their elderly neighbor Anderson served admirably in the Korean War; their only care is obtaining a portion of his inheritance when he passes away.

FIRE, FIRE

Beavis' fetishization of fire was a recurring symbol of the duo's utter lack of respect for societal values like responsibility and private property. In 1993, the *Baltimore Sun* reported that a 5-year-old Millennial set fire to his family's mobile home after being inspired by *Beavis and Butt-Head*.[40] In response, MTV agreed to pull the 7:00PM viewing of *Beavis and Butt-Head*, believing that this would reduce the size of the show's unsupervised child audience.

Parent groups and pundits seemed unable to accept that the real issue behind the preadolescent act of arson was the fact that no adults were around to stop it from happening in the first place. In any case, *Beavis and Butt-Head* drew creative inspiration from their own controversy. By July of 1994, the show aired an episode called "Generation in Crisis" that parodied the cultural conservatives who critiqued the show in endless newspaper columns and on talk-radio.

BLOWING UP THE NUCLEAR FAMILY

American conservatives who waged culture wars in the 1990s also found a relentless adversary in Matt Groening's animated sitcom *The Simpsons* (1989–present). First hatched as a segment on *The Tracy Ullman Show* (1987–1990), Groening's portrayal of a five-member family and its surrounding cast of characters in the fictional town of Springfield earned its own show in 1989.

Detractors could not credibly say that the show had no respect for family values: Homer, Marge, Bart, Lisa, and Maggie lived in a well-kempt suburb. They attended church regularly. And they literally upheld the conservative model of the nuclear family: Marge was a dutiful housewife, while Homer was a comfortably employed male breadwinner (at an actual nuclear power plant, no less). Adapting this familiar template allowed *The Simpsons* to spoof "family values" and the conservatives that touted them.

The 1991 episode "Homer Defined"[41] best represents the adversarial stance of *The Simpsons* in the culture wars. The episode ridicules the pervasive fear that media boogeymen (like Bart and Beavis) would steer children wrong. It also shows the societal search for "good role models" during the culture wars to be futile. In "Homer Defined," it is revealed that Homer isn't a heroic dad, but a bungling oaf who lucks into heroism despite his own stupidity. At the same time, it is revealed that neighborhood kids are not picking up their bad manners from Bart, but from being left unattended by their parents in front of the television. Mid-episode, Lisa Simpson burns culture warriors who place all their faith in the nuclear family's ability to prop-up heroes and exile bad influences: "A role model in my very own home," she says sarcastically; "how convenient."

A MUSEUM WITH A PULSE

Irreverent as the show's characters were, *The Simpsons* also celebrated the past and contributed to America's budding culture of pastiche. Most of the show's episodes contain nuanced in-jokes and cultural references that require deep familiarity with American pop culture of yore. *The Simpsons* anticipated the homage-heavy film *Pulp Fiction* (1994) and the Wu-Tang Clan's urban pastiche *Enter the Wu-Tang: 36 Chambers* (1993). Director Quentin Tarantino and rapper/producer RZA (of the Wu-Tang Clan) cultivated a friendship in the 2000s based on their shared love of sampling kung fu films.[42]

The notion that American culture would begin to obsessively mine the past for inspiration was a central thesis of Fredric Jameson's 1991 book *Postmodernism: The Cultural Logic of Late Capitalism*.[43] In *The End of History*, Francis Fukuyama concurred, writing that "nostalgia will continue to fuel competition and conflict for some time to come."[44]

Indeed, conservative criticism of America's youth frequently came coupled with appeals to the "simpler times" of the mid-20th century. In 1992, President George H.W. Bush expressed his wish that "American families be more like *The Waltons*, and less like *The Simpsons*."[45] The gist of Bush's unfavorable comparison was that *The Simpsons* represented a departure from the stolid "family values" represented by *The Waltons* (1971–1981).

CULTURE WAR CONTRADICTIONS

And yet no one had done more damage to the traditional nuclear family than American conservatives like Bush. In the 1980s, Ronald Reagan's trickle-down economics led to the defeat of organized labor and a decline in wages for American men. Corporations in search of cheap labor lured housewives into the workplace, and also took advantage of a regressive tax code that starved social programs which would have allowed one parent to stay at home to attend to young Millennials.

The fundamental contradiction of the conservative stance in the culture wars was that their own policies created a world where parents had to spend less time at home; the young Millennials and members of Generation X that these conservatives pretended to care about were therefore more likely to be influenced by "bad role models" like Bart and Beavis.

A real commitment to America's young Millennials in the 1990s would have meant a commitment to providing their parents a living wage, and access to much-needed social services. This would have ensured that parents could afford to spend more time with their children in the first place. But the conservative attack on liberal social programs continued into the 1990s. In 1994, Speaker of the House Newt Gingrich successfully introduced a senatorial bill called "Contract With America" that slashed cash welfare programs and abolished taxes on capital-gains.[46]

The welfare state and a progressive corporate tax rate had helped to undergird the mid-20th century golden age of capitalism that conservatives glorified. By not supporting those measures, conservative culture warriors revealed themselves to be ineffectual; and by railing against the impact their policies had on the family lives of young Millennials, they revealed themselves to be hypocrites.

ENTERTAIN US

Unattended Millennials were the products of American neoliberalism. The country's heavily commercialized pop culture apparatus swooped in to fill the void left by overworked parents. And marketers learned to appeal to Millennials as a distinct demographic with an exploitable consumer profile.

The first inklings of Millennial political activity would have to wait until Millennials came of age in the 2000s; but the 1990s saw their economic impact expressed in no uncertain terms. Under the influence of television, Millennials began to make their presence felt as consumers of popular culture. In the 1990s, Millennials spurred hundreds of billions of dollars of their parents' purchases, and made several billion more on their own.

As Mark Fisher writes in his 2009 tract *Capitalist Realism*, "Kurt Cobain seemed to give wearied voice to the generation whose every move was anticipated, tracked, bought and sold before it even happened."[47] The gravelly chorus of Nirvana's 1991 single "Smells Like Teen Spirit" heralded the arrival of America's kids and adolescents as consumers on the plane of American neoliberalism:

"Here we are now," growled Cobain. "Entertain us."

Chapter 5

American Siblings

During the so-called golden age of capitalism which lasted from 1945 until 1973, the wages of American workers rose in proportion to the country's productivity.[1] A consensus had been reached between government, organized labor, and big business: as long as profits increased, unions could barter for higher wages without too much fear of reprisal, and government could tax corporations heavily to subsidize the welfare state.

Mid-century stability arose from this consensus. Federal loans for schools and housing were made available to middle-class Americans, who were encouraged to purchase homes in suburbs created by the federal government. Widespread capitalist propaganda authored by the likes of DuPont and General Electric[2] coaxed adults into stuffing these homes with appliances, cars, and other consumer goods.

American men—whose unionized jobs generated the income these households depended on—were installed at the head of the mid-20th century family as sole breadwinners. Mothers, meanwhile, were wards of the market who waded through an endless constellation of commodity options to furnish their homes. Unprecedented post-WWII prosperity was a boon to lifestyle magazines like *Redbook*, *Life*, and *Vogue*.

The pop culture representations from this "golden age of capitalism" were glamorous. Male celebrities like Desi Arnaz, Gregory Peck, and Sidney Poitier symbolized the clean-cut conformity expected of American men. Elizabeth Taylor and Dorothy Dandridge were their female counterparts, offering images of domesticated complicity with the capitalist status quo.

But by the late 1960s, the social order these entertainers embodied began to decay. Rampant inflation resulted from

Lyndon B. Johnson's failed attempt to balance the expenditures of the Vietnam War with the costs of the welfare state. Wages hit an all-time high in 1973,[3] causing business activists to go on the counteroffensive against organized labor. Their political efforts culminated in the 1980 election of President Ronald Reagan; a former actor who first rose to national prominence as a corporate spokesperson for General Electric.

The welfare state underwrote mid-century prosperity. Ronald Reagan sacked it. An October 1st, 1981 article in *The Washington Post* announced "today marks the reversal of two great waves of government invention," as Reagan's $35 billion in cuts to the country's social welfare programs took effect.[4] Child nutrition programs—which benefitted young Millennials and members of Generation X—declined by 25%.[5] The withered welfare state left in Reagan's wake atrophied even further under President Clinton. In 1996, 68% of families with a child in poverty received Temporary Assistance for Needy Families; by the year 2000, that number would shrink to 45%.[6]

THE GENERATION AFTER

In their 1993 study *13th Gen: Abort, Retry, Ignore, Fail,*[7] demographers Neil Howe and William Strauss write that Gen-Xers were born between 1961–1981. This means the majority of them came of age as the social fabric of mid-century capitalism was unraveling in the 1980s and 1990s. Howe and Strauss waxed poetic on the sense that Gen-X had been born too late to enjoy the golden age of capitalism.

> *Imagine arriving at a beach at the end of a long summer of wild goings-on. The beach crowd is exhausted, the sand shopworn, hot, and full of debris. You step on a bottle, and some cop yells at you for littering. You feel the glare beating down on a barren landscape. This is how today's young people feel.*[8]

AMERICAN SIBLINGS

With a Millennial toddler sitting on his lap, Rapper Tupac Shakur once explained to an interviewer that his motto "THUG LIFE" was an acronym for "The Hate U Gave Little Infants Fucks Everybody."[9] Indeed, 1990s popular culture positioned Generation X as the deviant older sibling of Millennials. In films, television sitcoms, and cartoons, the trope of the troubled Gen-Xer was used as a cultural boogeyman. Generation X, it was feared, would pollute the purported innocence of young Millennials.

Rather than critique the socioeconomic climate that forced parents to spend more time at work, parents projected their fears onto various villains: child abductors, drug dealers, and other "bad influences" who could corrupt their unsupervised children. This culture war also involved pitting Generation X and Millennials against one another.

Many parents would not acknowledge that American neoliberalism was responsible for the destabilization of their families, and the exposure of latchkey Millennials to smutty entertainment. Instead, they made Generation X the villain in their morality play about the demise of American family values. Millennials, by the same token, were frequently positioned as a generation of gifted young heroes who needed to be shielded from bad influences.

GOOFUS VS. GALLANT

This good kid/bad kid dynamic was nothing new in American culture. First appearing in a 1948 edition of the magazine *Highlights for Children*, the "Goofus & Gallant" comic is an illustrative example:

The comic juxtaposed the valiant behavior of a child named Gallant with his sociopathic sibling Goofus. Gallant worked well with others, accepted responsibility for his shortcomings, and demonstrated a precocious level of social awareness. Goofus behaved in precisely the opposite fashion, often resorting to aggression and trickery to exploit the people in his life. In one comic from 1966, he makes a mess and leaves it for his mother to clean up.[10] In another, he "touches several cookies before choosing the one he wants."[11]

Goofus lived on as a signifier of bad behavior. A 1995 article in the *Los Angeles Times* showed that *Highlights* magazine still had a circulation of 2.6 million among its target audience of 12-and-under Millennials. If Goofus' shoddy behavior was a predecessor to the cultural framing of Generation X, then Gallant represented America's best hopes for its young Millennials:

In a 1994 episode of *Beavis and Butt-Head* titled "Patients, Patients,"[12] Beavis reads a copy of *Highlights* in the waiting room of a medical clinic. "Goofus is cool," the symbol of Generation X decadence declared.

5B

Baby Boomer popular culture is preoccupied with rites of passage. The protagonist of director Mike Nichols' 1967 film *The Graduate* is a wayward post-grad who finds his footing after a brief period of dissolution. And Bob Dylan's 1963 anthem "Blowin' in the Wind" questions masculine maturation in the cauldron of war and hard labor. When the song was placed on the soundtrack to the 1994 film *Forrest Gump*, it scored a linear story about a southern savant who lucks into military valor, corporate triumph, and pop culture immortality.

The suspense in these stories comes from the possibility that the protagonists will deviate from the path mid-century capitalism has paved for them, or die before they achieve their destiny. In each case, the advancement of the narrative coincides with a traditional rite of passage: a man joining the military, getting married, or finding a job. This dramatic trajectory was a reflection of the social stability of the golden age of capitalism. The development of the characters was tied to the transitional logic of the society they inhabited.

A LOST GENERATION

In her 2006 book *Generation Debt*, Anya Kamenetz describes five milestones of maturity: leaving home, finishing school, becoming financially independent, getting married, and having a child.[13] Kamenetz explains that the "socioeconomic upheaval of the past three decades" has resulted in mounting student debt and chronic underemployment for Americans aged 18–34. Epics like *The Graduate* and *Forrest Gump* show Baby Boomer protagonists speeding past the milestones of maturity; but many Millennials and Gen-Xers are "barely able to get out of the driveway."[14]

This generational contrast was reflected culturally. Where the march to maturity defined Baby Boomer culture, the embrace of narrative drift entered into representations of Generation X. Decentralized stories with no traditional "plot-points"[15] saturated the mainstream, as pundits painted Generation X as a "lost generation."[16]

NARRATIVE TUMBLEWEED

Two quintessential examples of Generation X drift were both released in 1991: Douglas Coupland's novel *Generation X: Tales for an Accelerated Culture*, and filmmaker Richard Linklater's feature *Slacker*. Linklater's plot-free film hovers around a single day in the world of Gen-X bohemians in Austin, Texas. The movie is composed of conversational vignettes that flow into one another. None of its characters have clear motivating actions or ambitions.

The structural entropy of *Slackers* is mirrored in Coupland's *Generation X*, whose main characters are four "refugees from history"[17] who flee steady employment and familial ties. Just as these Gen-Xers wander off the trodden path to adulthood, readers of the book are encouraged to divert their attention from the main text by Coupland's clever marginalia. The book's graphic design mirrors the Gen-X protagonists who "live marginalized lives on the periphery of society."

Much of 1990s pop culture responded to the same condition that created *Generation X* and *Slacker*. This condition was onset neoliberalism, and it included soaring costs-of-living, an uncertain economic horizon, and the anxieties of delayed adulthood. For minorities and the urban poor, these conditions were nothing new. But neoliberalism's "discovery" of dispriv- ilege as a resonant cultural template led to a slew of pop products that basked in Gen-X brokenness. Following the success of Fox's (all-Black) sitcom *Living Single* (1993–1998), NBC co-opted the show by creating (the all-White) *Friends* (1994–2004).

The latter show's theme song illuminated the dark socioeco- nomic backdrop of Generation X:

No one told you life was gonna be this way,
Your job's a joke, you're broke, your love life's D.O.A.
It's like you're always stuck in second gear,
When it hasn't been your day, your week, your month,
Or even your year.[18]

Narrative drift became a signifier of Gen-X cool in the 1990s. Storytellers attempting to capture the Gen-X condition under neoliberalism told stories about nothing. The wandering protag- onist in Joel and Ethan Coen's 1998 film *The Big Lebowski* is intro- duced alongside wayward tumbleweed in the movie's opening sequence. That same year, the last episode of the sitcom *Seinfeld* (1989–1998) aired. Each episode of that show consisted of nothing much but absurd social situations loosely tied together by lively banter about banal subjects.

In a 2014 *BuzzFeed* essay titled "Why Seinfeld is the Most Villainous Sitcom In Human History," Chuck Klosterman observes that *Seinfeld* was an insidiously nihilistic show about four self-centered, sociopathic characters. In *Seinfeld*, the setting of 1990s neoliberal New York is a silent demon that influences individuals to pursue petty power and pleasure at the expense of ethical culpability in the short-term commitments they entangled themselves in. In a 1992 episode titled "The Fix Up," character George Costanza is vehement that "hope is dangerous."[19]

The city that inspired *Seinfeld* to "celebrate meanness"[20] and chase "emotionless sex"[21] was also the city that bred the gangsta rap opus *Ready to Die* (1994). The vantage point of the album's narrator, Christopher "Notorious B.I.G." Wallace, was that of a self-described "stereotyped Black male" who refused legitimate channels of wealth accumulation in a rapidly stratifying city. Where Baby Boomer Bob Dylan's "Blowin' in the Wind" laid out the milestones of maturation, Wallace the Gen-Xer dwelled on underachievement and frustration. "I know how it feels to wake up fucked-up,"[22] raps Wallace on "Everyday Struggle"; "pockets broke as hell, another rock to sell."[23]

IN MY LIFETIME

Biggie was not alone. In 1994, Bill Clinton signed the Violent Crime Control and Law Enforcement Act, which provided $10 billion for the construction of prisons across the country.[24] The bill also ramped-up police surveillance and racial profiling. When coupled with Clinton's welfare cutbacks, the effects of this policy were devastating. Communities of color were more likely to live in neighborhoods with intense police presence, and more likely to be incarcerated for minor drug offenses.

Under these conditions, New York City rap thrived like a rose that grew from concrete. Gen-X rappers Nas and Jay Z reflected on hard times in the neoliberal metropolis in the classic albums *Illmatic* (1994) and *Reasonable Doubt* (1996). The albums languish in circular stories with squalor-set plots; the same day-to-day struggles, the same city blocks.

The year *Ready to Die* was released saw the debut of Ben Stiller's box office hit *Reality Bites*. The film begins with VHS footage of a graduating college student (played by Winona

Ryder) who delivers a blistering commencement speech. While representations of 90s power women like Hillary Clinton and Murphy Brown encouraged women to smash the glass ceiling, Ryder's character questions the value of climbing the corporate ladder at all.

And they wonder why those of us in our twenties refuse to work an eighty-hour week. Why we aren't interested in the counterculture they invented. How can we repair all the damage we inherited? Fellow graduates the answer is simple: I don't know.[25]

BROKEN GLASS, EVERYWHERE

Ryder's nonchalance was echoed in director Noah Baumbach's 1995 film *Kicking and Screaming*. The title of the movie is a reference to the fact that the film's characters are begrudgingly entering adulthood. One character has been a college undergrad for a full decade.

Kicking and Screaming winds in and out of go-nowhere vignettes and trivial conversations: during a post-baccalaureate literary seminar, a character calls attention to this aesthetic by critiquing a short story in which the "characters spend their time discussing the least important things."[26] The narrative drift at the heart of the film was a function of declining opportunities under neoliberalism: a 1990 Time/CNN poll revealed that 65% of Americans aged 18–29 agreed with the statement "It will be harder for people in my generation to live as comfortably as previous generations."[27]

Caught between the end of adolescence and an insecure adulthood, many Gen-Xers embraced an awkward interim existence. Adrift from attachment, pop culture showed them behaving in irresponsible, Goofus-esque ways. Rather than pick up a cup that has shattered on the kitchen floor, one of the college-age bros in *Kicking and Screaming* meticulously prepares a sign that says "BROKEN GLASS,"[28] and leaves the damage for someone else to repair.

THE KIDS ARE NOT ALRIGHT

The bad behavior of Baumbach's characters, the angst of Biggie's music, the nihilism of *Seinfeld*, and the nonchalance of Winona Ryder all had something in common: they fed into the worst fears Baby Boomers had for Generation X.

Generation X was born in a transitional period between the demise of one American epoch (Keynesian capitalism) and the arrival of another (neoliberalism). In the wake of this upheaval, they became a symbol of America's socioeconomic fall from grace, and its alleged moral decline. Baby Boomers brandished a negative image of Generation X to redirect socioeconomic anxieties into an attempt to save the children. Millennials were the idyllic younger siblings who needed to be protected from the corrupting influence of Generation X.

Director Larry Clark exploited America's moral panic about its youth in his disturbing 1995 film *Kids*. The 90-minute feature follows a gaggle of New York City teens as they roll blunts, fight, and have precarious sex. In the film's culminating scene, each of the (glaringly unsupervised) protagonists contracts HIV. A 20th anniversary retrospective about the film opined that "*Kids* represented a culmination of fears for cultural alarmists of the Clinton era."[29] In her 1995 review of the movie, Janet Maslin captured the generational interplay between Generation X and Millennials:

> *The very saddest of the lost characters in* Kids *are the little brothers, seen here sampling drugs, trying to keep up with the tough talk. They've barely reached puberty and are already drifting into the older boys' decadent extremes.*[30]

5C

Popular culture in the 1990s depicted the decadence of Generation X. The corollary to this narrative of moral decline was the depiction of child Millennials as gifted young heroes who would use their precocious talents to save society.

The Simpsons traced the template for this relationship between American siblings. Bart Simpson was a Generation X stand-in; a "focus for a moral panic about youth rebellion"[31] in America. In one episode, he hits his father over the head with a wooden chair after seeing a similar stunt performed by a professional wrestler; in so doing, he reinforced the popular notion that kids' intake of violent imagery needed to be policed. Lisa Simpson, by contrast, is a precocious 8-year-old with a demonstrated social sensitivity. She's a devout vegetarian, is civically engaged despite being too young to vote, and has an IQ of 159.[32] Her ostentatious intellect is what policy wonks had in mind for Millennials when they implemented reforms based on *A Nation at Risk*.

In his 2006 study *Watching with The Simpsons*, Jonathan Gray writes that "the hero's role in the sitcom version of nuclear family is to overcome villainy and affirm the strength of the family unit in overcoming all obstacles."[33] In this framework, Lisa is the hero of *The Simpsons*. The work of correcting Bart's excesses falls in her lap. When Bart turns their coauthored news program into a platform for base demagoguery in a 1998 episode called "Girly Edition,"[34] Lisa makes it her mission to expose him. As an adult in the 2000 episode "Bart to the Future," Lisa fixes the aftermath of a then-fictional Donald Trump presidency.

A bright, young Millennial, Lisa is the symbolic counterbalance to her sibling Bart's Gen-X shiftlessness. Both representations had a place on the battlefield of the American culture wars.

WE CAN BE HEROES

The process of Millennial myth-making seen in *The Simpsons* has deep roots in the way Americans have understood generations.

Generational theorists Neil Howe and William Strauss coined the term "Millennials," and applied it to Americans born between 1982–2004. In their 1991 book *Generations: The History of America's*

Future, they explained that Millennials were an archetypal hero generation whose job was to steward America through a series of crisis points, and onto a new high. Generation X, on the other hand, was framed by Howe-Strauss as a cohort of problem children who were born during a great unraveling of the American social fabric. As socioeconomic anxieties mounted in the last decade of the 20th century, the tendency to exorcise societal frustrations with unflattering portrayals of Gen-X intensified—as did the tendency to cast Millennials as a hero generation.

In 1990, cultural critic Fredric Jameson wrote that American cinema is a form of "compensatory wish-fulfillment."[35] Ever since they entered the American cultural mainstream during the Great Depression, movies have projected solutions to economic downturn and social instability. Shirley Temple rose to prominence as a child star in the 1930s during the deepest crisis the country had faced since the Civil War. Sixty years later, young Millennials in the mold of Lisa Simpson were made to solve the various malaises of American neoliberalism.

MILLENNIAL HERO NARRATIVES

The 1991 film *Curly Sue* is a quintessential Millennial hero narrative. Alisan Porter is cast in the film's titular role. Her curled locks and sassy mannerisms clearly allude to Shirley Temple. A completely illiterate transient, she dispenses ahead-of-her-years advice to her parents, and becomes a symbol of the untapped potential of America's poor children.

Sue's mother has died in the film's backstory. She roams the streets of Chicago with her adopted father. The two perform petty hustles to afford shelter and fast food, and their greatest heist comes when Sue uses her street smarts to defraud a corporate lawyer into providing her and her dad a place to stay. The film then leverages sympathies towards child poverty into an oddly patriotic celebration of the free market:

Lofty liberal government is explicitly cast in the film as corrupt and unable to understand the on-the-ground complications of private life, while social welfare takes place only in the feedback loops of financial success and generous philanthropy. In an angry rant, Sue's dad decries the "arm's length social reform" of do-gooder liberals. In another scene, Sue—unattended in front of the television—recites "The Star-Spangled Banner" that plays at the start of a Chicago Cubs game. At the anthem's crescendo, her belting voice echoes out of the halls and onto the desolate Windy City streets where Sue used to grovel for spare change. The rousing sequence places the burden of celebrating America on a young Millennial who has been utterly failed by it.

Inculcating young Millennials into supporting American capitalism started in the 1980s. The movie *Top Gun*, the television show *G.I. Joe*, and the video game *Contra* were Reagan-era capitalist propaganda. They promoted neoliberal notions of law and order to young Millennials at a time when law enforcement and the military were practically the only social programs seen as worthy of public support. The 1993 film *Cop and a Half* continued this cultural programming:

Cop and a Half follows an 8-year-old Black Millennial named Devon Butler. Butler is raised by his grandmother, who routinely leaves him home alone so she can work the nightshift as a nurse. A latchkey kid, Butler spends his spare time watching television. He is so influenced by reruns of the police procedural *Miami Vice* (1984–1992) that he gets scolded at school because he tries to discipline other children. Butler becomes an actual police officer when he extorts a local precinct into giving him a job. As a cop, he patches up domestic disputes and is instrumental in solving a high-profile murder case. As in *Curly Sue*, the Millennial hero narrative of *Cop and a Half* makes a young Millennial responsible for solving social ills—domestic abuse, street violence, organized crime—that were created before we were even out of the womb.

In the 1990s, American cities like Tampa, Florida—where *Cop and a Half* takes place—were ravished by neoliberalism. Deindustrialization, union busting, and depressed wages stoked the social pathologies of crime and unemployment. In his 1996 book *When Work Disappears*,[36] scholar William Julius Wilson described how communities hit hardest by socioeconomic downturn were forced to create opportunities through increasingly niche ways. Millennial hero narratives auditioned children to alleviate this condition. The films *Free Willy* (1993) and *Angels in the Outfield* (1994) both featured Millennial child protagonists who resurrected towns that had fallen on hard times:

Free Willy was set in Astoria, Oregon. In the 1980s, the city suffered greatly when the local Bumblebee tuna cannery liquidated thousands of jobs and closed shop. To generate revenue and attention, Astoria was forced to cultivate a cultural tourist industry; a process that included courting the film production *Free Willy*, in the hopes that it would provide local jobs and national visibility for the struggling community.[37]

Oregon's neighbor to the south, California, was hit so hard by the housing bubble crash of 1991 that Bill Clinton appointed a special advisor to deal specifically with reviving the economy of towns like Anaheim,[38] which shed thousands of construction jobs in the crisis.[39] While the Disney-produced film *Angels in the Outfield* was still in theatres, Disney purchased the actual California Angels, then coerced desperate Anaheim taxpayers into paying for the team's new stadium on the dubious promise that it would generate jobs.[40]

NEOLIBERAL FAIRYTALES

Both *Free Willy* and *Angels in the Outfield* made young Millennials responsible for revitalizing their struggling West Coast towns.

The child protagonist of *Free Willy* is a panhandling Millennial named Jesse who lives in an abandoned warehouse in Astoria, Oregon. Jesse has no blood family in his life, but sees himself in the familial loyalty of Orca whales. He refuses to let a local theme park commercialize his relationship with Willy the whale, despite the fact that the struggling town of Astoria was exploiting the sentimental narrative of *Free Willy* for its own commercial gain.

Angels in the Outfield, meanwhile, centers a hero Millennial named Roger who uses prayer to help a baseball team win games so they can remain in Anaheim and "create jobs." In the opening credit sequence, Roger rides through a ramshackle neighborhood with abandoned houses and a closed-down factory. *Angels in the Outfield* asks us to believe that appealing to angels—and not the creation of a federal jobs program—will solve this city's problems.

Free Willy and *Angels in the Outfield* are neoliberal fairytales. They only offer personal and sentimental solutions for political and structural problems. Like *Curly Sue* and *Cop and a Half*, their emotional appeal is based on employing child protagonists to save the world. But these films never ask why America was in such bad shape in the first place. Nor are the young Millennials at the center of these hero narratives allowed to grow into anything more than problem solvers for complacent parents.

THE DRAMA OF THE GIFTED CHILD

As Roxane Gay writes in her 2014 book *Bad Feminist*, "heroism is a burden. Heroes sacrifice their bodies and hearts and minds because heroism means the complete denial of the self."[41] In each 1990s Millennial hero narrative, youngsters put themselves in harm's way to save the broken world of their parents. The country they worked to save never rewards their efforts:

Despite having no reason to believe in the creed of capitalism, Curly Sue is a heroic arbiter of wholesome family values. "The proper way to start a family is with marriage," she cautions, instead of, say, decrying systemic poverty. And while Hillary Clinton was calling Black children "superpredators"[42] in 1994, Devon Butler was working overtime to keep Tampa's streets safe in *Cop and a Half*. Millennial hero narratives were not made to show children on a path to self-actualization—they were made to help adults feel better about passing their problems off to the next generation. In a nightmare scenario for any child of divorced parents, the 1998 film *The Parent Trap* outrageously makes a pair of Millennial twins responsible for repairing their parents' failed marriage.

The message of these films is clear: Make a mess. The kids will fix it.

All the while, as psychologist Alice Miller described in her book *The Drama of the Gifted Child* (first published in English in 1981 and reprinted in 1997), Millennials were growing up to be a generation plagued by imposter syndrome and anxiety; kids whose parents' unreasonable expectations were driving us to unsustainable heights of productivity followed by the inevitable crash of capitalist realism: resources are scarce; space among the elite is limited; and in the race to separate gifted kids from the pack of problem children, someone's child will be left behind. Adults fear it will be theirs.

Was the love that paternal/maternal capitalism had for young Millennials unconditional, or contingent on our performative achievement in youth athletics, talent shows, and science fairs? Shouldn't a country allocate resources to the welfare of its children simply because the future *en masse* is worth investing in, and not on the cruel and arbitrary basis of demonstrated "genius"? The mania for finding gifted children and heroes among the young was a way of legitimating brutal austerity measures that elevated 'exceptional' children while snuffing out the fortunes of others before they ever had a chance to flower.

THE PARENT TRAP

In the 1990s, Generation X was the symbol of this failed society. In mass media, they were made to represent all that had gone wrong since the demise of mid-20th century stability. Parents elected Millennials as a moral corrective. Millennial hero narratives like *Cop and a Half* and *Angels in the Outfield* allowed previous generations the luxury of sitting back, pressing play, and watching prepubescents solve poverty, crime, divorce, and unemployment. This required no civic investment in education — just a child's innate genius.

But Millennial hero narratives did not undo the straits of American neoliberalism, any more than Shirley Temple undid the Great Depression. Despite attempts to nominate young Millennials as a generation of *pro bono* social workers, America on the eve of the new millennium was still a country beset by socioeconomic insecurity. No amount of vilifying Generation X or valorizing Millennials could change this.

The cartoon *Captain Planet and the Planeteers* (1990–1996) showed a diverse team of Generation X and Millennial youngsters co-conspiring to rescue the planet from global warning. The show's celebration of "five special young people" was a rare positive portrayal of Gen-X, and a typical placement of Millennials on a pedestal. But as it became clear in the 21st century that America's gifted children needed a little help ushering in utopia, the narrative about Millennials began to change. Once heroic and talented, we were suddenly coddled and entitled. Formerly wise beyond our years, critics now complain that we refuse to grow up. In the space of a few short years, Millennials have become as much of a symbol of American decay as Gen-Xers once were.

Nonetheless, there was a time when our parents did paint us as pariahs — a period when, history will remember, we could have been heroes.

Chapter 6

Back To Work for the American People

For all the talk about Millennial adults being entitled and spoiled, we do a lot of work without pay. Interns and artists give their labor away for the "experience" and the "exposure." Temps labor for a portion of what their fulltime counterparts are paid. And freelancers do not enjoy the benefits packages reserved for employees. Meanwhile, Facebook and Twitter are social factories of memes and trends; assembly lines of cultural commentary that spectators pluck from, free of charge.

The morning after major cultural events like the Super Bowl and the Grammys, news websites often publish clickbait "articles" that are little more than litanies of jokes and gifs collected from Millennial tricksters on Twitter. International House of Pancakes and Denny's have used the compliment "on fleek" in their ad campaigns; the phrase was coined by Peaches Monroe, a Black Millennial who was not paid for this contribution to pop culture. As writer Doreen St. Felix pointed out in a December 2015 article in *The Fader* titled "Black Teens are Breaking the Internet And Seeing None of the Profits," Millennial creatives are accustomed to not seeing any of the ad revenue generated by their labor.

But without Millennials who convey cultural currency on social networking websites, capitalism would be in the dark about what's considered cool. Heavily tracked, targeted, and monetized, Facebook and Twitter are consumer focus groups that never finish; a medium where Millennials do the R&D work of major corporations without compensation.

WHAT A TIME TO BE ALIVE

Tech and hip-hop are the dominant cultural tributaries of the

Millennial generation; ever-flowing founts of fashionable language (slang), lifestyles (the sharing economy), and comedy. The number of popular hashtags on Twitter that are traceable to rap is too many to list in full: #YOLO, #swag, #squad, #NoNewFriends, #Lit, to name a few. An abbreviation of Drake and Future's 2015 mixtape *What A Time To Be Alive*, #WATTBA is used to tag stories and insights that highlight life in late capitalism. "To put the times in perspective," Twitter user @siyamali tweeted on one such tag on February 20, 2017, "I get annoyed when public transit doesn't have working wi-fi."

DOUBLE HELIX

Once upon a time in the mid-20th century, it was cinema and jazz—not the Internet and hip-hop—that were the prevailing cultural modes of capitalism's golden age. The two media were a creative double helix that provided the 'hip' lingo, images of glamor, and lifestyle expectations that defined the post-WWII period:

The film *The Man in the Gray Flannel Suit* (1956) displayed the gender roles of male breadwinners and their domesticated female counterparts under Keynesian capitalism. The prosperity of this period was predicated on constant military mobilization, and movies helped coax the public into supporting the Cold War: the James Bond franchise debuted in 1962 with the film *Dr. No*, a harrowing tale of international espionage. By producing propaganda films like *Why We Fight* (1942), Hollywood helped manufacture pro-capitalist sentiment.

Jazz was equally instrumental to capitalism's propagandistic pitch. Sponsored by the U.S. State Department, American composers performed benefit concerts to discourage developing countries from embracing socialism. Duke Ellington's stellar 1967 album *Far East Suite* was the result of one such tour. Blacks were deprived of basic civil rights in the 1960s; but the government's embrace of their music allowed America to seem tolerant. Louis

Armstrong's permanent grin was advertised worldwide as a sign that everything was alright.

Domestically, jazz scored America's happy march to post-WWII prosperity. The albums *Take Five* (1959) and *Kind of Blue* (1959) conveyed sophistication to an increasingly suburban population that craved entertainment with an edge.[1] "Crime jazz" emerged as a subgenre in the 1950s, describing the moody instrumentals that backed the murder mystery *Elevator to the Gallows* (1958) and the courtroom procedural *Anatomy of a Murder* (1959).

In tandem, cinema and jazz captured mid-century capitalism's cultural logic—the social order's tenants of paternalism and collaboration:

Directors John Ford and Alfred Hitchcock were the counterparts of capitalist patriarchs Henry Ford and Thomas Watson. As an industry that thrived on unionized labor and easily replicable creative formulas, film was a metaphor for America's industrial heyday. In the same era, Miles Davis and John Coltrane were masters of jazz because of their sensitivity to the collective dynamics of performance; similarly, the golden age of capitalism was a fragile consensus between big business, organized labor, and the federal government.[2]

GIANT STEPS

Jazz and cinema reflected the controlled spontaneity of mid-century industrial capitalism.[3] Times changed. The collapse of the studio system, the rising popularity of Polaroids, and the advent of VHS meant that the once-mystified process of image-making was being wrested from the hands of directors in the 70s. And the deaths of Duke Ellington (1899–1974) and Louis Armstrong (1901–1971) coincided with a marked decline in jazz's marketability. Jazz and cinema did not cease to exist in the 1970s. But because of deindustrialization, they no longer captured capitalism's cultural logic as completely as they once did. Hip-hop and personal computing took their place.

PAID IN FULL

"If blues culture developed under the conditions of oppressive labor," writes journalist Jeffrey Chang, "hip-hop culture would arise from the conditions of no work."[4] In deindustrialized areas from the South Bronx to Compton, hip-hop represented populations consigned to a policy of "benign neglect."[5] As the 1970s turned into the 1980s, rapping and DJ'ing created employment and wealth where none existed.

Eric B. and Rakim graced the cover of their 1987 album *Paid in Full* gripping fat stacks of green cash. The gold chains and champagne flaunted by LL Cool J were displayed in the same decade that spawned the television show *Lifestyles of the Rich and Famous* (1984–1995). With the television show *Yo! MTV Raps* (1988–1995), hip-hop slang and fashion became ubiquitous by the turn of the decade, as crossover acts MC Hammer and Vanilla Ice pimped the culture for maximum profit.

HIP-HOP NATION

Rap matured in the 1980s by corroborating the "greed is good" ethic of Oliver Stone's 1987 film *Wall Street*. In the 1990s, the music achieved unprecedented commercial success. Rap became the best-selling genre of music in 1998, pushing 70% of its product to White listeners. In 1999, Lauryn Hill landed on the cover of *Time Magazine* with the headline "Hip-Hop Nation."[6] The same year in the song "We Will Survive," New York rapper Nas reflected on hip-hop's improbable rise. "We in the 90s, and finally it's looking good," rhymed Nas; "hip-hop took it to billions, I knew we would."

HOW YOU LIKE THEM APPLES?

The development of hip-hop was tied to tech. During a blackout in New York City in the summer of 1977, looters raided electronic stores, taking turntables and drum machines back home, then selling them at a discount to neighborhood musicians. This boon of technology accelerated rap music's maturation in the Big Apple in 1977, making it a flashpoint in hip-hop history. That same year, the computer company Apple incorporated in Cupertino, California.

WHAT A FEELING

The technology behind personal computing and the Internet were pioneered when the mid-century welfare state provided American universities generous research grants. With Atari game consoles and the arcade games *Pong* and *Pac-Man*, the public rollout of digital technology occurred alongside deindustrialization in the 1970s and early 1980s. Forecasters painted tech as a force that could control-alt-delete the working class. But it was not until computers were branded as a teaching tool that they became a battleground in the culture wars.

Like rap, computers' appeal to kids is what made them dangerous—and also lucrative. In a 1983 promotional video featuring the hit single "What a Feeling" from the film *Flashdance* (1983), Apple marketed its Macintosh desktop as a teaching tool that could engage youngsters and save teachers time. The launch of the Internet in the next decade intensified fears that unattended young Millennials would seek out dirty pictures. Indeed, the Internet's arrival coincided with a porn renaissance: the 1996 biopic *The People vs. Larry Flynt* dramatized *Hustler Magazine*'s struggle against America's obscenity laws. Not to be outdone, the 1997 film *Boogie Nights* lauded the glory days of 1970s porn.

1997 also saw the Diamond Entertainment Corporation release the infomercial *Kids' Guide to the Internet*.[7] In the video, two parents leave their children unattended in front of the computer. When the father returns, he warns that "the Internet is not a regulated environment. Set up your Microsoft browser to only accept G-rated websites."

PARENTAL ADVISORY, EXPLICIT CONTENT

When parents wanted to police the eyes of young Millennials, they condemned the Internet. When they wanted to police our *ears*, they criticized hip-hop:

Miami rap group 2 Live Crew's 1989 album *As Nasty As They Wanna Be* flaunted songs with titles like "Me So Horny" and "Dick Almighty." In 1990, it was deemed legally obscene. Thanks to Second Lady Tipper Gore,[8] young Millennials got used to album covers with the alarmist label "Parental Advisory, Explicit Content" starting in 1996. Meanwhile, niche genres of smut proliferated online: snuff films, foot fetishism, historical rape fantasy, and more.

CASH RULES EVERYTHING AROUND YOU

On the surface, hip-hop and personal computing contradicted the wholesome mores and family values of the cultural conservatives who supported neoliberal policies. But no two industries were better utensils of neoliberalism than rap and the Internet:

The feud between Puff Daddy's Bad Boy Records and Suge Knight's Death Row Records amounted to a conflict between materialist millionaires who refused a peace-keeping merger; the hip-hop version of Microsoft vs. Apple. And for all his branding as a rap revolutionary, Tupac Shakur was a commercial spokesperson for St. Ides malt liquor.[9] At the same time, personal computing—as a means of production—became a staple industry of neoliberalism. Gone were the rigid days of reliable hours, clock-punching, and generous pensions which defined work in the golden age of capitalism. At startups like Amazon, exploited workers were expected to maintain open-ended schedules and constant availability, or else be ruthlessly replaced.[10]

Describing sample-based music made possible by digital technology, music critic Ann Powers has written that America's "ruling cultural metaphor is the network."[11] Social networks of laborers find leads for jobs on LinkedIn; and teams of freelancers commute digitally between gigs with clients on the cloud. Sociologist Richard Sennett described this new era of capitalism in 1998, saying that "the speed of modern communications has favored flexible specialization. In a large bureaucratic pyramid, by contrast, decision-making can slow down."[12] As Jonathan Crary surmises in *24/7: Late Capitalism and the Ends of Sleep*, rest is a luxury that many can't afford as capitalism moves at the speed of light. "I don't know how to sleep, I gotta eat, stay on my toes," rapped Jay Z in his 1998 hit "Hard Knock Life."

DIGITAL DASH

When Millennials reached adulthood, we stepped into this new world of work. Our music spoke to our condition, with hip-hop's hustler ethos pushing us to persevere past fatigue and failure. Materialistic and repetitive, the "Trap" genre of rap stylizes the monotony of low-wage labor that many Millennials are stuck in as students, unpaid interns, and workers in the informal economy who worry about runaway costs of living and rising rents. "I hustle the 1st to the 1st," complains Millennial rapper Future on "Digital Dash," a track from the mixtape *What A Time To Be Alive*.

6B

Rap and the Internet were not the only media that culture warriors attempted to censor in the 1990s. Born-again Christian and anti-obscenity crusader Jack Thompson rose to prominence by litigating a wide spectrum of villains who "peddled obscenity to children."[13] Thompson was the mastermind behind the legal condemnation of 2 Live Crew. Inspired by the 1989 film *Batman*, Thompson taunted his opponents by mailing them pictures of the winged crime-fighter;[14] that list of opponents included makers of the gory video game *Doom* and the racy film *The Basketball Diaries*

(1995), which Thompson alleged inspired a school shooting in Kentucky's Heath High School in 1997.[15]

THE LEFT FLANK OF THE CULTURE WARS

A self-professed "radical conservative Republican,"[16] Thompson was an archetypal culture warrior who spoke for conservative parents' groups, teachers' associations, and grandstanding politicians across the country.

But neoliberalism was a radical theoretical shift that also implicated Democrats and progressives. "The reinvention of left-wing politics in the 1990s," write Pierre Dardot and Christian Laval in their book *The New Way of the World*, "was only the most striking example of the domination of the new neoliberal rationality."[17] In the 1990s, Arkansas Democrat Bill Clinton won two presidential elections by echoing the rhetoric of "family values" and "personal responsibility" that Republicans perfected in the 1980s. At the center of his electoral success was the concern he showed for monitoring the images and sounds that America's young Millennials were exposed to.

In his 1996 electoral contest against Bob Dole, Clinton painted Dole as a purveyor of tobacco ads aimed at young Millennials.[18] Once elected to a second term, he denounced emaciated models like Kate Moss in the fashion industry's "heroin chic"[19] advertisements, which he accused of glorifying drug addiction. Clinton also criticized the pedophilic overtones of many Calvin Klein ads. With his endearing southern accent and sunny disposition, he represented himself as a compassionate culture warrior concerned about the country's young Millennials.

A TURNCOAT IN THE CULTURE WARS

Clinton's 90s speeches are filled with optimistic millenarian chatter about providing America's youth with a "bridge to the 21st century."[20] But Clinton was as responsible as anyone for subjecting Millennials to drugs, violence, and sex. As the president who famously went on MTV in 1994 to answer whether he wore boxers or briefs, he often exposed himself in ways that contradicted his stated aims.

Bill Clinton may have opposed Calvin Klein's glamorization of drug addiction. But this did not stop him from presiding over a spike in pharmaceutical ads that were aimed directly at consumers of all ages in the 1990s:

With the Reagan administration in the 1980s, pharmaceutical companies enjoyed a climate of deregulation that enabled them to push state-sanctioned drugs on the American public.[21] Clinton caved to the pharmaceutical lobby, opting to continue Reagan's deregulatory regime for American media: this led to the rise of "direct-to-consumer advertising" (DTCA)[22] for drugs. Ads for Rogaine, Prozac, and Viagra soon saturated television, which unattended young Millennials watched an average of 24 hours a week of in the 1990s.[23] By 1998, pharmaceutical companies were spending $1.3 billion on DTCA; up a staggering 2300% from 1991.[24]

On the 1992 campaign trail, Clinton castigated rapper Sister Souljah for making racially incendiary statements during riots that gripped Los Angeles in the wake of Rodney King's beating of 1991.[25] But Clinton was not a racially reconciliatory president. His policies disproportionately condemned nonviolent Black criminals to a separate fate from their White counterparts: In 1994, Clinton's Violent Crime Control and Law Enforcement Act allocated $10 billion for the construction of prisons. A 2001 Department of Justice report concluded that America's "prison population rose more under Clinton than any other president."[26] In 2015, even Clinton admitted his crime bill "cast too wide a net."[27]

Bill Clinton advocated a "V-Chip"[28] which would do the work of parents in censoring violence and obscenity on television. But this did not stop him from contributing to a climate of economic insecurity that led parents to spend more time at work. By making wage growth the prerogative of private industry and not substantive federal legislation, Clinton left wages up to the whims of the market.[29] Even with the paltry minimum wage hikes of the 1990s, real wages (the value of pay relative to the price of living and the tide of productivity) languished.[30]

Meanwhile, Clinton's welfare reform forced many parents to pick up part-time work in an economy that Alan Greenspan described as "persistently insecure"[31] in 1997. The net result of Clinton's economic record was a world where a surrogate network of schools, technology, and pop culture raised the children of always-at-work parents.

PORNOGRAPHER-IN-CHIEF

There was an irony about Bill Clinton's concern that young Millennials were being flashed obscene images on television and the Internet: namely, the fact that there was no bigger boon to the public's pornographic imagination than Clinton himself:

In 1995, a radically hostile Republican majority in the U.S. Senate froze all funds to the federal government. In the resulting government shutdown, the White House was forced to lay off dozens of salaried workers. They hired low-pay interns in their place—one of whom was a 22-year-old California native named Monica Lewinsky. Bill Clinton began a series of extramarital trysts with Lewinsky in the period spanning November 1995 to March 1997.[32] Once revealed, the lurid details of Clinton's private shortcomings became the public butt of pop culture comedy.

A 1998 edition of David Letterman's nightly "Top Ten" segment quipped that "Give me all your hot intern love" would be the first line of Lewinsky's hypothetical Harlequin Romance novel.[33] In March of 1998, the struggling talk show *Late Night with Conan O'Brien* was resurrected when O'Brien tackled the subject with a recurring gag called "The President in Crisis," in which a voice actor performs an uproarious impersonation of Clinton, popping Viagra and lying through his teeth about the affair.[34]

Also in 1998, Portland Radio station Z100 released a parody of The Notorious B.I.G's hit single "Mo Money, Mo Problems," retitling the song "Mo Booty, Mo Problems," and having a spirited Clinton imitator perform exclaim, "The GOP will never nail my butt,/ and speakin of butt, guess what I'm havin for lunch!"[35]

As millions of Millennials were hitting puberty in the 1990s, Clinton assured that we were awash in jokes about blowjobs, sperm-stained dresses, and cigar-aided cunnilingus.

FAMILY VALUES

Clinton was a family values Democrat in the culture wars. He could not afford to cede his territory as a moral authority. So he clung to his innocence vociferously, first denying his affair with Lewinsky in a White House speech on January 26th, 1998.[36] His performance was legendary. Eyes narrowed and voice strained, Clinton was vehement that he was being falsely accused. He punctuated his syllables with aggressive thumps on the podium, his tight fist and erect index finger driving the message home. *I did not. Have. Sexual. Relations. With that woman, Miss Lewinsky.*

BACK TO WORK FOR THE AMERICAN PEOPLE

Few recall the full context of that speech.[37] Sensing his own political vulnerability, Clinton preceded his deception with a policy speech about his "10-point-plan" to bolster education for young Millennials. Clinton could have called a press conference to affirm or deny the Lewinsky rumors outright. Instead, he calculatedly used his concern for Millennials kids as political cover.

"Tomorrow, in the State of the Union Address," began Clinton, "I will spell out what we seek to do on behalf of our children to prepare them for the 21st century."[38] Clinton then launched into a description of the Millennial latchkey condition under neoliberalism. His words echoed the 1993 Crash Test

Dummies single "Mmm Mmm Mmm Mmm," which features a verse about a young Millennial whose parents "made him come directly home after school":

> *Every child needs someplace to go after school. The hours between 3 and 7 at night are the most vulnerable hours for young people to get in trouble, for juvenile crime. Most of the kids that get in trouble [do so] before their parents get home from work. So in the adolescent years, it is important to give kids something positive to do.*[39]

Clinton concluded his remarks by exclaiming his pressing need to "go back to work for the American people." In so doing he was one of scores of parents who left young Millennials home alone to parse through what they saw in American media in the 1990s.

6C

I remember watching Bill Clinton's famous proclamation at home, alone, in front of the television. It was a familiar place to be. After my parents joined the burgeoning ranks of divorced or separated parents in the late 1980s, I moved to Seattle with my father in the spring of 1992. We were poor.

Growing up, my most prized memories were memories themselves: the endless parade of pop culture moments that were beamed into our little living room while my father was at work. Teenage Mutant Ninja Turtle action figures, Super Soaker water guns, and Pog milk-cap slammers were among the consumer goods that commercials on TV made me crave. So was the VHS for the 1990 film *Home Alone*—a Millennial hero narrative featuring a latchkey kid who saves the family home from a pair of burglars.

LITTLE TOWN, BIG TRAGEDY

I was home alone one fateful day in April of 1999 when news broke of a school shooting in a town I had never heard of. From that day forward, Columbine High School near Littleton, Colorado became the global signpost of a conversation about access to guns.

Because the massacre's perpetrators were a couple of near-Millennials who played the video game *Doom*, culture warriors seized the opportunity to beat their anti-obscenity drums: "What you are doing [by playing these games]," said Jack Thompson of the purported link between violent games and violent acts, "is rehearsing your physical revenge and violence against those whom you have been victimized by. And then you, like Klebold and Harris in Columbine, become the ultimate bully."[40]

DADDIES DIDN'T GIVE ATTENTION, MOMMIES DIDN'T CARE

Culture warriors were quick to castigate bad influences. But they did not call attention to the cause of the latchkey condition that exposed Millennials to these influences. Had Jack Thompson or Bill Clinton or Slade Gorton been really concerned about America's youth, they would not have stopped at criticizing violent video games or obscene music. They would have advocated for an increase in the federal minimum wage that could have allowed one or both parents to spend more time at home with their children. Culture warriors also could have advocated for paid sick, maternity, or paternity leave for America's parents. Or they could have expanded welfare benefits that would have put less pressure on parents to work part-time jobs or overtime. These programs could have been paid for by a higher corporate tax rate on billion-dollar companies like Nike and Calvin Klein.

But instead, culture warriors paid lip service to "family values," while sequestering the resources that these families would need to succeed. As Sydney Lewis wrote in her 1996 book *A Totally Alien Life-Form*, "The phrase 'family values' has been trotted out to denounce and defend all sorts of public policy agendas. It sounds surreal when falling from the lips of those who eviscerate the long-standing social safety nets that children rely on."[41]

The events that took place at Columbine High School on April 19th, 1999 were unspeakably tragic. They were also preventable. Michael Moore's 2002 film *Bowling for Columbine* portrays just how easy it was for unsupervised youths to access guns and ammo at Wal-Mart. Dylann Roof—a Millennial who gunned-down nine Black worshippers in a Charleston church in the summer of 2015—walked in their violent footsteps.

In their 1992 single "Jeremy," Seattle-bred rock band Pearl Jam was already calling attention to the plight of neglected young Millennials whose "daddies didn't give attention"[42] and whose "mommies didn't care."[43] In the song's narrative, Jeremy ends up shooting himself in front of his class. The attorney of a 16-year-old school shooter in Moses Lake, Washington claimed his client acted under the influence of the song "Jeremy" in 1996.

A (CULTURE) WAR ON YOUTH

Culture warriors pretended to fight for decency. In reality, they were waging war on the fortunes of America's future adults. With no formidable foes to fight abroad, culture warriors wielded their Cold War worldview onto Millennials and members of Generation X. "Some of the same resources once directed against an external Evil Empire," wrote Neil Howe and William Strauss, "are now being used against the generation coming of age. 300 FBI agents who once tracked foreign spies are now sleuthing around inner-city neighborhoods. And military bases are being retooled into prisons."[44]

In her 1998 book *A Tribe Apart*, Patricia Hersch adds that "over the years, the tone of discourse on adolescents has become shrill and frightened." Hersch continued:

Increasingly desperate attempts to understand adolescents fragment them into pieces of behavior that are "good" or "bad." Theories abound on how to fix them, as if they were products off an assembly line: just tinker with the educational system, manipulate the drug messages, impose citywide curfews, build more detention centers, be tough.[45]

MILLENNIAL ANGST

In the autumn of 1999, I watched on television as private security forces manhandled protestors—many of whom were teenagers and young adults—who objected to the WTO trade agreement that offshored tens of thousands of American jobs. WTO was one in a series of 1990s measures that—along with NAFTA and Clinton's repeal of Glass-Steagall—instituted a state of economic insecurity among the American middle class.

At the time, I did not understand the politics behind the WTO protests. But I identified with their angst. As Millennial kids, we were caught in an age cohort that adults wanted to be gifted children who over-achieved academically despite the fact that our schools were given fewer and fewer resources to succeed. The cartoon *Daria* (1997–2001) captured this condition.

A spin-off of *Beavis and Butt-Head*, *Daria* follows an alienated young Millennial in the titular role. Born in 1984, Daria Morgendorffer is a perpetually misunderstood high school student. Her aloof parents rely on hollow rituals and token praise to compensate for the negative effects that their career-centeredness has had on the family. Cut from the same precocious cloth as Lisa Simpson, Daria is more mature than the doting adults who don't know what to make of her intelligence:

"I don't have low self-esteem," Daria says when her parents send her to therapy. "I have low esteem for everyone else."[46]

Cartoon Network replicated the success of *Beavis and Butt-Head* and *Daria* with *South Park*, which follows a quartet of irreverent Millennial elementary school students. The show fictionalizes the upbringing of its main animator—Matt Stone—who once lived in Littleton and attended Columbine High School. As Stone's incendiary show earned the scorn of American culture warriors, it contributed to a post-Columbine climate that saw young Millennials—in the words of Michael Moore's documentary *Bowling for Columbine*—as "ticking time bombs."[47]

MISDIRECTED ANXIETIES

But in the last analysis of the 1980s and 1990s, Americans did not have to fear young Millennials, Generation X, or obscenity. They did not have to fear that young Millennials were growing to grow up lazy and stupid, as *A Nation at Risk* would have them believe. They did not have to fear foul language from Gen-X rebels like 2 Live Crew or Nirvana or *Beavis and Butt-Head*, as culture warriors would have them believe. And they did not have to fear missing out on the latest consumer craze, as Pepsi, the Spice Girls, or Lisa Frank would have them believe. On the eve of the new millennium, what Americans really had to fear was the runaway neoliberal status quo.

Americans, in the words of Chuck Klosterman, "failed to comprehend how they were trapped by the same system they supported."[48] Unwilling to face reality, Americans became infatuated with the disaster scenario of the "Y2K" bug. As Fredric Jameson once noted, "it's easier to imagine the end of the world than it is to imagine the end of capitalism."[49]

EXTINCTION LEVEL EVENT

But the arrival of the new millennium did not lead to the extinction level event that rapper Busta Rhymes predicted in his December 1998 album of the same name.[50] The cover of *Extinction Level Event* showed New York City engulfed in a spectacular plumage of fire and smoke. Two years later in their 2000 book *Millennials Rising*, Neil Howe and William Strauss wrote that the Columbine Massacre was the defining event of our generation. As of 8:45AM Eastern Standard Time on September 11th, 2001, their analysis was still correct.

A 15-year-old Millennial, I watched the curtain close on the 20th century in my hometown of New York City. In the shadow of the Twin Towers, I harbored a secret desire that the Y2K bug would obliterate my high school's academic records, and give me a reset on a school year where I was failing every class I was enrolled in besides P.E. and Creative Writing.

It was a cold night in lower Manhattan.

Part III: YOUNG ADULTHOOD

(2001–2011)

Destruction is a form of creation.
–Dialogue from the film *Donnie Darko* (2001).

Chapter 7

Live From Ground Zero

In 1989, the American recording industry conspired to release all albums on Tuesdays. No one knows exactly why.

Some have said that *Billboard* is to blame: the music magazine published its charts on Wednesdays, meaning that an album released on Tuesday could tally a full seven days of sales before being ranked alongside the competition. Others have estimated that the recording industry's institution of Tuesday releases was designed to protect vulnerable record stores. "One retailer might get an album on Monday morning," says Keith Caulfield, co-director of charts at *Billboard* in 2015; "but, a store a couple blocks down the road may not have got their shipment."[1]

Whatever the reason for their institution, record-release Tuesdays were a treasured day on the American pop culture landscape; a day when now-defunct stores like Sam Goody and Tower Records would be filled with eager consumers. September 11th, 2001 was one such Tuesday. The batch of albums released on 9/11 included work from headliners Mariah Carey and Slayer, as well as emerging rapper Fabolous. But no matter the status of the artist, their oeuvre was likely to be available illicitly on the Internet.

HIJACKED

In 1999, a couple of Gen-Xers named Shawn Fanning and Sean Parker founded Napster, a peer-to-peer downloading client that allowed anyone with a computer and an Internet connection to share and download music files. Replete with themed chat rooms that helped users bond over shared tastes, Napster was a giant record club that did not require anyone to buy records.

PEARL HARBOR

Music execs declined to work with this digital insurgency. "Their attitude was, they refuse to negotiate with terrorists," asserted Ali Aydar, Napster's Senior Director of Technology. Scholar Lawrence Lessig has called music piracy "culture's Vietnam."[2] And Sony executive Don Ienner compared Napster's effect on the recording industry to Pearl Harbor.[3] "What record companies have done is turned an entire generation of kids into electronic Hezbollah who hate these companies for ideological reasons,"[4] proclaimed writer John Perry Barlow.

When coupled with the proliferation of CD rippers and burning software, Napster visited havoc on the recording industry. At its peak in 2001, it had 60 million users who, according to the ransacked Recording Industry Association of America, contributed to a 39% decline in the sales of CD singles.[5] Record-release Tuesdays like September 11th, 2001 became dark days when the columns of the music industry's financial spreadsheets buckled because of boosted music and lost revenue.

A SHADY INDUSTRY

Dr. Dre, Eminem, and Metallica revealed their corporate commitments when they took legal action against Napster. "Metal and gangsta rap were against us," complained Sean Parker in the 2013 documentary *Downloaded*; "the two least likely genres to be suing us were."[6]

In the year 2000, Millennials and Gen-Xers using Napster took up 60% of all Internet bandwidth at Indiana University.[7] For millions of Millennials reaching young adulthood, their political identity-formation involved pushing back against an increasingly commercialized music industry. "It's the record companies who should hold the patent on cheating musicians out of money," quipped comic Jon Stewart in March of 2001. A decade later, *The Washington Post* called Stewart "Millennials' most trusted news source."[8]

CAPITALISM, RESILIENCE, AND POP MUSIC

Millennial teens who pirated records by Destiny's Child and Savage Garden on Napster were not the only Americans who were disaffected with capitalism:

At the turn of the millennium, the tech-centered job growth of the 1990s came to a crashing halt. The Dow Jones Industrial Average more than tripled its value in the period spanning January 1994 to March of 2000.[9] But in April of 2000, it shed more than 50% of its value.[10] 2.2 million jobs were liquidated, and the country was plunged into a deep "Dot Com" recession.

In his 2000 book *Irrational Exuberance*, economist Robert Shiller identified two mutually-reinforcing cultural determinants of this crash: the rise of the 24-hour news cycle that provided minute-by-minute updates on minor price fluctuations, and the spread of digital trading that allowed panicky shareholders to dump assets instantaneously.[11]

On the morning of Tuesday, September 11th, 2001, economically embattled Americans were still suffering from the economy's unexpected free-fall. In the recession-prone context of capitalism, consumer holidays like record-release Tuesday help to pad the fall of crashing markets. As musicologist Robin James writes in her 2015 book *Resilience & Melancholy*, Americans have been acculturated to capitalist narratives of trauma and redemption:

Resilience discourse ties pop music to neoliberal capitalism. Instead of expending resources to avoid damage, resilience discourse recycles damage into more resources. Resilience discourse follows a specific logic: first, damage is incited; second, that damage is spectacularly overcome, so that; third, the person who has overcome is rewarded with increased status, because: finally, and most importantly, this individual's own resilience boosts society's resilience.[12]

A BUSINESSMAN'S BLUEPRINT

Of all the records released on September 11th, 2001, none embodied the neoliberal resilience narrative better than Jay Z's *The Blueprint*. The 13-track rap classic defined the sound of urban music for a decade, introduced the world to producer Kanye West, and elevated Jay Z from an overexposed gangsta rapper with legal troubles to a global ambassador of hip-hop.

The cover of *The Blueprint* shows an authoritative Jay Z sucking a cigar in a corporate boardroom. Throughout *The Blueprint*, Jay Z's favorite subject is his own dominance as a businessman. "Put me anywhere on God's green earth, I'll triple my worth," he brags at the end of the second verse of "U Don't Know."

The creative key to *The Blueprint*'s triumphant tone is Jay Z's jubilation at having overcome adverse circumstances. This is a resilience narrative. Jay congratulates himself on his ceaseless work ethic—a character trait he used to overcome the collective trauma of deindustrialization and *de facto* segregation that crippled Reagan-era Brooklyn.

But Jay does not offer collective solutions to socioeconomic malaise. Politics are not a part of his blueprint. Instead, Jay has survived the ravages of neoliberalism because of his ability to turn losses into gains. "Lost 92 bricks, had to fall back," he raps on "Never Change"; "knocked a nigga off his feet, but I crawled back."[13] In the narrative of *The Blueprint*, resilience is the reason why Jay Z was able to ascend the capitalist summit.

If his song "Girls, Girls, Girls"[14] was any indication, Jay woke up on 9/11 wary of bootleggers on Napster, but nonetheless eager to see about the first-class flight his stewardess girlfriend saved for him.

7B

The Twin Towers of New York City's World Trade Center complex opened their doors on April 4th, 1973. That same year,

Welsh academic Raymond Williams was penning a theory of mass media that anticipated the spectacular demise of those buildings on September 11th, 2001.

Released in 1974, Williams' book *Television: Technology and Cultural Form* viewed TV as the cultural projection of American capitalism. "In the debate about relations between technology, institutions, and culture, television is outstanding," wrote Williams in the introduction to *Television*.[15] Before Williams, critics assumed that the isolated televised event was TV's primary text. A single episode of *Leave It to Beaver* or a broadcast of the nightly news was assumed to be at the center of the experience of watching television. Williams rejected this notion, writing that "ads, programs, and channel promos flow together as a seamless system."[16]

In Williams' lens, a commercial can say as much about the cultural spectacle of the Super Bowl as John Madden's play-by-play commentary on the game; and a network's bloc of primetime programming says more about its intent than a single scene from *Friends*. Describing a night of watching television alone for several hours, Williams was impressed by the seamlessness of the medium:

I cannot be sure what I took from that whole flow. I believe I registered some incidents as happening in the wrong film, and some characters in the commercials as involved in the film episodes, in what came to seem a single irresponsible flow of images and feelings.[17]

LIVE FROM GROUND ZERO

In many respects, September 11th, 2001 was without precedent. It was not, however, without context. Raymond Williams' notion of "flow" argues that the sideshows surrounding a television event are as important as the event itself. Adopting Williams' framework, the terrorist attacks of 9/11 must be seen in their full televised context[18] to understand how they landed on America's collective psyche: as the catalyzing act in a capitalist resilience narrative, and as the point-of-no-return in an international revenge fantasy.

When American Airlines Flight 11 collided with the North Tower of the World Trade Center at 8:46AM Eastern Standard Time on September 11th, 2001, it precipitated 93 consecutive hours of coverage on American network television. In that period, the average daily viewership of NBC, CBS, ABC, and FOX more than doubled. A moratorium on commercials was implemented on these stations for a short period of time; but within days, Americans learned to accept a side of advertisements and network promos alongside replays and analysis of the attacks. For the vast majority of Americans, 9/11 was a cultural event.

7:00AM

September 11th, 2001 started as another day in the 24-hour news cycle. The National Broadcasting Company's *The Today Show* entered the morning as the most-watched news program in the country. With its studios situated just four miles from "ground zero," the program's lead story on the morning of 9/11 was an athletic resilience narrative. Speculation spread that retired 6-time NBA Champion Michael Jordan would be returning to professional basketball after a 2-year hiatus.

NBC correspondent Bob Faw explains that Jordan's return presented America's recessed economy with an opportunity to rebound. "In Jordan's absence, NBA's television ratings slipped. Marketing experts say they'll climb if he returns," says Faw at 7:03AM, as images of Jordan's corporate sponsorships with Nike, McDonald's, and Warner Brothers are shown. *The Today Show* continued its search for capitalist comeback stories throughout the morning of 9/11.

7:13AM

With 93 minutes to go until September 11th became the bloodiest day on American soil since the Civil War, *The Today Show* host Matt Lauer returns from a commercial break with a story about what he calls America's "sputtering economy." NBC White House correspondent David Gregory tells Matt Lauer that Bush's visit to Booker Elementary School in Florida to discuss his educational initiatives "will attract very little attention" for Americans in the aftermath of the dot-com bust.

7:17AM

At 7:17AM, journalist Tim Russert tells *The Today Show* co-host Katie Couric that "there are natural cycles to economic growth and decline." All participants in this discussion take capitalism's volatility for granted. On *The Today Show*, no one questions why capitalism peaks unsustainably and then sheds millions of jobs in horrible recessions.

As Lauer and Couric casually discuss brutal austerity measures at 7:20AM, the unstated assumption is that Americans must accept the vicissitudes of capitalism without government support. Those who survive will then be able to spin resilience narratives that are then presented as "inspiration" to those who are still stuck in desperate straits.

Disaster is not a bug of neoliberalism; it's its main feature.

7:30AM

After the segment about the recession, *The Today Show* cuts to a lengthy break for local news and weather. Washington DC's NBC affiliate (WRC-TV) forecasts a "comfortably dry" day of bright sunshine. Pilots described the skies over New York City as "severe clear."[19]

When *The Today Show* resumes at 7:30, footage of the nearby Dean & Deluca building shows a scrolling headline ticker that reads "STOCKS CLOSE HIGHER." It's a fitting beginning to a segment in which Matt Lauer interviews General Electric CEO Jack Welch, who oversaw a 5200% increase in the price of General Electric stock from 1981 to 2000.[20] When Lauer confronts Welch about laying off 100,000 people at General Electric in a 4-year period, he callously responds, "We didn't get rid of people, we got rid of jobs."

Welch is certain that capitalism can correct itself with no regulatory intervention, even if he is uncertain of when or how this revival will occur. "I think the economy is close to the bottom. Where it swings back, I don't know," says Welch. In the 50 minutes from 8:00AM until *The Today Show* cuts to the enflamed North Tower at 8:50, narratives of resilience are at the core of several more segments.

8:14AM

Matt Lauer interviews Stanford University psychologist Laura Carstensen, who says that the main difference between "young people and old people is that young people allow bad moods to get them down for a week." The two agree that a resilient, *this too shall pass*-attitude is a mark of maturity. But the question is never asked: what exactly do young people and old people have to be so moody about?

Could it have been that the ups and downs of the American economy were being reflected in the personal struggles of an increasingly anxious population? Teenage Millennials worried about the unaffordability of college began recording dangerously high levels of stress at the turn of the millennium.[21] And the pension accounts of droves of adults evaporated in the dot-com recession. To compensate, already-busy adults became even more overworked.[22]

Nobody on *The Today Show* suggests a critical look at the pressures that lead to mood swings. Instead, personal mood management and medication are offered as solutions. Pharmaceutical ads air during the 9/11 broadcast of *The Today*

Show at 7:23AM, 7:54AM, and 8:24AM.

After the segment about mood swings ends at 8:14AM, a commercial for Stouffer's boxed dinners shows a group of young urban professionals complaining that their lifestyles leave them with no time for adequate nutrition. An ad for stomach medication airs 10 minutes later.

8:30AM

After an 8:30AM weather report in which weatherman Al Roker calls early 9/11 a "perfect summer morning," *The Today Show* runs a story about African-American resilience in the face of historical hate. "Our music is a canvas of our trials and tribulations," says singer Harry Belafonte about the box-set *The Long Road to Freedom*.

Black music like the spirituals of *The Long Road to Freedom* and the bombastic raps of Jay Z's *The Blueprint* serve neoliberalism. If individuals from historically marginalized groups can rise to the ranks of pop culture prominence, capitalism is able to appear as an inclusive and fair social order that rewards hard work. Blacks who cannot become success stories are stigmatized as somehow personally deficient.

As Nicole Aschoff writes in *The New Prophets of Capital*, "capitalism's ability to present legitimating principles that facil-itate the willing participation of society accounts for its remarkable longevity despite periodic bouts of deep crisis."[23] As of 8:45AM on September 11th, 2001, capitalism's main crisis was the dot-com recession; its new "legitimating principle" was the celebration of resilience, often embodied by Black entertainers like Harry Belafonte and Jay Z.

On *The Today Show*, trauma is an accepted fact of life in America. Recessions and massive layoffs will eviscerate jobs. Deindustrialization will leave the urban poor with few avenues to legitimate success. The ups and downs of the economy will expose Americans of all ages to anxiety and insecurity. The individual who can "rise above" these circumstances is celebrated for their resilience. Those who cannot perform this feat become the canvas that resilient individuals paint their greatness on.

8:46AM

When Katie Couric's interview with Harry Belafonte on *The Today Show* ends, it is 8:45AM. At 8:46AM, hijacker Mohammad Atta and his cohort of terrorists fly American Airlines Flight 11 into floors 93–99 of the 110-story North Tower of the World Trade Center. Viewers of *The Today Show* are as yet unaware of the attack.

8:47AM

When *The Today Show* returns from a commercial break at 8:47AM, Matt Lauer interviews author Richard Hack about his forthcoming biography of American aviator Howard Hughes.

A successful entrepreneur from the town of Humble, Texas, Hughes' life story (1905–1976) was a capitalist fairytale about innovation and resolve. A 20th century airplane magnate and media pioneer, his 1930 film *Hell's Angels* was a war epic that valorized combat pilots of World War I. It is widely credited with being an early ancestor of the "blockbuster" film that images of the terrorist attacks of 9/11 were compared to. In 1932, Hughes created Hughes Aircraft Company, an aerospace and defense contractor. He went on to acquire Trans World Airlines in 1939.

With his ties to the entertainment, weapons, and aviation industries, there might not have been a more fitting subject to anticipate *The Today Show*'s coverage of 9/11. As filmmaker Ric Burns noted in a 2003 installment of *New York: A Documentary Film*, "the symbols and instruments of globalization—skyscrapers, jets, and the mass media—would be turned back against themselves with a devastatingly lethal impact on September 11th."

At 8:51AM, Lauer interrupts the segment about Howard Hughes to "go live right now to a breaking story at the World Trade Center."

7C

At 9:01AM, *The Today Show* turned to NBC producer Elliot Walker for her eyewitness account of the first attack on the World Trade Center. "There must have been a 3-block cloud of white smoke," said Walker; "the air was filled with thousands of pieces of paper that were floating like confetti."

As Walker breathlessly explained the attack on the North Tower, United Airlines Flight 175 struck floors 75–85 of the South Tower at 9:03AM. *The Today Show*'s studio technicians can be heard braying in terror as shards of metal, debris, and yet more paper cascaded onto streets after the second attack.

"Paper was a constant presence on 9/11," remembered journalist William Langewiesche; "it rained down on New York, as if in mockery of the kind of business that was done at the World Trade Center."[24]

PAPER CHAMPIONS

For New Yorkers at the turn of the millennium, confetti was normally a welcome sight. In 1996, 1998, 1999, and 2000, the New York Yankees were triumphant in the World Series. In each of these years, their championship runs culminated in a ticker-tape parade down the city's "Canyon of Heroes" along Broadway in downtown Manhattan.

In previous years, the paper used in this confetti came from scraps discarded by Wall Street stock tickers. But the digitization of the stock exchange at the end of the 20th century made stock tickers obsolete.[25] So the confetti used in the Yankees' championship parades came to be sourced from shredded office paper, like the kind that fell from the World Trade Center on 9/11.[26]

AMERICA'S TEAM

When major league baseball play resumed on September 18th, 2001, it instituted the singing of "God Bless America" during the 7th inning stretch of all baseball games, and had American flags stitched onto the backs of team uniforms.

The baseball club from the beleaguered city of New York sputtered to the finish line of the regular season, then bounced back brilliantly in the playoffs. Following the inspired play of shortstop Derek Jeter, the Yankees bested the Oakland Athletics in the American League Division Series before crushing the heavily favored Seattle Mariners in the American League Championship Series.

With the Yankees squaring off against the upstart Arizona Diamondbacks in the World Series, the stage was set for the sports incarnation of New York City's post-9/11 resilience narrative.

SPORTS SELL CAPITALISM

While the Yankees were attempting a symbolic comeback on behalf of New York City, American capitalism was turning trauma into profit. Shortly before the World Series, America Airlines and United Airlines became corporate sponsors of the *MLB on FOX* telecast of the World Series.[27]

MLB on FOX belonged to the same media umbrella as Fox News, an incendiary right-wing channel on cable TV that experienced a renaissance after 9/11. Not coincidentally, *MLB on FOX* turned the World Series into a celebration of America's armed forces. "Through the years, baseball has inspired our nation," proclaimed Fox announcer Joe Buck during the *MLB on FOX* intro to Game One of the World Series, as images of American military valor flash across the screen.[28] "As a nation, we've been tested," Buck continued; "but America always gets up. So many Americans have fought for freedom."[29]

BLOODSPORT

President George W. Bush embraced the patriotic spectacle of the World Series to push his post-9/11 agenda to the America public. He travelled to the site where the Twin Towers collapsed on September 14th, 2001. "I can hear you," he exclaimed to the cleanup crew through a bullhorn; "and pretty soon, the people who knocked these buildings down are going to hear from all of us soon!"[30]

Months later, Bush flew to New York again to throw out the first pitch to Game 3 of the World Series. Rather than participate in the Game One festivities in Arizona, Bush decided New York was a better staging location for America's resilience narrative. Fox concurred. "What is a New Yorker?" asked a narrator with a heavy outer-borough accent during the *MLB on FOX* intro to Game 3 of the World Series. "Knock us down, and we'll not only get up, but fight twice as hard."[31]

America's post-recession fixation with resilience did not fade away after 9/11. Instead, it intensified—especially when the prospect of revenge became part of the picture. By valorizing the armed forces before any formal declaration of war had ever been issued, Fox's pre-game intros to the World Series fed the popular lust for post-9/11 revenge. Diamondbacks pitcher Curt Schilling further stoked the flames. In a *USA Today* editorial from fall of 2001, Schilling said his thoughts on 9/11 "steered towards revenge, retaliation, and retribution."[32]

Schilling pitched brilliantly in the World Series as the Diamondbacks defeated the Yankees in a thrilling Game Seven on November 4th, 2001. When the Super Bowl was played the following February, the NFL—*again* with the help of the Fox Network—furthered the narrative that baseball started. The patently violent game of football provided *NFL on FOX* an opportunity to sell out wholesale to America's post-9/11 embrace of militarized resilience.

PAID PATRIOTISM

Super Bowl XXXVI was played on February 3rd, 2002 between the St. Louis Rams and the New England Patriots. *NFL on FOX* began its telecast of the game with a pastiche of quotes from American politicians, including the famously belligerent Teddy Roosevelt's "We admire the man who embodies victorious effort."[33] Fox's production design of the Super Bowl broadcast emphasized war: military commandos were featured in cutaways between graphics, framing football as a game of strategy and conflict.

In an April 2008 *New York Times* article, it was exposed that the Department of Defense used Fox to fan the cultural embrace of the armed forces.[34] This propaganda mission involved populating the Fox News Channel with officers who were posed as neutral analysts, and stoking the American public's lust for revenge. As St. Louis and New England played Super Bowl XXXVI with commemorative 9/11 logos and flags on their helmets, the Patriots won the game 20-17 on a last-second field goal.

It was the first of five championships that New England won in a 15-year span from 2002 to 2017. The symbolism of a Patriot dynasty in the aftermath of 9/11 did not go uncapitalized on. A 2015 report by the U.S. Senate titled "Tackling Paid Patriotism"[35] revealed that from 2011 through 2014, the Department of Defense paid the New England Patriots $700,000 for pre-game and halftime ceremonies that celebrated the armed forces.

MILLENNIAL PATRIOTS

"We are all patriots," exclaimed Patriots owner Bob Kraft when New England defeated the Seattle Seahawks in Super Bowl XLIX in 2015. "And every true Patriot fan understands that our first Super Bowl was won at a unique time in our country."[36] The "unique time" Kraft spoke of was a post-9/11 climate where the pop culture embrace of war was at a fever pitch. This embrace had roots in changes to the American social fabric that began as the first Millennials were born in the 1980s:

In Reagan-era America, major corporations aimed hawkish
entertainment at young Millennials. As we saw in Chapter 2
("American Dad") the movies *Rambo* and *Top Gun*, and video
games like *Contra* were sponsored and funded by the federal
defense establishment, for the explicit purpose of raising young
Millennials as the next generation of soldiers. In the aftermath of
9/11, this pro-military propaganda enjoyed a second life. As
Deborah Jaramillo writes in her 2009 study *Ugly War, Pretty
Package*, "old toys received a boost from the buildup to war. Sales
of Hasbro's G.I. Joe line increased before and during the 2003
invasion of Iraq."[37]

MILLENNIAL CASUALTIES

In the period spanning March 2003 to December 2011, "Operation
Iraqi Freedom" raged in the Middle East. The average soldier's
age during the Vietnam War was 19; in Operation Iraqi Freedom,
it was 27. "A drafted army is not in Iraq and Afghanistan,"
remembered memoirist Paul Rieckhoff. "It's more of a professional force, so folks are staying in longer."[38]

But while the army-at-large in the 2000s was older than it had
been in previous decades, young Millennials accounted for a
disproportionate amount of its deaths: from 2003–2009,
combatants aged 18–24 comprised 53% of the casualties in
Operation Iraqi Freedom. For those aged 31–35 in the same
period, the figure was only 9%.[39]

"I get offended every time I hear folks—particularly politicians—talking about a generation that they think is the selfish,
Me Generation," said Missouri Secretary of State Jason Kander on
a December 2016 episode of the podcast *Keepin' it 1600*; "when I
was in the military, a large portion of the folks that I served with
were Millennials—and it's a volunteer military."[40]

While it's true that young people generally suffer more causal-
ities in war, this pronounced generational dynamic of death—

where the army is older but those who die are not—is in fact new. The phenomenon can be attributed to a few factors: 1) economic straits under neoliberalism that forced many Americans to pursue the armed forces as a career path, and 2) cultural determinants that encouraged Millennials to continually enlist in the military even as casualties rose and public opinion of the war plummeted.

The propaganda that attracted young Millennials in the 1980s proved successful in the 2000s. This propaganda was augmented in the 1990s with "advanced computing systems, computer graphics, and multiplayer networked systems"[41] that simulated warfare for young game-players. As the 2000s progressed, Millennials in the armed forces spearheaded digital, drone-led warfare. Their proficiency with these weapons systems were based on computer skills they learned while playing video games as youngsters.

THE WAR FOR HEARTS AND MINDS

Historically, the Pentagon has been the largest underwriter of computer graphics technologies. In the words of Colonel Casey Wardynski, "as the video game craze of the 1980s and 1990s exploded, the Pentagon realized it had to get Information about the army into pop culture."[42]

Professional sports also did their part to sell the War in Iraq in the 2000s. To score its *Sunday Night Football* broadcast in 2006, NBC enlisted composer John Williams, whose muscular scores were famous for mimicking the brassy fanfare of the military parade. In the same period, popular country musicians Darryl Worley and Toby Keith recorded the pro-war anthems "Have You Forgotten?" and "Courtesy of the Red, White, and Blue."

HARDER, BETTER, FASTER, STRONGER

In his 2002 book *Welcome to the Desert of the Real*, Slavoj Žižek wrote that the terrorist attacks of 9/11 presented America with an

opportunity to "humbly accept its own vulnerability."[43] In
Žižek's words, "[America could have] enacted the punishment of
those responsible for the attacks as a sad duty, not as an exhilarating retaliation."[44]

But America's resilience discourse did not allow for this kind
of reflection. Nor did it encourage Americans to think critically
about capitalism's role in causing the geopolitical instability that
created the terrorist scourge in the first place: In the aftermath of
9/11, producers of the movie *Rambo III* slickly deleted a title card
that dedicated the film to "the brave Mujaheddin fighters of
Afghanistan."[45] Ronald Reagan praised the villainized Taliban
terrorists as "freedom fighters," invited them to the White House
in 1983, and supplied them with the weapons they'd later use to
kill Millennial soldiers in the 2000s.[46]

9/11 could have become a referendum on the domestic instability of global capitalism, and the unforeseen consequences of
American military dalliances abroad. Instead, the trauma of 9/11
became the motivating event in a revenge fantasy. A disproportionately young and Millennial-filled military were the executors
of this revenge.

Meanwhile, capitalism—in words of Daft Punk's October 2001
single—had what it so desperately needed after the Dot Com
Recession: a crisis to help it emerge "harder, better, faster,
stronger."[47]

"We're going to rebuild," said New York City Mayor Rudy
Giuliani in the aftermath of 9/11; "we're going to come out of this
emotionally stronger, politically stronger, and we're going to
come out of this economically stronger, too."

Chapter 8

People You May Know

September 11th, 2001 found a 17-year-old Millennial named Mark Zuckerberg scrambling to help his classmates connect to the Internet.[1]

A high school senior at Phillips Exeter Academy in New Hampshire, Zuckerberg had taken a volunteer position as a tech proctor. "I was trying to link my computer to our school's new broadband system so I could communicate with my family, a classmate of Zuckerberg's later remembered. "In the midst of chaos, Mark was relentlessly focused on setting up my computer and getting me connected."[2]

9/11 was a generation-defining day that captured a Millennial luminary as he would come to be seen in the public eye: focused on a tech-oriented task, and committed to connecting a fractured world.

After graduating from Phillips Exeter Academy, Zuckerberg enrolled at Harvard University. Once there, he created Facebook: a self-described "social networking service" that allows its users to find, follow, and "friend" one another. Originally launched on February 4th, 2004 as "thefacebook.com," Zuckerberg's brainchild became an indelible aspect of the social experience of millions of Millennials.

THE FACEBOOK TRANCE

Unlike competitors such as Friendster, LiveJournal, and Myspace, Facebook was premised on the idea that an individual's real-life identity could be transparently expressed online. There was no hiding. Facebook forbade its users from creating pseudonyms. It made vital information like one's birthday, job, and city-of-residence part of its public record. And it encouraged users to upload "profile" pictures that represented their actual appearance.

By providing its billions of users a window into the private lives of one another, Facebook became political boilerplate in a national conversation about surveillance and social control in the post-9/11 United States. It was also enormously addictive. In 2009, Nielsen ratings reported that Facebook users—which included 85% of collegiate Millennials—spent more time per day on the service than Google, Wikipedia, Amazon, and YouTube *combined*.[3] As David Kirkpatrick writes in his 2010 book *The Facebook Effect*, employees of the company were dedicated to creating a "Facebook trance"[4] that ensnared users into idling away hours at a time on the website.

THE PUSSIFICATION OF THE AMERICAN MALE

Subsequently, 21st century conservative pundits who lamented the "pussification"[5] of American men in the post-industrial era often pointed to social networking as a culprit. By trapping men in front of the screen—the line of reasoning went, in countless op-eds and talk radio rants[6]—young men were pulled away from traditionally masculine pursuits like playing sports, eating steak, and changing flat tires. Based in large part on Reagan-era heroes like Rocky and Rambo, post-9/11 notions of masculinity were often tied to narratives of national chauvinism; tech-centered men were framed as less manly, and therefore less American. The 2004 film *Team America* parodied the linkage of patriotism and over-the-top masculinity with its crude anthem "America, Fuck Yeah."

ANTI-SOCIAL NETWORKING

Mark Zuckerberg was a triumphant symbol of the beta-male archetype that had been in the building since the 1980s. Classmates marveled at his ability to code in front of a computer for days on end in college. Like a modern-day monk, he wore the same outfit for countless days consecutively.[7] Zuckerberg's struggle to wrestle Facebook from a couple of Harvard jocks who claimed to've invented it became the stuff of cinematic legend: in the 2010 film *The Social Network*, a socially maladroit Zuckerberg (played by Jesse Eisenberg) is portrayed as saying, "I don't want friends"—quite the statement from a guy who became a billionaire by helping others make them online.

REVENGE OF THE NERDS

Mark Zuckerberg was born on May 14th, 1984. That same year, the debut of the film *Revenge of the Nerds* anticipated the neoliberal nerd prototype that Zuckerberg eventually epitomized.

Directed by Jeff Kanew, *Revenge of the Nerds* follows a gaggle of geeks who engage in a territorial dispute with football players at their fictional college fraternity. After learning resilience from also-marginalized African-American students, the nerds stage a revolt against their former tormentors. The film's preachy message—that "we all have something of the nerd within us"—is a rallying cry for those excluded from the cultural mainstream.

On the one hand, *Revenge of the Nerds* contained something like a countercultural message. As revealed in the 2001 PBS documentary *Merchants of Cool*,[8] Millennial teenagers in the 1990s and 2000s were exposed to a social hierarchy in American schools that hinged on commercialism: Access to consumer goods like soda, cars, and stylish clothes were markers of status among American teenagers. Students that didn't access these symbols of power became social outcasts in school.

As with neoliberal society at large, the size of the average public school's general population vastly outnumbered the amount of coveted spots atop the student body hierarchy. Thus, the high school experience for the vast majority of Millennial nerds, disadvantaged kids, and conventionally unattractive teens was marred by frustration and unhappiness. Inasmuch as it called attention to this social stratification and encouraged students to rebel against it when they became adults in college, *Revenge of the Nerds* was an insurgent counternarrative.

At the same time, capitalism thrives on identifying underexploited sources of profit. *Revenge of the Nerds* did not inspire revolt so much as it found America's 'inner nerd' and commercialized it. Just as capitalism re-branded in the wake of 9/11 with the help of its militarist resilience narrative, it also extracted opportunity from the social wreckage of the ostracized nerd. When Facebook became a publicly traded company on the New York Stock Exchange in 2007, Mark Zuckerberg became a billionaire.

NERDS OF A NEW GENERATION

Throughout the 1990s, scores of nerdy characters appeared on television in the form of Lisa Simpson, *Doogie Howser*, Steve Urkel (*Family Matters*), Mr. Spock (*Star Trek: The Next Generation*), and *Daria*.

In the 2000s, the films *Donnie Darko* (2001) and *Napoleon Dynamite* (2004) were cult classics that captured outcast male protagonists who did not fit into socially prescribed roles. Started by the movies *Funny Ha Ha* (2002), *LOL* (2006), and *Hannah Takes the Stairs* (2007), the so-called "Mumblecore" strain of independent film became the "genre of a generation"[9] by portraying socially awkward 20-somethings with a "true 21st century sensibility that reflected the minutiae of Myspace, and the voyeurism of YouTube."[10]

Socially excluded minorities and young women were encouraged by the film *Juno* (2007) and the television show *Ugly Betty* (2006–2010) to eschew traditional expectations of female behavior by presenting themselves as independent young women with intellectual pursuits. Meanwhile, the 2009 launch of Warby Parker was one example of a widespread "geek chic" fashion trend that turned bifocals, cardigan sweaters, and suspenders into fashion statements in the 2000s. Jay Z—who once sported jerseys in his music videos to look like a jock—suddenly bragged about "changing clothes" to reintroduce himself to a younger audience weaned on button-ups and skinny jeans.

TWEE THE PEOPLE

In 2003, an entry appeared on the website *Urban Dictionary* for the word twee: "something that is sweet, almost to the point of being sickeningly so."[11] The adjective was frequently applied to the British rock band Belle and Sebastian (*Dear Catastrophe Waitress*, 2003), and to the increasingly foppish films of director Wes Anderson (*The Life Aquatic With Steve Zissou*, 2004). Also in the 2000s, the cupcake—an icon of adolescent whimsy and youthful decadence—enjoyed a resurgence.[12] Buoyed by its presence on the television show *Sex and the City* (1998–2004), its ubiquitous presence at adult birthday parties and in hip 20-something neighborhoods symbolized the prolonged adolescence of Gen-X and Millennials.

GEEK CAPITALISM

To cultural conservatives, this activity was a crisis: America's youth had grown up to be a Peter Pan generation of gender confusion, where women worked and men wore mom-jeans. In actuality, pastel colors and effeminate skinny pants were a vehicle for capitalism to reproduce itself. The Nerd™ became a template through which resilient young Millennials of every color and creed asserted their idiosyncratic individuality with awkward speech patterns and pretentious cultural pursuits. At the same time, tech readied a new generation to partake in the next phase of American neoliberalism:

Members of the pro-business community such as venture capitalist Paul Graham weaponized the success stories of seemingly "self-made" geniuses like Mark Zuckerberg into arguments against providing social welfare.[13] It gifted children like Zuckerberg could succeed on the strength of their own wits and vision—the argument went—then Millennials had no excuse to not open their own businesses and also become billionaires.

The nerd was once the embodiment of social exclusion in the 1980s. Thirty years later, it had become a new face of neoliberalism. As Jodi Dean writes in her 2010 study *Blog Theory*, "geek norms emerge, claim neutrality and appropriateness, and then retreat, leaving in their wake a pro-capitalist, entrepreneurial, and individualistic discourse well suited for the amplification of neoliberal governmentality."[14]

AMERICAN HIGH SCHOOL[15]

In the 2000s, Mark Zuckerberg attempted to connect a world that was as segmented as ever. Decades of wealth stratification under neoliberalism divided Americans into haves and have-nots. Culture wars hosted the country's divisions on social issues such as guns, abortion, and the death penalty. During the polarized 2004 presidential election, the country devolved into separate flanks of blue states and red states. And in a 2006 article titled "Lunch Period Poli Sci,"[16] *New York Times* columnist David Brooks wrote that the prevailing metaphor for America's fractured politics was the high school lunch cafeteria: a Bunsen burner of social segregation that college-age Millennials had only recently escaped.

8B

The days immediately following 9/11 were probably the only time Millennials were alive during a political climate not defined by intense polarization. First devised by CNN to cover the Iran Hostage Crisis of 1979, the 24-hour news cycle blossomed into a platform for divisive spectacles. Anita Hill's contestation of Clarence Thomas' 1991 Supreme Court nomination, the OJ Simpson Trial of 1994–1995, and the lurid details of Bill Clinton's sex-life advertised America's race and gender divides, compelling viewers to pick sides as if they were watching sporting events.

By 2004, America's social rifts had grown so deep that media outlets began to speak of two Americas—a phenomenon historian Thomas Frank reflected on in his 2004 text *What's the Matter With Kansas?* "The red-state/blue-state idea was a standard element of the media's pop-sociology repertoire," wrote Frank. "It provided an easy tool for contextualizing small stories and spinning big ones. It justified countless *USA Today*-style contemplations of who Americans really are."[17]

GOLDEN AGE CONSENSUS

America was not always this way. From 1945 through 1973, the guiding logic of American political life was consensus. Political divisions obviously existed in this period: the complex interplay of radicals, reactionaries, conservatives, and liberals defined the politics of the tumultuous 1960s. But a legal-political apparatus was in place that at least conveyed the *appearance* that America was capable of solving its social issues using a functional, collaborative framework.

THE CENTER COULD NOT HOLD

If it ever truly existed, this consensus did not last long. In the late 1960s, the collapse of the New Deal Coalition of college-educated Whites, women, organized labor, and racial minorities led dissidents to seek shelter in isolated honeycombs. More importantly, the capitalist crises of the 1970s presented corporate interests with an opportunity to rewrite the American social contract:

Using behind-the-scenes pro-business activism and public propaganda, moneyed interests in the 1970s succeeded in pinning the unraveling of the American social fabric on dissidents, women, and organized labor. In 1972, wealthy CEOs formed the Business Roundtable, an interest group that lobbied the government to pass corporation-friendly policies.[18]

That same decade, conservative think tanks the Rand Corporation, the Brookings Institution, and the Cato Institute saw spikes in membership, as journalists and pundits trained in their ways began to spread the virtues of the free market in articles and on American airwaves. In January of 1980, neoliberal economist Milton Friedman was featured in a PBS documentary titled *Free To Choose*. By November 1980, Ronald Reagan rode into office as a champion of Friedman's policies.

THE NEOLIBERAL ECHO CHAMBER

It's impossible to overstate the success of the business counteroffensive in the 1970s and 1980s. In her 2010 study *Invisible Hands: The Businessmen's Crusade Against the New Deal*, scholar Kim Phillips-Fein assessed the neoliberal revolution's triumph:

> *By the early twenty-first century, the conservative movement transformed the tax code, government regulation of business, and the relationship between the federal government and the states. The political economy of the postwar period was sustained by the Keynesian belief that public policies should stimulate consumption while encouraging income redistribution. This vision no longer enjoys wide support in either political party.*[19]

Neoliberalism was the cultural water of Millennial fish. In the 1980s and 1990s, virtually all of American popular culture was an echo chamber for its values, saturating the public with free market ideology that framed race, gender, and class in capitalist-friendly terms:

Stories about disadvantaged ethnic groups emphasized individual success stories (Jay Z, Oprah Winfrey, Jennifer Lopez) over collective, structural changes to capitalism. Feminism was widely decoupled from the pursuit of policies that benefitted women, and identified with a celebration of corporatist ladder-climbing and consumer choice. Neoliberalism had even managed to turn its most obvious victims—White working class voters who suffered massive job losses with the onset of deindustrialization and devastating trade deals like NAFTA and WTO—into some of its most vehement advocates. In his 2013 book *Angry White Men*, author Michael Kimmel describes how the creation of conservative talk radio in the 1980s encouraged White voters to blame minorities and women—rather than major corporations—for their economic woes.[20]

All the while, conservative pundits posed as "neutral" sources of news and information on transparently biased stations like Fox News, and also on respectable-seeming networks like CNN. It took a series of technological breakthroughs in the 2000s to destabilize this state of affairs.

DIGITAL DISRUPTION OF AMERICAN MEDIA

The launch of YouTube in 2005 followed the advent of Facebook in 2004. Suddenly, citizens who were sick of the narrow discourse of neoliberal mass media could circulate their own social commentary in video form. The website grew into a repository for radical alternative news, and coverage of instances of police brutality, protests, and gender harassment that went ignored by corporatized news outlets.

Then, in April of 2006, Twitter launched. Together with the release of the iPhone in December of that same year, dissidents and discontents now had readymade organizing tools that facilitated the exchange of information and insights that could not find a home in the American mainstream.

In October of 2006, Millennial blogger Josh Wolf was jailed by a California judge for refusing to provide federal prosecutors footage he recorded of an anti-globalization demonstration in San Francisco. Wolf—a self-described "artist, activist, anarchist, and archivist"[21] who wore thick sideburns and even thicker hipster glasses—was a pioneer of Millennial dissatisfaction with the corporate media establishment.

AND THE WINNER IS...YOU.

In 2006, *Time Magazine* named "You"—as in, the digitized American public-at-large—its "Person of the Year" for "seizing the reins of global media, founding and framing the new digital democracy, and beating the pros at their own game."[23] This new world of Millennial media was structured like the networks that enabled it: open-ended, participatory, and collaborative. While the Internet is a petri dish for right-wing radicalism, it also amplifies intersectional dissent among progressives, people of color, sexual minorities, and more.

DIGITAL DEMOCRACY FTW

In their 2004 book *Multitude: War and Democracy in the Age of Empire*, political philosophers Antonio Negri and Michael Hardt eloquently summarized the new digital counternarrative that began bubbling up from below:

> There are two faces to globalization. On one face, Empire spreads its network of hierarchies and divisions that maintain order through new mechanisms of control and constant conflict. Globalization, however, is also the creation of new circuits of cooperation and collaboration that stretch across nations. This second face of globalization provides the possibility that [we'll] discover the commonality that enables us to communicate and act together. The multitude is thus composed potentially of all the diverse figures of social production.[23]

8C

In the same way that Bill Clinton's sexual misdeeds were a boon to Jay Leno and Conan O'Brien in the 1990s, the bungling jingoism of George W. Bush was heaven-sent manna to American counterculture in the 2000s.

RAP TAKES UP ARMS AGAINST WAR

Long lambasted by critics for its commercial tendencies, rap music took a turn for the explicitly political in the 2000s. On his 2002 follow-up to *The Blueprint*, Jay Z authored the poignant "A Ballad for the Fallen Soldier." Over melancholy production by rap powerhouse The Neptunes, Jay compares the bleak fate of young drug dealers in major cities with their enlisted counterparts in the military. In 2004, Jay Z's rap rival Nas took an equally pensive tone, using his single "Just a Moment" to commemorate those "trapped in the system" of desperate straits and premature death.

Meanwhile, Eminem's 2004 rager "Mosh" was perhaps the finest protest song of the 2000s. Released on October 26th, 2004 as part of the Puff Daddy-founded "Vote or Die" campaign, Eminem performs an impassioned takedown of the Bush regime's reliance on half-truths to justify a "War on Terror" that had needlessly stretched into Iraq and Afghanistan. With three seething verses, Eminem displays all of the lyrical virtuosity that made his anthem "Lose Yourself" a smash in 2002. The music video for "Mosh"[24] animates the intersections between economic desperation and military enlistment that led millions of Millennials and Gen-Xers to join the armed forces in the 2000s.

PEOPLE YOU MAY KNOW

Nearly 20 years after Chuck D likened hip-hop to a "Black CNN,"[25] a couple of comedians in the 2000s turned the news show format into a potent vehicle of protest: The television shows *The Daily Show with Jon Stewart* (1999–2015) and *The Colbert Report* (2005–2015) brutally undercut the politics of the Bush Administration, as well as the news outlets that legitimated its policies of constant war and corporate greed.

Stewart and Colbert had a clear ideological (progressive) slant, and packaged their shows into digitally digestible segments for consumption on the social networking websites that

Millennials inhabited. As a result, they became newsmen for a disillusioned generation that had no faith in traditional journalism to deliver an objective assessment of irrational times. Colbert and Stewart peddled jokes—but this was not fun and games: for their humor was a critical building block of resistance against the right-wing rule.

Comedy, like all of pop culture, is an innately political process of social production that draws distinctions between in-groups who are invited to laugh and out-groups who are laughed at. Celebrity entertainers Jay Z, Nas, and Eminem used their star power to drive a wedge in their own audiences, potentially alienating large swabs of their listeners over matters of political principle. Stewart and Colbert were similarly divisive: rather than play to the phantom center of the American political spectrum, they set up camp in the far Left and spoke to that audience by unceasingly ridiculing the Right. Intense partisanship was not a byproduct of Stewart and Colbert's comedy— it was the point.

The political economy of their humor belonged to a decade period where the political views of Facebook friends overlapped overwhelmingly, and Twitter bombarded users with opinion pieces that they already tended to agree with. If the 1970s saw the pro-business counteroffensive to the Keynesian welfare state, the 2000s hosted the digital counternarrative to the neoliberal status quo. As "digital natives"[26] who utilized these tools for entertainment and activism, Millennials were some of the first authors of this counternarrative.

A BRIEF HISTORY OF COMEDIC COUNTEROFFENSIVES

Humor had long been a strategy in the forging of cultural counternarratives. In the 1990s, *The Simpsons* anticipated the antics of *The Daily Show* and *The Colbert Report* by spoofing the nightly news in segments featuring a journalist named Kent

Brockman, who displayed a blatant lack of professional integrity. In 2004, Tina Fey and Amy Poehler were cast in the long-running *Saturday Night Live* "Weekend Update" sketch, where they posed as fictional anchorwomen who lampooned current affairs. But however accurately they parodied America's unscrupulous information economy, *The Simpsons* was a cartoon that could not capture reality completely. And *Saturday Night Live* relied on obvious impersonations that required audiences to suspend their disbelief. These shows may have satirized power. But in the words of cultural critic Chuck Klosterman, "they unintentionally reinforced the preexisting world [by not attacking the ideological foundations an institution claims to be built upon]."[27]

CLASS CLOWN

What differentiated Stewart and Colbert from their predecessors was their way of wading into confrontations with real-life villains. On the show's first episode after the terrorist attacks of 9/11, Jon Stewart delivered a meditation about freedom of the press in a country that would soon be at war.[28] In 2004, Stewart appeared on CNN's *Crossfire*, and lambasted the show's hosts for its "dog and pony show" debate format that polarized American political discourse.[29] Years later in 2009, Stewart criticized CNBC's Mad Money host Jim Cramer for his role in disseminating free market propaganda that led to The Great Recession.[30] These antics put Stewart in a seemingly impossible position: simultaneously a trusted news source, and a countercultural icon.

STONED SLACKERS AND A DOPEY SHOW

The typical episode of *The Daily Show with Jon Stewart* was comfortingly recognizable: a newsman (Jon Stewart) seated behind a desk in a studio, addressing the television audience while summarizing topics of current importance with the help of superimposed graphics and cutaways to relevant footage.

But subtle differences distanced *The Daily Show* from the hackneyed evening news format. The presence of a live studio audience, for example, provides television viewers cues to laugh, get angry, or become contemplative. Stewart's mannerisms, meanwhile, are far more expressive than any real journalist. His performed outrage and sarcasm invite the audience to become emotionally invested in ways that did not happen during a real nightly-news broadcast.

Pew Research Center's 2008 Media Consumption Study showed that 14% of 18–24 year-olds watched *The Daily Show* (as compared with only 4% of those aged 25 or older).[31] Another 46% of Millennials reported that they learned about politics by watching *The Daily Show*.[32] Millennials watched no other news program—real or satirical—more.

Because clips of *The Daily Show* also circulated widely via YouTube on social networks like Facebook and Twitter, it's hard to come by precise ratings data for the show. Many of the program's viewers were cord-cutting Gen-Xers and Millennial college students. This too was a marker of the show's popularity, as it became a social ritual for students at universities in the 2000s to locate a dorm room commons with a television, watch the *The Daily Show*, and laugh in groups.

"What's frightening is that you actually have an influence on this presidential election," opined Fox News firebrand Bill O'Reilly when Stewart appeared on *The O'Reilly Factor* in 2004; "you've got stoned slackers watching your dopey show every night and they can vote."[33]

TRUTHINESS HURTS

In contrast to Jon Stewart, Stephen Colbert did not subvert the archetype of the sober-minded news anchor. Instead, Colbert satirized outspoken conservatives like Bill O'Reilly by impersonating them. On *The Colbert Report*—a spin-off of *The Daily Show* that launched in October 2005—Colbert embodied an over-the-top stereotype of a reactionary conservative talk show host, forcing the caricature to crumble under the weight of its own absurdity and lies. Colbert's temperamental character was, in the words of media scholar Geoffrey Baym, "a foolish and deeply ironic personality who blatantly disregarded accuracy and political correctness."[34]

Colbert's comedic philosophy was encapsulated in his championing of the value of "truthiness"—a parody of the fact-deaf and incoherent anger displayed by conservative pundits Rush Limbaugh, Glenn Beck, and Sean Hannity. By refusing to respond to logic, spewing clearly confused patriotic propaganda, and shouting down his guests when they dared to make sense, Colbert was making fun of conservative talk show hosts who seriously engaged in such tactics in the name of serious reporting.

This shtick caught fire. Colbert garnered an audience of over one million viewers each night,[35] and earned him an acclaimed spot alongside Jon Stewart "as the Cronkite and Murrow for an ironic millennium."[36]

COURT JESTER

Colbert's coming out party was the 2006 White House Correspondents Dinner—the 92nd iteration of an annual event where members of the press, politicians, and select celebrities trade jokes and insults at one another's expense. In his 24-minute monologue, Colbert impersonated a staunch conservative, showing that the right-wing worldview was built on a fragile pile of fury and denial.[37]

C-SPAN cameras cut to President Bush laughing nervously nearby as Colbert compared his ability to rise above plummeting approval ratings to the sports film *Rocky*: "This is the heart-warming story of a man who was repeatedly punched in the face." With Bush bright red and a room full of conservatives on the ropes, Colbert went for the knockout by pounding Bush's post-9/11 resilience narrative.

> *I stand by this man. I stand by this man because he stands for things. Not only for things, he stands on things. Things like aircraft carriers and rubble and recently flooded city squares. And that sends a strong message: that no matter what happens to America, she will always rebound—with the most powerfully staged photo ops in the world!*[38]

Indeed, the manipulation of images and symbols was central to the Bush Administration's attempt to project moral authority in the 2000s. As Judith Butler wrote in her 2009 screed *Frames of War*, "throughout the Bush regime, we saw a concerted effort on the part of the state to regulate the visual field. The phenomenon of embedded reporting came to the fore with the invasion of Iraq, whereby journalists agreed to report only from the perspective established by military and governmental authorities."[39]

Images of the fallen Twin Towers and American military valor were key components of a post-9/11 resilience narrative that hinged on achieving revenge. Colbert spoofed this alchemy of conservative policy and media manipulation in his 2006 diatribe.

A LEFTIST ECHO CHAMBER?

Less than 48 hours after being posted, various clips of the Colbert performance had been viewed 2.7 million times on YouTube, and occupied the first, second, and third slot of the site's "Most Viewed" video list.[40] Three weeks later, audio of the speech became the number one most purchased album on iTunes. Millennials, who in 2006 accounted for a disproportionate amount of YouTube traffic and iTunes downloads, had a major role in powering these figures.[41]

Some have come to the conclusion that "the boom in satire TV during George W. Bush's historically contentious presidency in the conservative 2000s"[42] was not necessarily good for the budding political maturity of Millennials. This fear—rooted in postmodern anxieties about the blurring of fact and fiction—was not without merit:

In 2006, researchers Jody Baumgartner and Jonathan Morris discovered that Millennial watchers of *The Daily Show with Jon Stewart* did not differ significantly from non-watchers, except inasmuch as these Millennial viewers had an inflated sense of their own awareness about political issues. Baumgartner and Morris concluded that "any learning which may occur as a result of exposure to *The Daily Show* does not seem to translate into more political participation, and may in fact engender greater feelings of political cynicism."[43]

COOL KIDS

For a generation that grew up with an unforgiving social hierarchy in high school, Colbert and Stewart couldn't overpower the jocks that steered American foreign policy, and so instead settled for ridiculing them in the cafeteria of public opinion. Simply watching these shows earned viewers social capital with one another; a chance to finally be seen as "cool" in the great high school of American politics, despite doing nothing substantive to change the status quo that exiled them in the first place. Jodi Dean refers to this new complacency as "communicative capitalism"[44]—the contemporary web of communications that ensnares passive users in wires of enjoyment and surveillance, and stifles real resistance.

YES WE CAN (LAUGH OUR ASSES OFF)

But *The Daily Show* had an impact beyond encouraging Millennials to burrow into the echo chambers of social networking. In the 2000s, a new progressive front was learning to articulate their demands by laughing at the people who stifled them.

As critical theorist Nancy Fraser has written, the Internet beehives where Jon Stewart and Stephen Colbert vids were shared were "discursive arenas where members of subordinate social groups invented and circulated counterdiscourses to formulate oppositional interpretations of their identities, interests, and needs."[45] This was no truer for any group than for Millennials.

Sensing the importance of cashing in on Jon Stewart's cultural cool, an Illinois Senator named Barack Obama made his first of several appearances on *The Daily Show* as a presidential candidate in 2007:

"We've been having a wonderful time travelling across the country, getting these enormous crowds," Obama told Stewart. "We've been seeing a lot of young people. And that's what's most excited about this campaign: people who haven't seen a lot of inspiration in politics suddenly taking this seriously."[46]

Chapter 9

All Millennials Are From Akron

As Americans born between 1982 and 2004, Millennials matured in the generations after the high-watermarks of mid-century liberalism: the Civil Rights Act of 1964, the Voting Rights Act of 1965, and the Immigration and Naturalization Act of 1965. After decades of discrimination and xenophobia, these reforms created unprecedented pathways for racial minorities and immigrants to participate fully in American society. African-American representation among the ranks of homeowners and the college educated surged, while American universities absorbed skilled laborers from Africa, Asia and Latin America.

Combined with the shrinking fertility rates of American Whites, this new era of minority visibility was an irrevocable demographic shift. As a result, Millennials are the most diverse generation in American history: in 2014, the U.S. Census reported that 50% of Millennials are part of a "minority" ethnic group.[1] Even as Millennials came of age during the onset of American neoliberalism, Millennial diversity is a last vestige of mid-century social reforms.

SNORTING THE COLOR LINE

The gradual inclusion of racial minorities and immigrants presented America with a cultural contradiction. On the one hand, legislation and mass media clearly acknowledged differences between American ethic groups: Civil Rights reforms were necessary because specific groups were historically disadvantaged, while sitcoms like *Good Times* (1974–1979) and *The Jeffersons* (1975–1985) were clearly Black-themed.

On the other hand, suggesting that differences between ethnic groups had to do with genetics or inherent cultural tendencies was met with criticism from newly empowered minorities who, after decades of discrimination, were justifiably wary about being misrepresented by mainstream media. This tenuous middle ground—between the acknowledged reality of America's racial situation and the country's hesitance to describe it in stark terms—was fertile ground for transgressive comedians.

In the 1970s, cocaine-addled comedian Richard Pryor rose to fame by making his rendition of the Black experience unflinchingly intelligible in coarse terms. His legendary 1974 comedy special *That Nigger's Crazy* is a fireball of harsh truths about interracial love, police brutality, and cultural differences told in incendiary language. Chris Rock carried on the tradition in the 90s by describing internal differences among African-Americans that respectability-obsessed representations of the Black middle class shied away from.

In the 2000s, no comic abused the politically correct climate of "post-racial"[2] America as routinely as Dave Chappelle: a Black comedian who, like Jon Stewart and Stephen Colbert, was buoyed by Millennial audiences. "When you mention Chappelle's name among young folks," the Civil Rights-era comic pioneer Dick Gregory opined in 2005, "it's like mentioning Jesus in a Christian church."[3]

BLACK JESUS

After a string of forgettable film appearances in the 90s and the memorable comedy special *Dave Chappelle: Killin' Them Softly* (2000), Chappelle first forged his Millennial following with *Chappelle's Show* (2003–2006). On it, he combined the observational genius of Jerry Seinfeld with the statement-making ambition of Chris Rock. In the words of scholar Bambi Haggins, the result was a hit series that "enjoyed dual credibility through ties to the Black intelligentsia and [suburbia's] White slackers of Generation Y."[4]

One of Chappelle's most popular skits was "the racial draft":

a sketch in which each race is allowed to pick a public figure to become part of its culture. In another sketch, Chappelle performs as the fictional character Clayton Bigsby—a blind Black man who rises to power in the Ku Klux Klan because no one can see his dark skin beneath his White sheets. Antics like these highlighted both the artificiality of race and its undeniable concreteness. The message resonated with the most diverse generation ever. In 2004, it was reported that *Chappelle's Show* was the highest rated program in its timeslot among 18–34 year-olds, who helped home media sales of the show's first season become the best-selling television-series DVD of all-time.[5]

Chappelle's humor was confrontational and always topical. His aesthetic was reminiscent of the rap artists he affiliated himself with. Acts such as Mos Def and De La Soul appeared on *Chappelle's Show*, highlighting the cross section between their socially conscious rhymes and his socially subversive material.

Chappelle's status as hip-hop's Comedian-in-Chief was solidified in the 2005 film *Block Party*, a Michel Gondry-directed concert documentary where Chappelle hosted politically outspoken acts such as The Roots, dead prez, and Kanye West. The spectacle of *Block Party*—a showcase of all-Black artistic talent held in a rapidly gentrifying section of Brooklyn— indicated that America's self-satisfied narrative of post-9/11 national unity contained deep fissures beneath the surface.

I DON'T SEE COLOR

The Nation writer Mychal Denzel Smith has written that: "White Millennials are a product of a failed lesson in colorblindness."[6]

After the contentious climate of 1960s politics and protests, the nation came to an unstated collective decision to not revisit the traumatic times that saw Black leaders get gunned-down for daring to oppose domestic racism and capitalism. With its rosy-eyed portrait of racial reconciliation, the cultural strategy of colorblindness showed up as a soothing salve to frayed collective nerves. Adherents to the disingenuous logic of colorblindness pretended to not see color as a self-satisfied attempt at abdicating responsibility for inequities and racial disparities. Its cultural incarnations were television shows like *I Spy* (1965–1968) and the movie *Silver Streak* (1976), where Black comedians were paired with White actors in buddy comedies to demonstrate hokey racial harmony.

Though colorblindness was first cultivated in liberal and academic circles in the late 60s and mid-70s, American conservatives learned to get in on the game. By using loaded buzzwords and dog-whistle appeals, GOP politicians advanced neoliberal policies that disadvantaged minorities and cultivated support from racist voter blocs without seeming to be racist themselves. At the dawn of the Reagan Era in 1981, conservative strategist Lee Atwater summarized the link between the rhetoric of colorblindness and neoliberalism:

> You start out in 1954 by saying, "Nigger, nigger, nigger." By 1968 you can't say "nigger." That backfires. So you say stuff like "states' rights" and "cutting taxes." You're getting so abstract now [that] these things you're talking about are totally economic things, and a byproduct of them is that Blacks get hurt worse than Whites.[7]

In his 2016 memoir *Invisible Man, Got the Whole World Watching*, Denzel Smith argues colorblind logic was not dislodged until Hurricane Katrina "[made] our national conversation on race concern itself with questions of inequality and government neglect."[8]

BLACK 9/11

A category 5 weather event dubbed "Katrina" by the World Meteorological Organization, Hurricane Katrina visited 170+ mile-per-hour winds on the American southeast. When it reached landfall in the Gulf of Mexico on August 28th, 2005, the storm wreaked most of its havoc on Black, brown, and poor residents. In its wake, Katrina claimed 1,245 lives and caused $108 *billion* worth of property damage. A major metropolitan area and a beacon of American arts and culture, the city of New Orleans became the eye of the media storm surrounding the spectacle of Hurricane Katrina.

News cameras captured dispossessed families flooding into the Superdome for shelter. Surrealist images of toilets and pickup trucks lodged atop trees circulated in print and online. In the storm's aftermath, New York Knicks point guard Stephon Marbury cried inconsolably at a press conference while pledging $1 million in charity to help clean up the wreckage.[9] Months later in a first-person retrospective published by *Dime Magazine* in February of 2006, famously insular Los Angeles Lakers superstar Kobe Bryant described the storm as motivation to embrace his Black identity.[10]

GEORGE BUSH DOESN'T CARE ABOUT BLACK PEOPLE

A Fox News broadcast on the eve of the storm showed an anchor warning that "people who ignored the evacuation orders or for some reason didn't get them are simply going to have to rescue themselves."[11] Indeed, in an editorial for *The Guardian* from September of 2005, scholar Cornel West wrote that "the hurricane was the naked manifestation of America's social policy towards the poor, where the message for decades has been: You are on your own."[12]

Perhaps the most memorable critique of the American social order that hosted the disaster of Katrina came from Kanye West. On a live telethon for the American Red Cross broadcast by NBC on September 2nd, 2005, West was paired with actor Mike Myers to crowdsource cleanup funds. Myers read a sappy introduction from the teleprompter. But West deviated from the script:

"America is set up to help the poor, the Black, and the less well-off as slowly as possible," stated West, firmly but nervously; "when you see a Black family [in the news] it says they're looting, [but] when you see a White family it says they're looking for food."[13] After a stiff interruption by Myers, West delivered a cutting statement that slashed its way into pop-culture immortality:

"George Bush. Doesn't care about. Black people."[14]

TRAGEDY TO TRIUMPH

In her 2010 tome *Shock Doctrine: The Rise of Disaster Capitalism*, Naomi Klein observes that "in [the week after Hurricane Katrina], the Louisiana State Legislature was crawling with corporate lobbyists helping to turn New Orleans into a city with lower taxes, fewer regulations, and cheaper workers."[15] New Orleans' public schools were given over to privatized interests that created a charter system, and lucrative contracts totaling $3.4 billion in value were given to defense and construction firms.[16] In a November 2005 editorial in the *Wall Street Journal*, a neoliberal architect used the catastrophe to advocate that more charter schools be built in New Orleans.[17]

When the New Orleans Saints defeated the Indianapolis Colts in Super Bowl XLIV in February of 2010, the nation was joined in celebrating the city's post-Katrina resurgence. An Associated Press news report valorized the team as "symbolic of New Orleans' resilience in the face of disaster."[18]

A decade after Hurricane Katrina, President Barack Obama visited New Orleans in August 2015 to celebrate what he called "the extraordinary resilience of the city and its people."[19]

"We've been going through a national recovery, but there's a specific recovery going on right here in New Orleans," Obama said. "You are an example of what is possible when people come together to build a better future, brick by brick, block by block."[20]

9B

Obama's lyrical hues of hope made him appealing to Millennials. His optimistic worldview—pulled from Cold War stoic Reinhold Niebuhr and Civil Rights gradualist John Lewis[21]—contained a futurist thrust that posited generational endurance as the path to achieving leftist political goals.

In a campaign trail interview from January 2008 that circulated widely on YouTube, Obama fancied himself as a transformative figure *ala* Ronald Reagan.[22] By invoking the president who had the single biggest impact of the cultural and political terrain of American Millennials, Obama presented himself as a generational equivalent for progressives; a chosen one who would initiate a right-to-left shift in the country's political paradigm. In his stump speeches and campaign appearances, Obama used his trademark eloquence—as well as social networking outreach and Internet fundraising—to tie his candidacies to youth and rejuvenation.

Millennials were infatuated with Obama's message, and with Obama the messenger. His multiracial phenotype mirrored the generation's diversity, as a CBS News writer noted in 2008 that Obama's features "seemed beamed from a post-racial future."[23] Later in 2008, artist Shepard Fairey colorized Obama's compulsively watchable face, placing it atop the words HOPE and PROGRESS in posters that were increasingly visible in gentrifying cities where college-educated Millennials and the urban poor came to live in close proximity to one another.

The Obama Effect on American politics was real. ABC News reported in 2009 that turnout among Millennial (18–24 year-old) African-Americans in the 2008 presidential election had increased by an astounding five million votes over the demographic's 2004 turnout.[24] In his successful first bid for the presidency, Obama captured the support of 66% of voting Millennials of all races.[25]

THE NEXT GENERATION

Over the years, the phrase "next generation" appeared in scores of Obama's speeches. Upon his acceptance of the DNC presidential nomination in August of 2008, he urged America to "come together as one American family to ensure that the next generation can pursue their dreams."[26] In his first Presidential Weekly Address on January 24th, 2009, he promised to provide a $2,500 tax credit to four million students, and "triple the number of fellowships in science to help spur the next generation of innovation."[27] At a speech to the National Wireless Institute in February of 2011, he praised college students at Northern Michigan University for "partnering with various companies to build a high-speed, next generation wireless network"[28] in four days without raising tuition. These shout-outs were not just gestures. They provided cover and legitimacy for Obama's political agenda.

OBAMA IS FOR THE CHILDREN

As we've seen in Parts I and II of this book, Ronald Reagan and Bill Clinton used anxiety about young Millennials to justify retrograde measures in law enforcement and economic policy. Obama instead used generational rhetoric to signal the dawn of a new era of progressivism. In his 2016 State of the Union Address, Obama opined, "I don't want to talk about next year. I want to focus on the next five years, the next 10 years, and beyond. I want to focus on our future."[29]

SPORTS CZAR

Obama's embrace of professional sports was key to his politics of generational endurance. In 2008, he took Chris Rock's advice that he had to deliver a decisive "knockout" of Hillary Clinton in the presidential primaries "because contenders can't win on points."[30] Once in the White House, he talked trash to Kobe Bryant and Celtics guard Rajon Rondo, and played competitive basketball regularly. Obama called himself a "game-day player"[31] while preparing for debates against Mitt Romney, and likened his reelection in 2012 to a Michael Jordan repeat.

Obama's athletic affiliations helped build his cultural brand as perhaps the coolest president since Kennedy, or at least Clinton. But his sporty showcases also indicated something else: the fact that his worldview was a competition-centric relic of the University of Chicago—the same school that incubated the neoliberal revolt against mid-century Keynesian capitalism. Obama taught there for 12 years. As Pierre Dardot and Christian Laval note in *The New Way of the World: On Neoliberal Society*, neoliberalism celebrates "the man of competition. Competitive sport is the great social theatre that displays the modern gods, demi-gods, and heroes."[32]

WE CAME HERE TO COMPETE

For decades in the mid-20th century under the leadership of Milton Friedman, the University of Chicago was a resilient school of radical neoliberal economists who existed outside of the establishment mainstream. While collaborative Keynesianism was the governing logic of the post-WWII era, intellectuals at the University of Chicago polished their anti-regulation, antigovernment arguments. Friedman and his intellectual offspring updated the social Darwinism of America's robber baron era, forging a survivalist worldview that celebrated competition and stigmatized welfare as weak.

"Our basic function," Friedman declared, addressing himself to other neoliberal radicals who were marginalized under Keynesian capitalism, "is to develop alternatives to existing policies, to keep them alive and available until the politically impossible becomes the politically inevitable." Milton Friedman preached the need to use global crises like coups, terrorist attacks, and environmental catastrophes to implement neoliberal, market-friendly reforms. In this respect, he was the godfather of the capitalist resilience narrative. His teachings had a reach as far as capitalism's tentacles:

A pack of Friedmanite disciples famously travelled to Latin America to spread the gospel of neoliberalism in the late 1970s, telling a group of Chilean centrists "we came here to compete, not to collaborate."[33]

OBAMA AND NEOLIBERALISM: A MIXED LEGACY

Barack Hussein Obama was born on August 4th, 1961 to a Black father from Kenya and a White woman from Kansas. His socioeconomic legacy has been mixed.

On the one hand, Obama shredded the core tenants of neoliberalism in his 2012 campaign against wealthy republican Mitt Romney. "If you were successful, somebody gave you some help," Obama said at a campaign stop in Virginia; "there was a great teacher. Somebody invested in roads and bridges. If you've got a business, you didn't build that."[34] Obama later observed that fiscal conservatives under the influence of philosopher Ayn Rand's celebration of selfishness were immaturely consumed by a "you're-on-your-own vision of society."[35]

At the same time, Obama was quoted on the 2008 campaign trail as saying, "I'm a pro-growth, free-market guy. I love the market."[36] To prove it, he chose University of Chicago economist and Milton Friedman eulogist Austan Goolsbee as his top economic advisor in his first term as president.

Obama's rhetoric about race also tended to echo that of American conservatives. When discussing social pathology facing disadvantaged Black families, Obama tended to emphasize "personal responsibility" and "initiative" over structural issues like poverty and lack of access to education.[37] Years before asking Michael Jordan for campaign donations in his runs for president, then-Senator Obama lambasted Black children who spent money on Air Jordan sneakers instead of books in an ESPN segment from 2002.[38]

Unfortunately, Obama's zeal for critiquing the criminal and pathological tendencies of Black fathers did not extend to disciplining Wall Street for creating the fiscal calamity of 2008. Obama refused to prosecute a single trader, banker, or executive in the aftermath of the Great Recession, saying on a March 2009 episode of *60 Minutes* that "we can't govern out of anger."

FIX IT!

Obama's conflicted relationship to neoliberalism was never more obvious than in his handling of the 2008 financial crisis. While his presidential hopes were as yet unrealized in September of 2008, global capitalism was rocked by news that the global investment firm Lehman Brothers went bankrupt.

It gradually came to light that the post-9/11 economic recovery was based on a deregulated housing market. The documentary films *Capitalism: A Love Story* (2009) and *Inside Job* (2010) explained that predatory lending agencies extended the promise of cheap homeownership to opportunistic Americans while trading mortgage debts on a shady market of collatorized debt obligations.

An uproarious 2008 "Weekend Update" skit on *Saturday Night Live* reflected America's bewilderment at the causes of capitalism's crash. In the recurring gag, Kenan Thompson plays a fictional economist named Oscar Rodgers, whose solution for the Great Recession is, simply, to "FIX IT!":

> *It's a simple 3-step process:*
> *Step 1: Fix!*
> *Step 2: It!*
> *Step 3: Fix it!*
> *Then repeat steps 1 through 3 until it's been FIXED!*[39]

BOOMERANG CHILDREN

Barely out of their caps and gowns, graduating Millennials were left to rummage through their disinheritance, as America shed 8.4 million jobs between 2008 and 2009. By 2010, an article on Slate.com titled "The Visit That Never Ends"[40] highlighted Millennials as "boomerang children" who returned home because of the financial downturn. The Great Recession presented Obama with an opportunity to consummate the countercultural appeal he cultivated with Millennials, if he could only corral capitalism after the crash.

AMERICA ON THE REBOUND

With the wind at his back, Obama quietly lobbied sitting duck President George W. Bush to authorize a federal bailout for struggling automotive giants GM, Ford, and Chrysler in the autumn of 2008. Once in office in 2009, he also signed the American Recovery and Reinvestment Act, providing $830 billion of federal spending to social programs, tax rebates, unemployment benefits, and education initiatives.[41] Shortly thereafter, Obama pledged to "invest in students rather than subsidize banks"[42] by allocating billions of dollars for Pell Grants and student loans which disproportionately *advantaged* Millennials of color. "These are programs that help people who need the help the most,"[43] explained Obama. When he was up for reelection in 2012, Obama could scarcely be heard giving a speech where he didn't credit himself for helping the economy rebound after the Great Recession.

JOBLESS RECOVERY

But what was at the center of Obama's post-recession recovery? CQ Researcher estimates that between 2008 and 2012, jobs in the relatively low-paid "temp" fields increased by 41%.[44] Meanwhile, a joint study by Harvard and Princeton economists revealed that an astonishing 94% of the 10 million new "jobs" created during the Obama era were temporary contract positions in the gig economy.[45] Many of these jobs were filled by Millennials who were nominally employed for working even a single hour a week (and who cruelly found themselves kicked off of still-needed unemployment assistance as a result).

EVERYDAY WE'RE HUSTLING

By the end of the 2000s, pop culture representations like the television shows *How to Make It in America* (2010–2011) and *Girls* (2012–) focused on the struggles of enterprising Millennial young adults who lived in increasingly unaffordable cities. Strapped with student debt and stretched thin by go-nowhere gigs and temp work, Millennials who hustled everyday scarcely had time to pontificate about what the symbolic achievement of a Black presidency really meant.

9C

While Hurricane Katrina was raging and America was still a few years away from electing its first Black president, I was in college struggling to pay rent, and working my first of many service-industry gigs. Times were so hard financially that I was even forced to drop out of school for a time—living near campus and working odd jobs by day, and reading American History tomes like *Anti-Intellectualism in American Life* at night to stay sharp for the time I had the chance to re-enroll. That opportunity never came. I left school for good in the Spring of 2008 with enough credits to nominally satisfy my History Department's under-graduate degree requirements, but not enough to earn a full Bachelor of Arts from the University of Washington.

CRAP JOB

Back in August 2005 I had accepted a gig as an ice cream scooper at the music festival Bumbershoot. Beneath the sweltering sun and the Space Needle, I served festivalgoers while a nearby busker played a janky rendition of the Beatles' "(Money) Can't Buy Me Love" repeatedly on his decrepit saxophone. In four consecutive days of 14-hour shifts, not one of the hundreds of people I interacted with at my ice cream stand mentioned Hurricane Katrina to me. My apartment did not have a television, and by the time I was done with work I didn't have the energy to do anything besides sleep.

Upon finding out about the storm days later, I wondered in retrospect if the ample tips I received were my customers' attempt to purchase racial and generational reconciliation. *We allowed Reagan to sack the social safety net that young people and minorities like you depend on. And Katrina is a real bummer. We are so, so sorry. Here's a dollar.*

In her 2006 book *Generation Debt*, Anya Kamenetz writes that low-wage "[crap jobs] are a generational rite of passage."[46] While I once believed that I was being singled-out as a service worker and later as a freelancer, I came to see that my adventures in the land of low-wage labor were a part of a generational condition.

THE UPHILL CLIMB

College was an anxiety-inducing obstacle course for me, just as it is for millions of other Millennials who have just enough privilege to attend. Between excelling at classes, making friends, pursuing love interests, chasing scholarships, working, and tending to aging and sick relatives, the amount of responsibilities we handle in these years is mind-boggling. And we've been asked to do it with fewer resources than previous generations, who enjoyed the promise of free education and near-full employment under Keynesian capitalism.

On the cultural terrain of neoliberalism in the 2000s, success stories of resilient, high-achieving students are used to guilt those who struggle. Social networking websites intensify feelings of depression and anxiety, as we witness others selectively edit their lives on Facebook and Twitter to omit all signs of strife. In this setting, the culture of resilience valorizes the act of overcoming; but it also prevents a critical look at why life has to be such an uphill climb in the first place.

IT'S NOT YOUR FAULT

A son of Trinidadian immigrants and a Millennial born in 1989, *Jacobin Magazine* editor Bhaskar Sunkara asserts that young people must reject the culture of personal shame, and realize that our socioeconomic woes are structural, not personal. His remarks from a 2014 episode of *The Tavis Smiley Show* echo a moving scene from the 1997 film *Good Will Hunting*, where a psychiatrist played by Robin Williams explains to a wayward youth that his hardscrabble upbringing is "not his fault":

> *Americans were told that if you work hard, you'd be given a nine-to-five, a pension, and a safe retirement. Now people are working harder and harder, but wages have stagnated. People are filling the gap with loans, with credit, with two or three jobs. And people are realizing it's not their fault. Austerity, cutbacks, layoffs—it's not your fault. They know that they're following the rulebook, but they're seeing generationally that they're not getting even what their parents and grandparents got.*[47]

MILLENNIALS RISING

By the late 2000s, a cultural profile of the Millennial generation began to emerge. Against the backdrop of the fallen Twin Towers, America's post-Katrina, recession-era culture revealed an unprecedentedly diverse and tech-friendly generation. A 2010 study by Pew Research Center described Millennials as the most socially progressive and distinctly disadvantaged generation in recent memory.[48] By decade's end, business texts began circulating the idea that Millennials "prefer praise over pay"—clearly a canard to justify wage exploitation.

Popular culture reflected the straits of America's maturing Millennials. Issa Rae launched the YouTube sensation *Awkward Black Girl* in 2011, before going on to stylize the adverse impact chronic joblessness has on relationships in the 2016 HBO drama *Insecure*. Riding the wave of outspoken 80s feminists, Lena Dunham rose to prominence with her 2010 independent film *Tiny Furniture*, then went on to advertise herself as "a voice of a generation" in the television show *Girls*. Animating gender norms resulting from the demise of mid-century capitalism, Lady Gaga became an androgynous sex symbol and champion of gay pride.

Television actors America Ferrara (*Ugly Betty*, 2006–2010) and Aziz Ansari (*Parks and Recreation*, 2009–2015) illustrated the generation's diversity with depictions of white-collar people of color employed in predominantly White professions. And actor-turned-rapper Aubrey Drake Graham parlayed buzz from his online mixtape *Comeback Season* (2007) into the platinum album *Thank Me Later* (2010), then became the soundtrack for a digital social scene of short-term relationships and broken commitments (see Chapter 10, "Millennial Man"). Meanwhile, hulking Millennial athlete LeBron James was making it a personal mission to solve the ravages of recession in the region hit hardest by it.

ALL MILLENNIALS ARE FROM AKRON

Born LeBron Raymond James on December 30th, 1984 in Akron, Ohio, James had been tapped as a sports savior since before he could legally drive, vote, or drink. While still a teenager at St. Vincent-St. Mary's Catholic School in 2002, a *Sports Illustrated* cover story titled "The Chosen One"[49] announced that James had the potential to rank with NBA greats Michael Jordan and Magic Johnson.

The son of a teenage mother and an absentee father, James was one of millions of Millennials who had a childhood filled with high expectations in the midst of widespread institutional decay. What's more, his upbringing in Ohio—a political battleground state whose travails under neoliberal capitalism reflect widely on the condition of Millennials as a whole—gives his public sports saga resonance. In his 2016 book *But What If We're Wrong*, Chuck Klosterman wrote that "Ohio is a wonderful place to ponder the state of American democracy because you're constantly being reminded that America is where you are."[50] Indeed, several great American cultural crosscurrents came together in James' career in Cleveland:

The spectacle of LeBron James' Cleveland ties were a quintessential example of what scholars Kirk Boyle and Daniel Mrozowski have termed "bust culture"[51]—a strand of entertainment that centered the recession's effects on American citizens. As in the television shows *American Greed* (2007–) and *How to Make It in America* and the films *100% OFF: A Recession-Era Romance* (2012) and *Detropia* (2012), capitalism's depressed state was a silent character that influenced the decisions of actors on the screen. In the same period, the blogs Abandoned America, Architecture of Doom, and Ruin Porn made a spectacle out of social decay. From 9/11 to Hurricane Katrina to the Great Recession to the BP Oil Spill of 2010, America in the 2000s was obsessed with stories about post-traumatic survivalism. In his quest to deliver an NBA championship to Cleveland, Ohio—an economically depressed city that suffered deindustrialization in the 1970s, and recession in the 2000s—James' career became an archetypal resilience narrative. Broadcasters could seldom make it through a Cleveland Cavaliers game without uttering bromides about *"what this city has been through over the years."*

Moreover, the fact that James was a Black employee in a field dominated by primarily White employers meant his career was a simile of Millennial labor in the neoliberal economy. Judgments that critics levied at James for simply seeking the most advantageous work environment found an echo in ageist (and racist) criticisms of "entitled" Millennials who don't know "the meaning of hard work." Indeed, the inflammatory rhetoric of the typical anti-Millennial diatribe was first rehearsed on "lazy" people of color who look for "handouts." James was a multimillionaire, but this did not shield him from being exposed to the same insults that Millennials and people of color at all levels of the class strata are unfortunately familiar with.

Being the most diverse generation in American history includes suffering the social stigmas and justifications of wage exploitation that have historically accompanied the minority experience in the United States. Anti-Millennial sentiment— coupled with our country's fixation on personal resilience—is therefore a vehicle for intensifying the austerity measures and disprivilege facing American minorities who are told to "suck it up" under neoliberalism. At the same time, White Millennials who experience chronic joblessness, trouble renting apartments, and the cycle of debt are only becoming acquainted with conditions that their counterparts of color have always known.

This late capitalist cauldron of generalized socioeconomic depression, racial animus, and generational antagonism was the melting pot in which LeBron James' career was created.

FREELANCER

James' athletic feats in the 2000s were legendary. A 6'8" 250lbs. specimen, his combination of size and speed defied conventional divisions of basketball labor. Players of his stature are typically confined to the area underneath the basket; but James' athleticism allowed him to freelance as both a guard and a forward. He was just as likely to grab a steal on the perimeter as he was to dart to the basket for a devastating block.

In their 2006 study of business management texts *The New Spirit of Capitalism*, sociologists Luc Boltanski and Eve Chiapello note that "flexibility"[52] and "adaptability"[53] are coveted traits for downsizing companies in search of workers who can fulfill multiple roles. As a result, millions of Millennial temps, interns, and freelancers are all too familiar with the fact that their undervalued (and often uncompensated) efforts are indispensable to the enterprises they work for. James was the basketball embodiment of these socioeconomic principles: as long as he was on the roster to hide his squad's weaknesses, his singular gifts allowed his team owners to skimp on talent acquisition and competent coaching. Soon after being drafted by the Cleveland Cavaliers in 2003, James repeatedly dragged mediocre teams to championship contention.

While James became rich as a professional basketball player, his salary in the 2000s was but a fraction of the Cleveland Cavaliers' total worth as a franchise—a franchise that he was singularly responsible for resurrecting.

DIVISION OF LABOR

Great basketball teams like the 1980s Los Angeles Lakers or the 1990s Chicago Bulls had historically been built with the financial resources of an (always White) patriarchal team owner, the intellectual design of a (usually White) head coach, and the physical labor of (mostly Black) athletes. Individual basketball players could be brilliant, but brick ceilings of class and race blocked even savvy businessmen like Michael Jordan or Isaiah Thomas from meddling with team management. No such barriers applied to LeBron James.

Aided by digital tools that allowed him to diagnose player tendencies, James developed a reputation as a masterful appraiser of talent who could anticipate plays before they happened, and recall sequences of plays years after they occurred. He routinely overruled hapless head coaches like Mike Brown and David Blatt, and served as an ersatz general manager to Cleveland Cavaliers team-owner Dan Gilbert. Had these hijinks not resulted in wins, James would have become another story in a legion of complaints about me-first Millennials with no respect for authority. But James' inverted pyramid of leadership produced success. His subversion of the traditional basketball division of labor corroborates a February 2016 article in *Millennial Magazine* titled "Your Boss Fears You, So Leverage It!":

That's right he/she knows that you demand work that has meaning, are wildly influential on social media, and will leave for greener career pastures the minute they present themselves. These trends are reshaping today's workplace.[54]

PARTICIPATION TROPHY

When LeBron registered 45 points in a valiant playoff defeat against the juggernaut Boston Celtics in the 2008 Eastern Conference Semifinals, it seemed only a matter of time before his anointment as basketball royalty would be consummated in a championship. A Nike ad campaign titled "We Are All Witnesses" cast James as a once-in-a-generation talent on the brink of basketball immortality.

But as the 2000s came to a close, disappointments that once seemed like cute stepping-stones became an annual tradition for James. After the Cavaliers were trounced by the underdog Orlando Magic in Game Five of the 2009 Eastern Conference Finals, James left the court without consoling his teammates or shaking his opponents' hands. A year later when the Boston Celtics dealt the Cavaliers yet another premature playoff exit, cameras captured James hastily discarding his jersey in a hissy fit.

Snapshots like these contributed to a growing cultural narrative that painted "coddled" Millennials like James as work-averse whiners who were weaned on participation trophies in youth athletics, and therefore did not ever learn to struggle for victories of substance. The point was rarely made that those trophies were about making *the* parents of young Millennials feel better about their child not being the next Michael Jordan.

THE DECISION

Anti-Millennial criticisms and public castigation of James' short-comings as an athlete finally coalesced in his 2010 resolution to leave the Cleveland Cavaliers for the Miami Heat. James announced this decision in a 2-hour long ESPN television special titled *The Decision*. In signing with the Miami Heat in the summer of 2010, James actually took a significant pay cut. He also donated all proceeds from *The Decision* to an Akron Boys & Girls Club. Nonetheless, news cameras captured Clevelanders burning James' jersey in the streets. Cavaliers team owner Dan Gilbert called James' actions a "cowardly betrayal [from a] former hometown hero."[55]

POSTINDUSTRIAL PICK-AND-ROLL

James' relocation was devastating to Cleveland sports fans—and not just psychologically. In an article titled "The Global Circus: International Sport, Tourism, and the Marketing of Cities," David Whitson and David Macintosh assert that sports are "a form of public assistance to private accumulation, a postindustrial variant of traditional subsidies to industry."[56] LeBron James' economic impact on the region of northeast Ohio has been estimated at as much as $500 million. By leaving, it was as if a factory plant had shuddered its doors.

For an area used to corporations relocating for greener pastures on the cutthroat socioeconomic terrain of neoliberalism, James was cast as yet another civically disloyal business entity. James was the basketball version of General Motors fleeing Flint, Boeing flying from Seattle, or Sprint booking it out of Kansas. His visibility made him an easy target for socioeconomic anxieties that were rooted in the dynamics of corporate capitalism. Because he is a Millennial, he became a symbol of everything older pundits thought was wrong with America's 80s babies.

[OBLIGATORY MENTION OF NARCISSISM]

Reflecting on *The Decision*, sportswriter Bill Simmons decried LeBron as a member of the "me-me-me generation"[57]—a label borrowed from a 2013 *Time Magazine* story about Millennials.[58] In his scathing 2011 book *The Whore of Akron*, journalist Scott Raab blasted James as a "feckless child"[59] and an "entitled narcissist"[60] who betrayed Cleveland after the "socioeconomic Katrina of deindustrialization."[61] To be sure, James' preening behavior often played into these criticisms: in an Instagram post on March 1st, 2015, an emo LeBron stares glumly at himself in a mirror, writing a caption where he summons himself to be "the greatest I've ever seen!"[62]

FREE AGENT NATION

But what pundits failed to grasp was that James was a member of a generation that inherited three decades of neoliberal policies. By the 2000s, America had become what author Daniel Pink described as a "free agent nation"[63] — a place where loyalties are fickle because finance capital was more mobile than ever. In the mid-20th century, Keynesian capitalism tamed big business with progressive taxes and strong unions. Neoliberalism removed the regulations that made this possible. As a result, states like South Carolina — that could court corporations with the lowest taxes and the cheapest wages — were enfranchised. Those that could not, like Ohio, suffered.

A LITTLE CHILD SHALL LEAD THEM[64]

But if previous generations could not keep their social order under control, the least they could do to compensate was wage a culture war against "entitled" Millennials who merely made choices in the socioeconomic context handed to them.

For 20 years going back to films like *Home Alone* (1990), *Curly Sue* (1991), *The Parent Trap* (1998), and *Harry Potter and the Sorcerer's Stone* (2001), Americans consumed cultural representations that nominated Millennials as gifted children who would save the world from the ravages of neoliberalism. James' great cultural crime was in refusing the Millennial savior narrative hoisted on him by Cleveland, opting instead to win a bunch of championships with his best friends while looking at a sunny beach in Miami.

In the end, LeBron James was being criticized for his seeming lack of resilience in a culture context that was obsessed with that quality. But the question is rarely asked: why are Americans culturally conditioned to meet mounting odds with individual resilience, as opposed to collective correction of capitalism?

MILLENNIALS EMERGE

The first Millennials reached adulthood in the 2000s. Diverse and disprivileged, we died disproportionate to our numbers in Iraq and Afghanistan after 9/11. We went into debt for the crime of attending college. We posted our petty glories on Facebook, wasted time on YouTube, organized on Twitter, and entertained the world with sports and music that made the body politic dance. Presidential candidates appealed to us as an electoral force, while capitalism repaired itself on the backs of our often-as-not unpaid labor. All the while, pundits called us entitled and self-centered. But were it not for Millennials, many would not know the meaning of resilience. And resilient we were. Because resilience was all that many of us had.

Part IV: ADULTHOOD

(2012–present)

I'm really scared for my generation. Instead of kids going out and making their own moments, they're just taking these images and living vicariously through other people's moments. It's a scary simulation life that we're living in.[1]
–rapper, Drake.

Chapter 10

Millennial Man

In October of 2008, the *Wall Street Journal* published an excerpt of author Ron Alsop's book *The Trophy Kids Grow Up*, announcing that "with [America's] financial system in crisis mode, companies are facing the challenge of how to manage the new crop of millennials in the workforce."[1] Released weeks later in November of 2008, Alsop's book[2] said that "there is truth to the negative perception that Millennials are fickle,"[3] and argued that "a strong sense of entitlement is one of the most striking characteristics of millennials."[4]

By 2011, Alsop's ideas formed the basis of a TED Talk by marketer Scott Hess, who proclaimed that "Millennials are [seen as] entitled, lazy, and just not fit to live."[5] Hess concluded that previous generations are jealous of Millennials because "they have extended their adolescence." The sentiment was echoed in 2015 by cultural critic Chuck Klosterman, who wrote that "the prolonging of adolescence and the avoidance of adulthood"[6] is a defining factor of life in the 21st century.

PROLONGED ADOLESCENCE, PROLONGED EXPLOITATION

As American capitalism regenerated in the aftermath of the Great Recession, some of the defining myths about Millennials made their first mainstream appearances. For companies looking to cut costs after the recession, cultural stories about Millennials provided the ideological basis for how capitalism would treat Millennial temps, interns, and fresh-faced employees: as an incompetent source of cheap labor. Business literature praised the technological prowess and independence of Millennials, while simultaneously claiming that they were tactically inept and needed to be constantly supervised. Negative portrayals of Millennials as a Peter Pan generation that refused to grow up emboldened employers who didn't want to pay us the wages that would allow us to do so.

THE CULT(URE) OF MASCULINITY

The idea that Millennials were coddled perpetual adolescents emerged during the Great Recession. It was also a function of ideas about masculinity that Americans had been telling themselves for the previous century.

In the early 20th century, America underwent a series of technological and demographic changes that led to concern among civic leaders that men were becoming weak. In the years spanning 1890–1920, Americans separated themselves from their agricultural origins, as millions of citizens moved to cities with dazzling new amenities like automobiles, electricity, and movie theatres.[7]

Teddy Roosevelt called for a restoration of the country's masculine character through war,[8] and fraternal organizations like the YMCA endorsed gender-segregated sports to incubate rugged individualism.[9] Basketball was invented in 1891, boxing achieved legitimacy when it was included in the 1904 Summer Olympics and used as a training technique for American soldiers during WWI, and the National Football League formed in 1920.

Meanwhile, popular books by Jack London and Rudyard Kipling celebrated the survival of the fittest, and the philosophy of Herbert Spencer was invoked in defense of wealth stratification under capitalism's Darwinian, dog-eat-dog social order. Scholar Christopher Oldstone-Moore notes that men in this period grew mustaches as an outward sign of "fierceness and discipline."[10]

This cult of masculinity has endured. Performative masculinity in team sports is still a proving ground for American men. Guys who can't so much as change a flat tire (let alone cut down a tree) sport lumberjack flannel and beards. And cruel ideas about lazy poor people who lack initiative legitimate cuts to social services. For a capitalist country weaned on a century of stories about self-reliant men and self-made millionaires, the greatest insult that could be hurled at men of a certain generation was to call them coddled and weak.

ENTITLEMENT PROGRAM

And yet the myth of the entitled Millennial does not square with the facts of life under late capitalism. It is Baby Boomers, and not Millennials, who are far and away the most entitled generation in American history. Simply by virtue of being born during a federal policy of full employment, aging, sick, and widowed Boomers have come to expect Social Security payments that are many times greater than if they invested the Social Security taxes withheld from their paychecks in U.S. Treasury bonds or high-performing index funds.[11] What's more, the Social Security taxes taken from the paychecks of Millennials who entered the workforce in the 2000s and 2010s go mostly to support the "silver tsunami"[12] of aging Baby Boomers.

In other words, Boomers receive benefits that far exceed the amount they actually worked for on their own. There is nothing wrong with this. But, to be sure, it is the literal definition of "entitlement." In his 2004 book *On Borrowed Time*, Neil Howe explained how Social Security gave Boomers a massive retirement cushion at the expense of Millennials:

> *The American concept of "entitlement" is inherently prejudicial against the young. We are quietly expecting them to pay as much as one-third of their paychecks before the middle of the next century to finance our own retirement and health-care programs. We are failing our children.*[13]

AND THEN A HERO COMES ALONG

Neil Howe's book *On Borrowed Time* was named after a 1939 movie about an abandoned child who came under the care of his grandparents. It's a feel-good story about intergenerational caretaking.

Like Shirley Temple's performances in *Bright Eyes* (1934) and *The Little Princess* (1939), *On Borrowed Time* provided an emotional lift to economically insecure audiences during the Great Depression. Decades later in the 2000s and 2010s, another genre gave Americans wracked by war and recession some much-needed hope: superhero films.

Beginning with the 2002 rendition of *Spider-Man*, the superhero film came to define cinema in the new millennium. Installments of director Christopher Nolan's *Dark Knight Trilogy* dominated box offices in 2005, 2008, and 2012, while the Marvel Cinematic Universe used *Iron Man* (2008) to launch an epic anthology that culminated in *The Avengers* film of 2012.

Be it the vigilante violence of Batman or the unilateral altruism of The Avengers, superhero movies all exhibited the same strand of masculinity: that of the Alpha Male who divorced himself from institutional solutions to societal problems, and instead took matters into his own hands. A century after Teddy Roosevelt proclaimed himself "a strong individualist by personal habit and conviction,"[14] cinema's expression of this ethos was the exceptional superhero to whom laws and due process did not apply. In 2016, filmmaker John McTiernan called superhero films part of the "cult of hypermasculinity."[15]

HERO GENERATION

Skeptics have also seen these films as a model of Millennial entitlement; the cinematic wet dream for a generation of perpetual adolescents who grew up idolizing *G.I. Joe* and identifying with Harry Potter. "In a superhero film, you're awesome. [But] not because you did something special," writes journalist

Joe Queenan. "Superhero movies are made for a society that has given up. It's the dream of this fame-hungry generation."[16]

Coincidentally, Neil Howe has described Millennials as a "hero generation" whose job was to steward the country past crisis points of the 21st century. "Early in life, a hero generation becomes the target of passionate adult efforts to encircle and protect the child," wrote Howe in his 2000 book *Millennials Rising*. "Millennials are America's latest generation with hero potential."

10B

John McTiernan's complaint about "hypermasculinity" was hypocritical. After all, he was the director behind the macho 80s action films *Predator* (1987) and *Die Hard* (1988). These films followed the success of Sylvester Stallone's performances as Rambo and Rocky, and anticipated the first modern Batman reboot in 1989. As the first Millennials were born in the 1980s, Reagan-Era entertainment valorized hero masculinity in all its steroidal forms.

TOO MANY CREEPS

But the 1980s also saw several countercultural currents of masculinity: that of the nerd who never fit in socially; of the creeper who couldn't compete for the affection of women through conventionally suave means; and of the calculated sociopath who substituted brains for brawn.

The 1984 film *Revenge of the Nerds* features a group of geeky outcasts who spy on a sorority with surveillance cameras and commit rape-by-deception of a cheerleader. A year earlier in 1983, the all-female dance-punk band Bush Tetras scored a minor hit with their wary song "Too Many Creeps,"[17] while Michael Jackson crooned, "See that girl?/ She knows I'm watching,/ She likes the way I stare" in his hit single "Human Nature."

By 1986, the sci-fi horror film *Night of the Creeps* made zombies a metaphor for this troubling new mode of masculinity. With the demise of male breadwinner roles and the rise of female empowerment in the 1980s, something about traditional masculinity seemed dead on its feet. So popular culture showed that men with no redeeming qualities could have their way using trickery, deceit, and persistence.

SLAP ON A SMILE

As the sitcom *Charles in Charge* (1984–1990) came to a close, television offered a slew of shows based on similar premises: beta-males in awkward social circumstances who blurred the lines between acceptable and deviant behavior by appearing to be sensitive and emotionally available.

The sitcom *Step by Step* (1991–1998) featured a Gen-X surfer-dude named Cody who dispenses life-affirming advice to members of his large blended family while repeatedly hitting on his step cousin. *Family Matters* (1989–1998) centered a nerd named Steve Urkel's unwanted and increasingly conniving sexual advances on his next door neighbor.

Meanwhile, *Blossom* (1991–1995) cast teen heartthrob Joey Lawrence as a womanizing jock with soft side: the show's theme song contained the lyrics "Stop all your fussing, slap on a smile [...] Don't fight the feeling, you know you wanna have a good time."[18]

IDGAF

By the 2000s and 2010s, this trend towards lowkey toxic masculinity did not relent. Instead, the violent tendencies of 80s macho men were augmented onto the beta-male model. All across the resurgent medium of serial television, shows centered calculated criminals and fragile-minded murderers: Walter White in *Breaking Bad* (2008–2013), Don Draper in *Mad Men* (2007–2015), Marlo Stanfield in *The Wire* (2002–2008), and Joffrey Baratheon in *Game of Thrones* (2011–).

Once upon a time, Americans looked to shows like *Full House* (1987–1995) and *The Cosby Show* (1984–1992) for wholesome father figures. In the new millennium, audiences seemed to want something else: confirmation of the suspicion that the men in their midst were pure poison.

In his 2012 book *Why We Love Sociopaths: A Guide to Late Capitalist Television*, media scholar Adam Kotsko describes the dynamic between awful males and the audiences who loved them.

We live in a world where we are constantly exhorted to "network," to live by the maxim that "it's all about who you know." The sociopaths we watch on TV allow us to indulge in a kind of thought experiment, based on the question: "What if I really and truly did not give a fuck about anyone?" And the answer they provide? "Then I would be powerful and free."[19]

BLURRED LINES

In 2013, singer Robin Thicke—son of *Growing Pains* (1985–1992) sitcom star Alan Thicke—released the smash single "Blurred Lines." The track is an anthem of toxic masculinity.

Thicke sings from the perspective of a sexually frustrated male who is courting a married woman; he attempts to convince her that, deep down, she does not want to be "domesticated" because it's "in [her] nature" to be "an animal." With Pharrell Williams' help, Thicke croons the song's rapey chorus in sultry tones saturated with dick-centered sensitivity: "Good girl!/ I know you want it,/ I know you want it." In the song's hook, Thicke goes on to lament the "blurred lines" that prevent his seedy intentions from being expressed in unadulterated fashion. "Blurred Lines" is weapons-grade male entitlement wrapped in an attractive package.

(BETA-)MALE PRIVILEGE

The pussy-hungry plot of "Blurred Lines" is echoed in comedian Aziz Ansari's web television series *Master of None,* which debuted on Netflix in 2015. Ansari serves as the show's writer/director, and also plays the role of its main character, Dev, who struggles to chase professional and romantic opportunities in a culture that has stereotyped Indian-American men as asexual and passive.

By positioning himself as a victim of historic inequities, Ansari's privilege is given license to express itself in commitment-averse and frequently creepy ways. At the conclusion of an episode titled "Hot Ticket,"[20] Dev grows frustrated when a girl with whom he has no relationship or romantic chemistry declines to give him a hug. In another ("Parents"),[21] he blows off his immigrant parents when they ask to go see an X-Men film with him, and complains about having to help them with technology.

Dev is a Millennial male with searing ambition and a sense of male entitlement to match. But in a city full of professional rivals and sexual competition, he is master of no one and nothing. *Master of None* finds him marauding between the world his masculinity suggests he is entitled to enjoy, and the glaringly finite limits on what he has to offer the world in return.

DATE CAPITALISM

Aziz Ansari is the author of the 2015 book *Modern Romance,* an impressively thorough investigation of Millennial experiences with dating and relationships.

Where previous generations found the pool of available sexual partners constrained by geography and social norms, Millennials are awash in options. Drawing on focus groups and interviews with leading technology scholars like Sherry Turkle, Ansari masterfully shows how dating apps like Tinder and digital communication via text and Twitter have changed how men and women court (and don't court) love interests.

In a chapter titled "Choice and Options," Ansari writes "that's the thing about the Internet: It doesn't simply help us find the best thing out there, it has helped produce the idea that there is a best thing [and that] there are a bunch of inferior things that we'd be foolish to choose."[22] It's telling that Ansari chooses to refer to sexual options as "things." The word choice equivocates carnal connection with capitalist accumulation. Additionally, the advent of more "choices and options" for consumers was the public cover of Milton Friedman's austerity measures that treated everything from schools to hospitals to prisons as a business with a profit margin. It was only a matter of time before the logic of endless privatization came to pervade our personal lives.

In a similar mold as his character Dev, Ansari was motivated to write *Modern Romance* when a woman he hoped to hook-up with suddenly stopped returning his texts. But to get a new girlfriend, a Millennial man of capitalist means only needs Google or an iPhone.

YOU'RE DOING IT WRONG

If this digital landscape of short-term relationships and noncommittal sex in *Modern Romance* had a soundtrack, Canadian musician Aubrey "Drake" Graham would provide it.

Born on October 24th, 1986, Graham first reached the public eye when he played a preppy upstart named Wheelchair Jimmy in the television show *DeGrassi: The Next Generation* (2001–2015). From the start, Graham's persona seemed dialed into post-Columbine Millennial zeitgeist: his character was rendered a paraplegic by a school shooting in the show's 4th season in 2004. After a brief stint as a phone scam operator in the mid-2000s, Graham—known by the mononym Drake when his first mixtapes surfaced in 2006—began his rise as the emblematic rapper of the Millennial generation.

"We live in a generation of not being in love and not being together," purred Drake on his 2011 single "(You're) Doing It

Wrong." In a 2011 blog post, he expressed concern that Tumblr was ruining Millennials because it made them live vicariously through the experiences of others, instead of "creating moments of their own."[23] On his 2013 "From Time," he explained, he "want[s] to take it deeper than money, pussy, vacation,/ and influence a generation that's lacking patience."[24] Drake exhaled "I speak on this generation, but can't change it alone,"[25] on the 2015 "6PM in New York."

IF YOU'RE READING THIS IT'S TOO LATE CAPITALISM

By speaking to a digitally meditated sensibility of doubt and male entitlement, Drake became a representative musician of the Millennial generation. In a world where hundreds of potential sexual partners are available inside of one's phone, Drake stylized the indecisiveness that comes with endless options.[26] His hits "Marvin's Room" (2011) and "Hotline Bling" (2015) are confessions of horny uncertainty aided by the alienated intimacy of 21st century technology. A former phone scammer who hustled unsuspecting strangers into transmitting their banking information to him over the telephone in the mid-2000s, Drake's ability to perform self-interested sincerity with his voice is unmatched in pop music.[27]

SOMETHING THAT BELONGS TO ME

As music writer Mark Fisher wrote in his review of Drake's album *Nothing Was the Same* (2013), "Drake's signature move [is] the transition from rap to singing, the slipping down from ego-assertion into a sensual purring."[28] Like the nerd's natural intelligence, the geek's myopic focus, or the athlete's situational grace, Drake's ability to project vulnerability is something like a superhero's superpower: a skill that becomes the pretext for a life of exceptionalism and unaccountability. Indeed, critics concerned about Millennial "entitlement" should start here: with passed-down codes of masculinity that still associate manhood with unconditional access to women's bodies.

"I should be downtown, on the way to you,/ You got something that belongs to me," he cawed like a modern-day Nat King Cole on "Feel No Ways" (2016). On "Hotline Bling," he tells another paramour "all I do is wonder if you're bending over backwards for someone else [...]/ doing things I taught you, getting nasty for someone else."

The way Drake sings these lyrics—so full of transparent yearning and contrived pain—is almost enough to make the listener forget the message behind them: that it hurts him to see women enjoy freedoms and act on urges that have nothing to do with him.

LOOKING FOR REVENGE

For all the fragile manhood displayed in "Hotline Bling," Drake frequently pulls back the mask of masculinity. On "Too Much" (2013) he describes his struggle to care for sick and aging relatives. On 2015's "You & The 6," he raps, "I used to get teased for being Black, and now I'm here and I'm not Black enough."

Like Dev, Drake uses his disadvantages—being of mixed-race in a genre dominated by darker men, his vulnerability—to give himself a moral blank check for misogyny and materialism. "Three years ago I was after pussy, trying to make up for all the years when no girl would talk to me,"[29] Drake admitted to *Rolling Stone* in 2014. When spoken instead of sung, sentiments like these reveal a sordid side to Drake's much-celebrated "sensitivity."

And these sentiments have been immensely popular. In the year of Drake's birth (1986),[30] *Billboard* charts saw 31 #1 records by 29 separate artists. By 2015, decades of media consolidations that eliminated independent radio made this kind of diversity impossible. In all 52 weeks of 2015, there were only eight separate #1s produced by a paltry six artists. That year, *all 17 tracks* of Drake's mixtape *If You're Reading This It's Too Late* charted in the top 100. This is what "revenge" looks like for nerds like Wheelchair Jimmy.

HERO MASCULINITY

Under the semblance of sensitivity, the masculinity of Drake's discography traced that of the superhero: the larger-than-life sociopath who was above society, and bigger than the social bonds that keep the rest of us under wraps. The affect resonated. To prepare for his performance as a heartless banker in the 2013 film *Wolf of Wall Street*, actor Jonah Hill revealed via Twitter that he listened to Drake to "get pumped."[31]

"No new friends, no new friends," Drake crooned on the 2013 track "No New Friends." Another song from that year's *Nothing Was the Same* saw him gloss over his privilege—the influence of his mother, the mentorship of Lil Wayne, his corporate sponsorship from Sprite—and pretend as if he alone was the reason for his success: "I came up, that's all me/ No help, that's all me,/ All me for real!" he bragged on "All Me."

Incidentally, "All Me" features a spoken intro from Aziz Ansari's performance as a stand-up comedian in the film *Funny People*. "I'm really stepping up my game," boasts Ansari. "These bitches gotta start paying me for this!"[32]

10C

By the time Drake's fourth studio album *Views* hit iTunes in April of 2016, he was at the height of his celebrity. Financial backing from Apple[33] and a flawless victory in a rap battle against Meek Mill propelled the Canadian crooner to the top of pop music. Toronto was his hometown, but he may as well have purchased real estate on top-40 radio and *Billboard* charts. Along with Millennial counterparts Taylor Swift, Justin Bieber, Rihanna, and Adele, Drake had become a member of America's pop music elite. With few rivals left in the world of music, Drake turned to the world of sport for competition.

SO SYNONYMOUS

When LeBron James' Cleveland Cavaliers visited his Toronto
Raptors for Games Four and Six of the 2016 Eastern Conference
Finals, *NBA on ESPN* cameras captured Drake egging on the
crowd and aggravating James. The Raptors fell to the Cavaliers.
But the point was made: as big businesses on the terrain of
spectator capitalism, the competitive fervor of rap and basketball
echo another. In his 2010 track "Thank Me Now," Drake rapped,
"I swear rap and sports are so synonymous,/ Cause we want to be
them, and they want to be us."

I'M COMING HOME

Perhaps Drake saw himself in LeBron James. Both were
Millennial "boomerang children" who returned home after time
away. After bouncing around in Memphis and Houston earlier in
his career, Drake spoke of buying a home in Toronto and
embracing his roots there in a 2016 interview with Zane Lowe.

Meanwhile, James found redemption as a hometown hero in
Cleveland. After winning two championships with the Miami
Heat in 2012 and 2013, James announced his return to the
Cleveland Cavaliers with the 2014 *Sports Illustrated* essay "I'm
Coming Home,"[34] which took its name from a 2010 P. Diddy track
featuring Millennial songstress Skylar Grey.

Both James' and Drake's stories dovetailed with a 2015 Pew
Research Report[35] which tied the Millennial boomerang
phenomenon to economic downturn: to the 26%[36] of Millennials
who lived with their parents in 2015, home is where the heart
(and the cheap rent) is. At the same time, for cities struggling
under the weight of austerity, cultural ambassadors like Drake
and James are economic assets:

The *Toronto Star* has placed the figure for Drake's fiscal
footprint in Toronto at a staggering *$3 billion*.[37] For James—who
pledged $41 million towards a college fund for Cleveland-area
kids in 2014[38]—the figure is $500 million. "Maybe some of the

kids I sponsor through my foundation will realize that there's no better place to grow up than Northeast Ohio," wrote James in his *Sports Illustrated* essay. "Our community, which has struggled so much, needs all the talent it can get."[39]

HOMETOWN HERO

LeBron James eventually tasted championship triumph in Cleveland. After falling to the Golden State Warriors in the 2015 NBA Finals, the Cavaliers won an epic rematch the following year. In the summer of 2016, framers of popular culture offered differing interpretations of James' triumphant return to Cleveland. In typically blustery fashion, *Jacobin Magazine* declared that "after decades of capitalist assault, Cleveland needs a political alternative [more than it needs] a championship."[40] In a caustic article in *The Ringer* titled "No Country for Old LeBron,"[41] Twitter trickster Jason Concepcion (@netw3rk) cast James as an aging Millennial with a receding hairline who was attempting to squeeze the last few wins out of a waning career.

Lost in the cultural chorus was the fact that James' way of achieving his coveted Cleveland championship provided a progressive example of how masculinity could be lived under late capitalism.

SUPERMAN SYNDROME

For the entirety of his career in the 2000s and 2010s, James was a "pass first" player in a sport that valorized individual gunners who wowed crowds with stellar one-on-one play at the expense of teamwork. The 1994 basketball documentary *Hoop Dreams* features a scene where an angry coach lambasts a young player for passing to an open teammate instead of taking a contested shot at the basket.

While selfless teammates like James were stigmatized as weak, superstars like Michael Jordan and Kobe Bryant were celebrated as basketball superheroes because of their trigger-happy antics and isolationist ways. T-shirts from the Chicago Bulls' 1996 championship run branded Michael Jordan as a basketball "Superman." Later on in the 2000s, Kobe Bryant created a superhero alter-ego called "The Black Mamba."

HERO BALL

Players who did not indulge in what ESPN sportswriter Henry Abbott has called "hero ball"[42] were seen as weak. In a cultural climate that associated the scorer of the most points (and the alienator of the most teammates) with superior manhood, guys like James who set up teammates and shied away from hogging the ball got routinely castigated by sports pundits like Skip Bayless. What's more, James' way of switching teams during NBA free agency was seen as another sign of weakness.

The chorus[43] of former NBA greats who criticized James for joining star player Dwyane Wade in Miami included Michael Jordan, Isaiah Thomas, and Larry Bird. All of them were equally hard on Kevin Durant for joining Stephen Curry and the Golden State Warriors in the summer of 2016. A recurring theme in the critiques coming from former players was that players of Durant and James' generation were "different" (read: less competitive) because they wanted to join with other stars instead of beat them.

Broadcast journalist Stephen A. Smith opted to attack Durant's basketball manhood directly, calling his relocation to Golden State "the weakest move [I've ever seen] as a superstar."[44] As Captain America was dominating the box office and a megalomaniacal Donald Trump was claiming to know more about the military than actual generals in his 2016 presidential candidacy, James and Durant were being criticized for placing teamwork before personal glory.

In film, politics, and sports, the cultural consensus in the mid-2010s seemed to be that real men don't collaborate or ask for help to achieve their goals.

INCLUSIVE MASCULINITY

And yet signs of what scholar Eric Anderson has called "inclusive masculinity"[45] were visible in the 2010s. This new style of masculinity included the intelligence of the 80s nerd, the sensitivity of the 90s man, and even some of the scheming tendencies of the 2000s sociopath. But it employed these traits as part of a team-centric framework designed to reach shared, consensual, collective goals (as opposed to individualistic, imposed-upon desires). LeBron and Kevin Durant were not afraid to ask for help. As men, this made them exceptional.

James once described the 2004 Olympic basketball team as a "shit show"[46] because he was stuck on a team with hero-ballers Stephon Marbury and Allen Iverson. In the ensuing decade, his great cultural contribution to American masculinity was in showing that one could be the best at something, but still have a beta-mentality; terrific people, but not terrible teammates.

In his 2000 book *Millennials Rising*, Neil Howe explained that this emphasis on teamwork became a hallmark of James' generation. Perhaps it was a result of our networked upbringing on the Internet and social media, or the outcome of youth sports' commercial boom in the 80s and 90s. In any case, as the 2000s wore on and professional sports became populated mostly by Millennial males, several franchises represented the team-centric ethic that was reflected in James' style of play.

WE'RE ALL WE GOT, WE'RE ALL WE NEED

In their 2015 championship run, the Golden State Warriors culled inspiration[47] from the Seattle Seahawks, an NFL juggernaut in the mid-2010s that had appeared in the previous two Super Bowls, winning one in 2014. Both the Warriors and Seahawks developed reputations as tech teams based on their use of unorthodox technology-centered training methods, and their geographic locations.

Like Google and Amazon, Golden State and Seattle were über-competitors in a profession defined by competition. But these were not traditional teams built around an anonymous assortment of role players and one or two superstars who took all the credit. Instead, Golden State and Seattle wove trust and collaboration into their competitive fabric.

When the Seahawks hit a mid-season slide in 2015, players attributed it to a momentary lapse in their team-first philosophy, which resulted in "trust issues."[48] Coincidentally, members of Seattle's vaunted defense chanted, "We all we got, we all we need!" to one another before taking the field. Meanwhile, a 2016 article in the technology review *CNET* titled "Golden State Warriors use tech to their on-court advantage,"[49] praised the team for their "unselfish play" and assist-heavy offense. The Seahawks and Warriors were superteams. But they didn't play (super-)hero ball.

Perhaps this ethic of collaboration was a holdover of the 1960s. Under Keynesian capitalism in the mid-20th century, government fostered the climate and funds necessary for teams of programmers to execute the research and development behind the Internet. Thus—even though marketing schemes by corporations like Microsoft and Apple sell the Internet as the ultimate playground for individualism—the structural reality behind tech is teamwork. At its core, the Internet is nothing but a diaspora of computer users agreeing to rely on one another for information.

NOT A PERFECT GAME

Neither tech nor team sports are a utopia. In the Bay Area and Seattle, tech companies that have a record of employment discrimination against minorities are also partially responsible for rampant gentrification. As curators of news and social interactions, Facebook and Twitter have been slow to curtail online abuse and misogyny, while Amazon's labor practices are famously harsh on their workers.[50]

At the same time, sports are a capitalist simulacrum where

hierarchies of race and class are reproduced, and misogynist behavior is excused. When a tape of Donald Trump celebrating sexual assault was released in October 2016, Trump defended himself by saying the remarks were "locker room talk."[51] So to suggest that tech or team sports in and of themselves can help to usher in a cultural shift away from problematic modes of masculinity is to ignore facts.

BIG DUMB ATHLETES

But by uploading some of tech's spirit of collaboration into their competitive endeavors, players like LeBron James and teams like the Warriors and Seahawks at least provided an antidote to the "All Me"-mode of masculinity, exemplifying something markedly more progressive. Not coincidentally, the Seattle Seahawks have earned a reputation for being the most politically outspoken team in professional sports.

Cornerback Richard Sherman has called the U.S. "a country built off slavery"[52] while repeatedly calling attention[53] to the NFL's hypocrisy in regards to labor exploitation and player safety. Meanwhile, Seahawks wide receiver Doug Baldwin testified before a legislative task force on the use of deadly force in policing in Washington State in November of 2016, saying that cops are enabled by the law in engaging in "reckless behavior."[54] Baldwin has also tweeted that "classism is the number one enemy to democracy. And in America it is destroying the American dream. The 1% of the 1% buy politicians and write policies."[55]

This is some pretty heady stuff from a couple of big dumb Black athletes. Along with San Francisco 49ers quarterback Colin Kaepernick's protests during the national anthem in the 2016 NFL season and LeBron James' support of #BlackLivesMatter,[56] the 2010s have seen an encouraging trend of male athletes using their platforms for more than self-aggrandizement.

A BRAND NEW BALLGAME

The rising popularity of soccer in the United States can also be understood in these terms; as part of a generational shift away from individualist hero-masculinity.

In 2004, Chuck Klosterman wrote that soccer was a "non-competitive"[57] sport for a judgment-averse generation of Millennial athletes who were given participation trophies simply for putting their uniforms on. The dynamics of soccer are no doubt incomprehensible to Americans who are too intoxicated by the pace and marketing of hero-driven films: the sport emphasizes strategy and sustained intensity over raw athleticism and instant gratification. It is common to hear soccer-haters say the game "doesn't have enough action," as if they would rather be watching a Michael Bay film.

As Eric Anderson wrote in a paper titled "Theorizing Masculinities For a New Generation," the soccer pitch is a site for "increased emotional intimacy, tenderness, and social inclusivity [among young men]."[58] For Anderson, the Millennial embrace of soccer is a sign of receding homophobia ("homohysteria"), and an increased comfort with homoerotic behavior:

> In times of homohysteria, men must adhere to extremely rigid body language and must present themselves as heterosexual [...] All of the youth that I study are distancing themselves from conservative forms of muscularity, hyperheterosexuality and masculinity. My theory argues that with decreasing stigma against homosexuality, there no longer exists a hierarchical stratification of masculinities. Instead, decreasing cultural homophobia permits various forms of masculinities to exist without hegemonic dominance of any one type.[59]

SOMETHING THAT YOU'LL NEVER UNDERSTAND

Early 2016 saw the deaths of two famously androgynous Baby Boomer males who did much in their day to plant the seeds for the cultural shift that Eric Anderson describes: David Bowie and Prince. In his groundbreaking MTV music videos, Bowie appeared in makeup and drag, while Prince projected an unhinged sexuality that transcended socially constructed categories of gender. "I'm not a woman, I'm a man, I am something that you'll never understand," he sang on his 1984 song "I Would Die 4 U."

A NEW CREED OF MASCULINITY

The passing of Prince (1958–2016) and Bowie (1947–2016) heralded a coming crisis in healthcare. As the massive Baby Boomer demographic gets older and fades, the deaths of more and more celebrity Boomers will grab headlines. The 2015 boxing film *Creed* anticipated this crisis:

Creed—which *The New York Times* called a "Millennial update"[60] of the *Rocky* series—features a young Black boxer named Adonis Johnson who seeks training from Rocky Balboa. Once a physical specimen in previous Rocky films, Balboa is now 70 years old and brain damaged from repeated blows to the head. In *Creed*, he is diagnosed with cancer. Adonis then wields his strength to help Balboa back to health.

In showing how Adonis nurses Balboa while training for a heavyweight bout, *Creed* blends the blue-collar bruising of boxing with the pink-collar profession of caretaking. The film is an emotionally volatile vortex of violence and vulnerability. It reflects widely on an economy where one of the fastest growing professions among Millennials is in-home caregiving: a job that is as physically demanding as it is emotionally taxing.[61]

MILLENNIAL MAN

Between the silver tsunami of aging Baby Boomers in need of healthcare, the social injustices of capitalism, and the ravages of climate change, the challenges facing Millennials in the coming decades are as steep as they are complicated. Life in the 21st century can resemble a dystopic Hollywood disaster scenario. But in desperate times, only cynics reserve the luxury of holding out hope for heroes; and only the self-interested use crises to feign sincerity.

While self-interested men use crises to feign sincerity and pose as the answer to all our problems, exemplars of inclusive masculinity show that men can forge forward while using their emotions to fuel new and better notions of power. A new fraternity might be founded on the basis of acknowledged vulnerability and emotional transparency. With the constraints of hero masculinity no longer in place, perhaps we'll be free to undo the strictures and social codes that expect us to be strong without complaining, and to battle without bonding.

Until then, the absolute least that men could do—for women and for one another—is make the climb together. As Adonis tells Rocky in *Creed*: "If I fight, you fight."

Chapter 11

Millennial Woman

Movies like *Man of Steel*, *Spider-Man*, and *Iron Man* wean viewers on the entitlement of masculine superheroes. These are characters that ignore the law. They perpetrate vigilante violence. And they're responsible for unseen amounts of property damage.

A disaster expert at Watson Technical Consulting estimated that the culminating battle of the 2013 film *Man of Steel* would—if real—be responsible for an estimated $700 billion worth of destruction to New York City. As scholar Jean Boampong has written, "fans pack theatres to see larger-than-life action, but the subsequent decimation is generally glossed over."[1]

Audiences rarely see who is responsible for cleaning up the wreckage left in the wake of heroic men and their acts of courage.

THE GREATEST STORY NEVER TOLD

A 2004 episode of the cartoon *Justice League Unlimited* (2001–2006) titled "The Greatest Story Never Told"[2] shows what happens when the expectation of unaccountable male heroism is frustrated. The episode centers on an upstart superhero apprentice named Booster Gold, who is disallowed from participating in glamorized combat by senior superheroes Green Lantern and Batman. Boost is assigned crowd control duties. At one point while stewarding bystanders away from a battle royale, he is reduced to returning a lost teddy bear to a child.

This work—the work of keeping crowds safe and retrieving lost belongings—is important. It is the unseen labor that allows fighting scenes to hit the screen without having collateral losses complicate the moral message of superhero movies. Marvel Comics even tried to make the work of superhero caretakers visible in the short-lived 1988 series *Damage Control*. But in the cultural logic of the contemporary superhero narrative, Booster experiences having to perform this unfashionable work as a kind of emasculation.

In "The Greatest Story Never Told," Booster's proximity to children—and especially women—leads him to feel like a professional failure. He is embarrassed when children don't want his autograph, and relies on an Asian-American doctor named Dr. Simmons for emotional support. Simmons provides Boost with the technical wizardry he needs to discover his latent potential as a man who lacks confidence, and also presents herself to him as a romantic option.

The "never told story" of the episode is how Simmons musters the emotional reserve to prop up the male protagonist without ever complaining or asking for credit. She is the episode's true superhero. Her superpower is her ability to manage the fragile emotions and expectations of entitled men.

THE SECOND SHIFT

As writer Everett Maroon notes in a *Bitch Magazine* article from Fall 2016, "female superheroes' powers are more passive, focused on communication or healing."[3] Meanwhile, the 2003 docu-series *Profiles from the Front Line* showed how cleaning, housework, and cooking followed female enlistees all the way to Afghanistan. In a segment from the show titled "Mission: Breakfast,"[4] cameras followed an African-American cook who ensures that soldiers are happy and fed.

As the first Millennials were born in the 1980s, American women were economically enfranchised in unprecedented fashion. Offshored industrial jobs and an expanding service sector opened up opportunities for female employment that had not existed during the days of male breadwinners in mid-century capitalism. Unfortunately, this economic enfranchisement did not come with an accompanying social revolution in attitudes towards women. American supermoms were still expected to labor long hours in the workplace, then come home to put in a "second shift"[5] of cooking, cleaning, and caretaking.

In the closing decades of the 20th century, men were rarely the sole providers of income in a given household. But many still conducted themselves with an air of privilege and a sense of entitlement to women's labor. This condition was reflected in the 2014 pilot of the television series *Halt and Catch Fire*, when fictional tech genius Gordon Clark leaves his working wife to take care of the kids while he chases glory in the burgeoning computing industry of the 1980s.

DAUGHTERS OF AN AMERICAN REVOLUTION
A century earlier in 1877, suffragist Susan B. Anthony predicted that American women would be stuck in this predicament:

> *Even when man's intellectual convictions shall be on the side of [granting] freedom and equality to women, the force of long existing customs and laws will impel him to exert authority over her.*[6]

When the Millennial daughters of American supermoms matured into young women in the 21st century, many found themselves embroiled in the post-recession doldrums of low-wage labor and freelance exploitation. Additionally, many Millennial women worked in their private lives to placate men who have little to offer, but still behave as if women owe them romantic attention.

LABOR OF LOVE
Back in 1983, sociologist Arlie Hochschild coined the term "emotional labor"[7] to refer to the work that women do to cater to men who feel entitled to their time and affection. Her description forecasted the droves of Millennial women who work as secretaries, baristas, and servers. As Millennial British feminist Laurie Penny has written, "girls are much more employable than young men in shitty, less-than-subsistence-level service jobs because

[they're] better at pleasing other people and plastering on the pretty grin even when we're screaming inside."[8] Penny continued:

> Girls are better at emotional labor, not because there's anything in the meat and matter of our living cells that makes us naturally better, but because we're trained to it from birth. Trained to make others feel good. Trained to be feisty, but not strong. To be bubbly but not funny.[9]

In her lucid 2016 study *Labor of Love: The Invention of Dating*, author Moira Weigel describes how the hook-up culture of young women is a function of this new economy of short-term contracts and unstable professional engagements. For Weigel, dating apps like Tinder and OkCupid require the same performative hi-jinx as job-finding sites like LinkedIn and Fiverr: "If marriage is the long-term contract that daters hope to land, dating itself is the worst, most precarious form of contemporary labor: an unpaid internship."[10]

FEELING THEMSELVES

With the ravages of neoliberalism and sexism raining blows on their romantic relationships with men, many heterosexual Millennial women seek shelter and solidarity in female friendship. In 2008, pop megastar Beyoncé celebrated "Single Ladies" in a song whose title was later appropriated by author Rebecca Traister's 2016 study *All The Single Ladies: Unmarried Women and the Rise of an Independent Nation*.

Traister wrote of a cultural landscape in which "a revolution in the expansion of options"[11] helped women avoid the "single highway of early heterosexual marriage and motherhood." By then, the 2014 music video for rapper Nicki Minaj's "Feeling Myself" showcased her and Beyoncé as carefree Black girls, scarfing fast food and shooting water pistols with no concern for male attention.

BOSS BITCHES

In the 2010s, more pop culture than ever passed cartoonist Alison Bechdel's "Bechdel Test": an informal rubric that assesses whether a given cultural product "has two women in it who talk to each other about something besides a man."[12]

The sitcom *2 Broke Girls* (2011–) centers the travails of two Millennial women whose differing class backgrounds informed their contrasting responses to the Great Recession. The 2012 film *Frances Ha* is an autopsy of a faltering female friendship that sends actress Greta Gerwig into financial disarray. Debuting on Comedy Central in 2014, the sitcom *Broad City* follows two self-proclaimed "boss bitches"[13] who battle precarious employment situations in their semi-lesbian quasi-marriage to one another.

These films and shows indicate a generational condition where bonds between Millennial women are crafted in the crucible of low wage work and rising rents in American cities. They are edgy—and even countercultural—to the extent that they show women who shine without the shackles of male expectation. They also demonstrate the effects of poverty-level wages on the declining fortunes of Millennials.

TRICKLE-DOWN FEMINISM

At the same time, many portrayals of Millennial women on film and television reproduced capitalist hierarchies of class and racism. In its first season, Lena Dunham's show *Girls* featured no main characters of color, despite being set in the diverse city of New York. A Millennial born in 1984, Dunham used her platform as a writer-director-actor on *Girls* to be the "voice of a generation"[14] of assertive women. The sad defect of her lily-White faux-universalism was that Millennials are in fact the most diverse in American history.

By presenting mostly-White young urban professionals gallivanting in gentrified settings, Dunham participated in a tradition of symbolically erasing people of color on television that goes back at least as far as 90s shows like *Friends* and *Seinfeld*. Was the 21st century counterculture of Millennial feminism that Dunham represented a force for female empowerment? Or was it a tool for the continued upward mobility of wealthy White women?

11B

Bitch magazine co-founder Andi Zeisler has been plumbing pop culture for answers to problems facing American women since 1996.

In her 2016 text *We Were Feminists Once*, she reminisces about rallying to create a publication that analyzes the ways women are portrayed in media. "We were omnivorous pop-culture consumers," wrote Zeisler, "and the point of *Bitch* was to take pop culture seriously as a force that shapes the lives of everyone. I always believed that the realm of popular culture was where feminism would truly change hearts and minds."[15]

Twenty years after the founding of *Bitch*, Zeisler's enthusiasm for pop culture as a force for good has been tempered. On the one hand, she's lived to see feminism become pop culture. This phenomenon seemed unthinkable as America emerged from the vicious misogynist backlash of the 1980s. By 2014, Beyoncé famously appeared before the word **FEMINIST** at the 2014 MTV Video Music Awards, and celebrities like Taylor Swift—who once renounced the f-word—came to flaunt it.

On the other hand, it seemed to Zeisler that feminism's heavy commercialization was watering it down. Hence, women like Lena Dunham could claim to speak for all women while only letting one kind of woman speak in her films and television shows. "I've seen this called 'pop feminism,' 'feel-good feminism,' and 'White feminism,'" wrote Zeisler. "I call it market-place feminism. It's decontextualized. It's depoliticized. And it's probably feminism's most popular iteration ever."[16]

GOOD NEWS/BAD NEWS

Zeisler's concerns about the brand of feminism popularized by Millennial celebrities echoes the work of sociologists Eve Chiapello and Luc Boltanski:

In their 2006 tome *The New Spirit of Capitalism*, the duo explains that capitalism appropriates rebellion before it can become revolution. Progress is strategically granted on the fronts of aesthetics and representation, while advances in the redistribution of wealth and political power is stalled. The result is a world where an African-American president presides over a criminal justice system that disproportionately targets African-Americans, and conservative women like Sarah Palin and Michele Bachmann rise to fame in a political party that is defined by anti-feminist policy.

In *We Were Feminists Once*, Zeisler writes that feminism's relationship to capitalism "[has] become a constant game of Good News/Bad News":

> As we celebrate the increasing number of female TV show-runners and writers, Senate Republicans have unanimously voted against closing the gendered wage gap. As our magazines documented every step of Caitlyn Jenner's transition, an anti-discrimination ballot measure in Houston was defeated thanks to TV ads that painted transgender women as child predators. As we binge-watch a Netflix series about life and love in a women's prison, dozens of Black women have died in police custody in recent years, with no explanation as to why.[17]

Zeisler's description is an incisive framework for interpreting the work that prominent Millennial women have been doing on the front lines of America's ongoing culture war against women's liberation.

TAYLOR SWIFT (b. December 13th, 1989)

A Millennial singer-songwriter, Taylor Swift is perhaps the textbook example of marketplace feminism. A Pennsylvania native who relocated with her parents to Nashville to embark on a career as a country musician as a teenager in the mid-2000s, she originally brandished a soft-spoken "sweetheart" image that catered to her conservative fans in breadbasket regions of the country. As recently as 2012, she declined to call herself a feminist, saying that she "doesn't really think about things as guys versus girls [because my] parents brought me up to think if you work as hard as guys, you can go far in life."[18]

After being radicalized by a friendship with none other than Lena Dunham, Swift came out as an avowed feminist in 2014. She decried double standards in music that allow men to express themselves emotionally while calling women "crazy" for doing the same, and cautioned women against letting entitled men claim an unearned share in their success.[19] Her new defiance coincided with a shift from the stylistic and regional confines of country music to the prog-pop of her 2014 breakout opus *1989*.

Taylor Swift raising the mainstream visibility of feminism is the good news. The bad news is that the archetype of the lanky blonde that she embodies has long been a locus of depression and anxiety for women who do not fit capitalism's narrow ideals of beauty. Swift has upheld these mass-marketed aesthetics.

Swift's 2015 music video for "Wildest Dream" was a colonial fantasy that featured no people of color despite being shot in Africa. And when Nicki Minaj castigated the MTV Video Music Awards on Twitter in summer of 2015 for only celebrating "women with very thin bodies,"[20] Swift took the structural critique personally and accused Minaj of "pitting women against each other." In erasing women of color from her music videos and using the pretext of feminism to bicker with Black women about an experience she knows nothing about, Swift seemed to absorb quite a lot from her friendship with Lena Dunham.

ALI WONG (b. April 19th, 1982)

An Asian-American writer and stand-up comedian, Ali Wong has worked as a writer for the groundbreaking television sitcom *Fresh Off the Boat*. When it debuted in 2015, *Fresh Off the Boat* was one of the first programs in television history to star an Asian-American family, harkening back to Margaret Cho's *All-American Girl* (1994).

Wong was featured in the 2016 comedy special *Baby Cobra*, in which she performed her raunchy and provocative stand-up shtick while seven-and-a-half months pregnant. In *Baby Cobra*, Wong used a torrent of profanity and vulgar imagery to rage against stereotypes that portray Asian-Americans as passive and asexual.

Wong's courageous way of performing while visibly pregnant was the good news. The bad news is that at the time of her performance, the United States was still the only advanced industrial society that did not federally mandate paid maternity leave. Images of hardworking pregnant moms complement neoliberal notions of individual grit that prevent the welfare state from mobilizing to provide resources to women and families.

Paid maternity leave is a staple of any seriously feminist political platform. But in *Baby Cobra*, Wong distanced herself from feminism, saying that women's empowerment comes with duties and responsibilities that women shouldn't want. "I don't want to lean in. I want to lie down!" she exclaimed, referencing Facebook COO Sheryl Sandberg's 2013 book *Lean In*: "I think feminism is the worst thing to ever happen to women."[21]

Meanwhile, Wong's raunchy sense of humor may be the result of internalized sexism. In her 2005 study *Female Chauvinist Pigs*, Ariel Levy writes that "the post-feminist Female Chauvinist Pig (FCP) has risen to an exalted status. If Male Chauvinist Pigs were men who regarded women as pieces of meat, the female chauvinist pigs outdo them [by] making sex objects of other women. Why try to beat male chauvinist pigs when you can join them?"[22]

AMERICA FERRERA (b. April 18th, 1984)

Honduran-American actress America Ferrera was the star of the television sitcom *Ugly Betty* (2006–2010). Cast in the titular role of Betty Suarez, Ferrera played a socially awkward 22-year-old who struggles to find employment and respect in the glossy world of New York City fashion magazines. In the series pilot, Ferrera's character finally scores a job, only to be verbally abused and overworked by her boss, Daniel.

Ugly Betty eventually delivers a stirring monologue that resonates with cash-strapped Millennials who also take care of aging relatives.

> *What are your problems, Daniel? Which model you're going to sleep with? Try spending the day on the phone with some HMO getting them to cover your [parents'] prescriptions, or lining up a job because you have to help pay their rent the next month!*[23]

The good news is that America Ferrera's character in *Ugly Betty* is substantially scrappier and more resilient than the average diatribe about fickle and entitled Millennials would have us believe. Her visibility as a Latina on television is also significant, because portrayals of the generation frequently lack diversity.

The bad news is that "diversity" can be the basis for business as usual.

Under capitalism, the increased visibility of women and racial minorities is often leveraged to make society appear more progressive than it actually is. As feminist Zillah Eisenstein has written, "the manipulation of race and gender as decoys for democracy reveals the corruptibility of identity politics."[24]

In July of 2016, America Ferrera appeared alongside Lena Dunham at the Democratic National Convention. The two spoke lovingly of presidential candidate Hillary Clinton: a former senator who in November of 2015 bragged about authorizing funding to "build a barrier"[25] that would keep illegal immigrants like Betty Suarez's family out of the United States.

THE PINKPRINT

Millennial women's cultural contributions in the arts and entertainment run concurrent to setbacks for women in the realm of politics and power. Often times, success, celebrity, and cachet for American women mean celebrating the same structures of power that dominate and oppress women globally:

Lindy West's glowing September 2016 endorsement of Hillary Clinton's candidacy in *The Guardian* made no mention of Clinton's support for the 2003 Iraq War—a fiasco which cost trillions of dollars that could've been used for women's social programs domestically, and that exposed countless Iraqi women and girls to rape at the hands of American soldiers. Lena Dunham's support of Clinton was equally indulgent. At a 2016 pro-Clinton campaign event, Dunham exclaimed, "the idea that Hillary Clinton has somehow not done enough for women is offensive to the core of my being."[26] For a certain strain of feminism, substantive critique of Clinton's record was tantamount to sexism.

A NIGHTMARE DRESSED LIKE A DAYDREAM

Criticizing women's responses to oppression is tricky terrain. As Jennifer Pozner writes in her 2010 book *Reality Bites Back*, "media respond [to signs] that women might be on the verge of achieving progress by condemning not only their ability to succeed, but also [by] condemning the notion that they should want to do so at all."[27] At the same time, feminism will have betrayed its origins as a liberatory project if it allows itself to become a vehicle for policies and practices that hurt women. What good was it for feminism to gain the world if it forfeited its soul?

11C

In her 25 years in the national spotlight, Hillary Clinton has been pilloried for not putting in the emotional labor expected of female performers. When she was a first lady, senator, Secretary of State, and presidential candidate, Clinton's sexist detractors called attention to her shrill voice, her unpleasant demeanor, and her calculating ways. These insults strayed from a serious assessment of Clinton's political career. They also undersell her formidable gifts as a master of public policy and a career politician of withering ability.

THE BITCH AMERICA NEEDED

Clinton's 2016 appearance on *Broad City* and her Instagram selfies with Millennial singer Katy Perry were designed to make her appear more likeable to voters. America's cultural standards did not allow women to be smart without being seen as cunning, or assertive without being called bitchy.

In a searing *New York Times* op-ed from September 2016 titled "The Bitch America Needs,"[28] Andi Zeisler announced, "there are so many ways to be a bitch when you're Hillary Clinton. You can be too loud, too ambitious, too emotional, not emotional enough."[29] A Hillary Clinton victory at the ballot box in November 2016 would have been a public vindication in the private struggles of millions of women who couldn't win with chauvinist pigs.

WORK, WORK, WORK, WORK, WORK, WORK

Unfair expectations exist for female entertainers of all kinds: secretaries, service workers in coffee shops, politicians, and pop stars. As Steven Shaviro writes in his 2010 tract *Post Cinematic Affect*, "[pop culture figures] circulate endlessly among multiple platforms. Their performances are at once affectively charged and ironically distant."[30]

Shaviro's words bring to mind Arlie Hochschild's 1983 book

The Managed Heart, in which she described airline stewardesses who suppress their outward reactions in order to appear accessible and affable to passengers. For Hochschild, repressing emotions and redirecting stress constitutes a form of labor—"emotional labor"[31]—that women in capitalist societies are practically required to contribute.

Millennial women in particular are disproportionately employed in fields like caretaking, food service, and customer service. The emotional labor that these fields require—the labor of seeming kind, smoothing over awkward situations, and legitimating the frustration of others—is echoed in the work of female entertainers. In her 2016 single "Work," Millennial singer Robyn Rihanna Fenty sang, "I wake up and act like nothing's wrong/just get ready for work, work, work, work, work, work."[32]

FIERCE ENOUGH TO BE YOUR ACCESSORY

For a time, near-Millennial Beyoncé Knowles-Carter (b. September 4th, 1981) embraced the expectations that came with being a female entertainer. While her early work as a member of the girl-group Destiny's Child flaunted a Spice Girls-style of female liberation, Knowles-Carter's career for much of the 1990s and 2000s was largely devoid of controversy or confrontation. Songs like "Crazy In Love" and "Be with You" framed her as an accessory-wife to rap mogul Jay Z. Beyoncé's hospitable southern drawl and inoffensive song material made her a sex symbol that didn't challenge the expectations of lecherous male viewers or politicize her work.

SOMEONE WHO BELIEVES IN THE EQUALITY OF THE SEXES

With the election of the country's first Black president, Knowles-Carter's career started to take a political turn in 2008—the year she released the song "All The Single Ladies." In January of 2009, she sang at Barack Obama's inauguration ball. With the line "I buy my own [and] if he deserve it, buy his shit too," she brandished a new independence in the 2011 hit "Countdown."

By 2013, Knowles-Carter—who now refused to do interviews—refuted pandering marketing schemes by releasing her album-video *Beyoncé* on iTunes with no promotion. The *Beyoncé* cut "Flawless" featured stirring narration by Nigerian author Chimamanda Ngozi Adichie, who asserted that "[a feminist is someone] who believes in the social, political, and economic equality of the sexes."[33]

Beyoncé's burgeoning radicalism reached full bloom with the 2016 hit "Formation," a single from her forthcoming album *Lemonade*. The song celebrated female economic independence and solidarity among Black women. When Knowles-Carter performed it at the halftime of Super Bowl 50 on February 7th, 2016, she did so in Black Panther garb that underscored her support of the #BlackLivesMatter movement. In the midst of a spate of police killings of African-Americans, news broke that Knowles-Carter had been quietly bailing protestors of police brutality out of jail.

The once-silent southern belle had matured into a symbol of defiance. As writer Tamara Winfrey Harris notes in a 2016 *Bitch Magazine* article, "It's not until women have the power of adulthood that we're able to break out and reclaim ourselves as who we really are."[34]

HOW IT FEELS

Beyoncé was not alone in the cultural orbit of outspoken female creatives. In the mid-2010s, many Millennial women in the public eye had fewer and fewer "fucks to give"[35] about putting in the emotional labor—the "work, work, work, work, work, work"— required to seem unthreatening and respectable. The new nonchalance contrasted greatly with the brand of corporatized feminism that endorsed staying silent to smash glass ceilings in the 1980s and 90s.

An angsty Millennial born in Barbados, Rihanna has made a career out of what music critic Robin James calls "directionless drift and melancholic *meh*."[36] Her 2015 single "Bitch Better Have My Money" was unapologetically agitated, while *The New Yorker* called her 2016 album *ANTI* "a testament to her cavalier approach and unyielding rejection of artifice."

Rihanna's unfiltered expression was echoed in the web series *The Mis-Adventures of Awkward Black Girl* (2011–2013), which follows a woman named "J" (played by Millennial actress and author Issa Rae) as she deals with racism, sexism, and romantic tension in the workplace. Rae went on to helm the 2016 TV show *Insecure*, for which Solange Knowles (b. June 24th, 1986) served as a musical director after releasing her landmark album *A Seat at the Table* (2016). On "Cranes in the Sky," Knowles sang about the stress on her mental health resulting from the double bind of racism and sexism:

I tried to drink it away,
I tried to put one in the air.
I tried to dance it away,
I tried to change it with my hair.
I tried to keep myself busy,
I ran around in circles,
Think I made myself dizzy.
I slept it away, I sexed it away
I read it away,
Away.

Millennial poetess Jenny Zhang shares Solange's radical transparency, with her masterful 2015 poem "How It Feels"[37] detailing her struggle to climb out of bed in the midst of a crippling bout with depression. Similarly, Millennial actress Aya Cash plays the clinically depressed-but-working-through-it character of Gretchen on the television show *You're the Worst*.

MILLENNIAL WOMAN

For all of liberalism's narratives about gender progress and equality, women still assume the bulk of society's caretaking burdens. Artists like Rihanna and Jenny Zhang speak to the emotional toll that millions of Millennial women pay at the intersections of low wage service work and unfair romantic expectations; because young women are still coerced into catering to the egos and emotions of men while letting their own labors in work and love go largely uncompensated, their work is radical.

The advent of neoliberalism occurred alongside the sexual revolutions of the 1970s. As an ideology and economic system, it has cunningly used the rhetoric and symbols of female liberation to compel women to work twice as hard: as underpaid workers in the private sector, and as overworked wives and lovers in their private lives. Whether it's pantsuits or aprons, the exploitation of female labor is a scarlet letter sewn onto all of capitalism's material relations. Radical female entertainers force society to calculate a woman's worth by inspiring their listeners to refrain from extending their emotional labors to parties that will not properly value them. As a social statement, Solange's record *A Seat at the Table* was a musical invoice for centuries of unpaid physical and emotional labor contributed to capitalism by its female participants.

The problems posed by defiant female entertainers of a certain generation are so unsettling to the neoliberal status quo that *even other women* feel threatened by the outspokenness of their female counterparts. Much as the Black Power message of Malcolm X and the Black Panthers disturbed both the Black and White bourgeoisie, Beyoncé is a frequent target of criticism from (primarily White) women who object to the way she flaunts her body, riches, relationship, and political stances. Defiant Millennial pop stars of color such as Nicki Minaj and Cardi B therefore illuminate America's gender disparities while simultaneously highlighting the racial foundation that those disparities take place on top of.

The visibility of entertainers such as Rihanna and Beyoncé subverts the aims of marketplace feminism using the very means of marketplace feminism: spectacle, corporate triumph, and sex appeal. Marketplace feminism behaves as a system where women leverage their assets into the accrual of social and fiscal capital. To the (very large) extent that it does not actively advocate redistributing resources or attention to less advantaged women who have not made this climb, marketplace feminism is—at its core— conservative. By hailing from historically marginalized communities and centering the lives and images of those populations in their music, outspoken female pop stars draw sharp lines in the sand between a) women who are fine stepping over other women to achieve a limited feminism for a few, and b) women who insist that the liberation of all women is a necessary condition of a true feminism.

THE LIMITS OF POP FEMINISM...

But for all the brilliance of Millennial women in the sphere of pop culture, the predicaments facing women under capitalism will have to be solved politically. As Andi Zeisler writes in *We Were Feminists Once*, "the issues that feminism confronts—wage inequality, gendered divisions of labor, institutional racism, and bodily autonomy—[can't be solved by marketplace feminism]. Those who hoped that the marriage of pop culture and feminism would yield progressive fruit might have a lot to answer for."[38]

...AND THE LIMITS OF CULTURAL HISTORY

Something similar maybe said of the Millennial condition as a whole. We might comb magazines, television shows, professional sports, and music for inspiration; but the best they can do is fashion new symbols for our real-world struggles to build a better world than the one our generation inherited.

YOU'RE NOT A FEMINIST

The 2015 film *Grandma* features a scene where a renegade septuagenarian excoriates a bookstore coffee shop manager for exploiting her female Millennial employees. While trying to pawn copies of the first editions of Simone de Beauvoir's *The Second Sex* and Betty Friedan's *The Feminine Mystique*, she exclaims, "You're not a feminist—I bet it's illegal what you pay these kids!"

Grandma's notion is radical. It proposes that faux-feminist virtue signaling or even the presence of women is not enough to qualify as substantively feminist. The rhetoric and the symbols have to be accompanied by attention and resources that actively correct sexism, and alleviate the actual pressure facing women.

In this spirit, perhaps the most radical yet readily attainable solution to sexism and wealth disparities comes from Baby Boomer feminist Nancy Fraser: Fraser has advocated the "universal caregiver model."[39] The idea assumes that all workers also have caretaking responsibilities, and posits that the state should compensate them with a guaranteed minimum income that allows people to care for sick and aging relatives, start families, and raise children without worrying about their bills. A policy along these lines would relax the burden of caring for aging Baby Boomers—a burden that will fall disproportionately to female Millennials (of color, specifically). It could also turn care work into a site of professionalism and income, rather than a drain or a source of shame. More than anything, it monetized forms of emotional labor that women are expected to contribute to society for free.

For the argument is often made that women are better than men at managing the domestic sphere—better at cooking, cleaning, and resolving conflict. If true, this is all the more reason to compensate that expertise with cash.

LOVE AND WORK

Millennials do an amazing amount of caretaking in any given day. We provide tech support to confused elders, prepare and deliver food, and provide entertainment. In a way, all of society is a domestic sphere, with more and more of the public becoming dependent on Millennial labor in all of its guises. When unrewarded and uncompensated, that labor can be a source of anger and resentment; when respected and recognized, it can be a labor of love.

In the 2015 film *The Intern*, an elderly character played by Robert De Niro nags Millennial go-getter Anne Hathaway for a gig that will give him a new lease on life. As an actress, Hathaway seems to've been plagued by Hillary syndrome: the reputation for being dislikeable has undermined an accomplished career. Undeterred by the commandeering ways of Hathaway's character, De Niro becomes a secretary of her emotions.

"Love and work, work and love," he says at the start of the film. "That's all there is."

Chapter 12

The Millennial Agenda

When Barack Hussein Obama rose to the Presidency in 2008, the point was often made that his path was paved by a generation of "respectable" post-Civil Rights Era pop culture representations of African-Americans. With entertainers like Tiger Woods and Michael Jordan capitulating their way into middle America's living rooms—the line of reasoning went—an equally articulate politician with a similar knack for appearing nonthreatening parlayed their gains on television's box of light and wire into a triumph at the ballot box.

BLACK HOLE

"If you're searching for reasons why it became possible for Barack Obama to make his run at the presidency," wrote columnist Mike Bianchi of the *Orlando Sentinel* in November of 2008, "look no further than the golf course, basketball court, or football field."[1] As America's airwaves became tuned to the sight of acceptable-seeming Black Americans like the Winslows on *Family Matters* and corporatized athletes like Grant Hill, our culture became our politics. Barack Obama swept into office as a photogenic, family-friendly symbol of racial reconciliation.

So we can survey the cosmos of American culture for the causes behind our country's brightest political star in recent memory. But that means we'll also have to embark on a similar search to explain the electoral arrival of Donald Trump: a black hole of attention-seeking behavior who once predicted he'd shuttle to the presidency by commanding headlines and compromising the country's establishmentarian orbit. "I'm going to suck all the oxygen out of the room," Trump once told a political consultant in 2013. "I know how to work the media in a way that they will never take the lights off me."[2]

POLITICS ARE POP CULTURE

Presidential elections are quadrennial occasions where politics merge with popular culture. In primetime, politicians air self-promotional advertisements that compete with commercials for cars and dish soap and sexual performance-enhancing pharmaceuticals, showcasing themselves and their visions as preferable products on the marketplace of ideas. In speeches and rallies, candidates access cultural scripts that describe a national "mood," and advance policies that address it.

The winner of this competition is not just the one who convinces the most people that their vision for the republic is the best, but also the one who most effectively uses their airtime to diagnose the state of the country. In this exercise, Donald Trump had a leg up. He had already made himself a living room fixture as the host of the hit NBC reality show *The Apprentice*.

In the words of Amelia Bonow, Millennial feminist and founder of the #ShoutYourAbortion hashtag, "political change is the manifestation of cultural change that has already taken place."[3]

FROM ARCHIE BUNKER TO DONALD TRUMP

The normalization of Trump that *The New Yorker* author Hua Hsu warned of in the aftermath of the 2016 presidential election actually began decades earlier. While Hillary Clinton faced an uphill climb in her quest to convince the country that women could run the free world, Trump enjoyed the benefit of decades of lovable television bigots. A stellar 2016 pencil graph by artist William Powhida titled "Is Donald Trump an Existential Threat? Or Just A Major Asshole"[4] places Trump on the same cultural continuum as Archie Bunker and Homer Simpson.

Of course, it would be the most crude and inaccurate culturalist analysis to pin a Trump Presidency on television alone.

Leftists in search of answers to electoral defeat would do better to remedy voter suppression in key swing states, as well as the Democratic Party's historic failure at fusing the politics of the working class with those of people of color and the growing population of maturing Millennials. Nonetheless, Trump's triumph—predicted as it was by *The Simpsons* in the year 2000[5]—felt like a bizarrely familiar post-truth farce for politics in a postmodern era.

The ludicrously dark vision of America's inner cities that Trump painted on the campaign trail was first painted by the debut of the television show *Cops* in 1989. And his transparently contrived economic populism was a copy of man-of-the-people movies like *Mr. Smith Goes to Washington*. Meanwhile, the too-good-to-be-true assertion that he alone can fix America's problems—a proposition that President Obama called a throwback to the days when colonial America still believed in the divine right of kings—seemed right out of the playbook of fascistic superhero films where power is concentrated in the hands of a privileged few; Trump quoted Batman villain Bane's speech in the 2012 film *The Dark Knight Rises* during his 2017 inauguration address, saying his plan was to raid Washington's power and give it "back to you, the people."

A chameleon of late capitalist populism, Trump accessed these cultural scripts, posing as the answer to all of America's problems. Trump used Survivor's "Eye of the Tiger" as entrance music at rallies to make himself look like a self-assured winner. He sought the endorsement of boxer Mike Tyson to look like the fighter who could "MAKE AMERICA GREAT AGAIN."

"NEEDED ME"

In her 2016 single "Needed Me,"[6] Rihanna sang, "know you hate to confess, but baby you needed me" to an unnamed lover who takes her for granted. Indeed, Millennials and women were two political stopgaps who were supposed to stop Trump's from reaching the White House. But pop culture provided clues that Hillary Clinton was not an appealing candidate to these demographics.

BROKEN BLOCS

As Tamara Draut writes in her 2007 book *Strapped: Why America's 20- and 30-Somethings Can't Get Ahead*, Millennials grew up under Ronald Reagan, in the era of "latchkey self-sufficiency"[7] and the arrival of neoliberalism. With their parents away at work and depending on pop culture as a surrogate supervisor of their children, young Millennials were exposed to neoliberal propaganda like *G.I. Joe* and *Top Gun*.

The proximity of Millennials to this culture of pro-capitalism punctures the notion that the generation should have been inherently immune to the appeals of Trump, or any other conservative. *Bloomberg* reports that Donald Trump secured 48% of the White vote in the 18–29 group (compared to 43% for Hillary Clinton).[8]

Meanwhile, in the most discussed demographic development of the 2016 election cycle, exit polls showed that Trump captured 53% of the electorate's White women.[9] Where their counterparts-of-color voted as a bloc for Clinton, White women enthusiastically embraced a self-avowed sexual predator. In October of 2016, Trump's candidacy seemed all but sunk when *The Washington Post* released the infamous rape tape of Trump proclaiming he "grabbed [women] by the pussy"[10] without consent. It turns out that America's culture of misogyny had long since regularized this sort of behavior—even and especially among White women.

For media critic Jennifer Pozner, Trump's central role in the reality television show *The Apprentice* furthered a culture filled with distrust, judgment, and racial stereotypes among women who compete for masculine attention. "Reality TV lays the groundwork of jealousy and insecurity by telling women that every other female is their natural adversary,"[11] writes Pozner in her 2010 book *Reality Bites Back: The Troubling Truth about Guilty*

Pleasure TV.

In this survivalist context, Hillary Clinton—a hyper-articulate woman with a history of achievement in male fields, a sexually-coveted husband, and a reputation for being untrustworthy—was the most likely candidate to get voted off the island. At the same time, Trump's support among White women who shared his racist views may have been anticipated by Sarah Paulson's chilling performance as a plantation wife in the 2013 film *12 Years a Slave.*

THE OBAMA COALITION

The cultural determinants for Trump's rise were complicated and deep rooted. But the demographic future of the republic does not belong to conservative Millennials, to racist White women, or to the 63%[12] of White male voters who supported Trump. Instead, a viable path to victory for the American Left depends on a progressive vision that does not pit the interests of Millennials, people of color, and the working class against one another.

The diverse population of economically insecure Millennials employed in precarious fields of work can drive a new Left turn in American politics. On a November 16th, 2016 post for radical publisher Verso Books' blog, political theorist Mike Davis wrote that "the Black turnout in Milwaukee, Detroit, and Philadelphia alone would explain most of Clinton's defeat in the Midwest, as would the lack of enthusiasm amongst Millennials."[13] Davis continued:

The downward [economic] mobility of graduates, especially from working class and immigrant backgrounds, is the major emergent social reality, not the plight of the Rustbelt. Trumpism, however it evolves, cannot unify millennial economic distress with that of older White workers, while Bernie Sanders showed that heartland discontent can be brought under the umbrella of a "democratic socialism" that reignites New Deal hopes for an Economic Bill of

Rights. With the Democratic establishment in temporary disarray,
the real opportunity for transformational political change belongs to
Sanders and Elizabeth Warren.[14]

Had Hillary Clinton retained The Obama Coalition of working
class minorities, college-educated Whites, and Millennials that
ushered Obama into office in 2008 and 2012, she easily would
have been voted President-elect on November 8th, 2016. Instead —
as Obama campaign architect David Plouffe predicted in
September of 2016[15]—Clinton succumbed to low voter turnout
among the social base she needed to mobilize most.

POLITICAL PRIORITIES

Seen this way, the comparatively low voter turnout among the
social base of minority, college-educated, and Millennial progressives is a much bigger area-of-improvement than the centrist
White voters that candidates usually obsess over. And the culture
of political disengagement that so often passes as cool is among
is a bigger problem than even neo-Nazi vectors like 4chan or
Breitbart.

#BLACKLIVESMATTER, AND VOTING DOES TOO

An eloquent spokesperson for the #BlackLivesMatter movement,
San Francisco 49ers quarterback Colin Kaepernick was eager to
point out that he did not vote in the 2016 presidential election
because he did not think his vote mattered.[16] But Trump's win of
Kaepernick's own home state of Wisconsin was decided by a
smaller margin (27,000 votes) than the amount of voters
reportedly barred from casting a ballot by the state's restrictive
voter ID laws (300,000).[17]

It's hard to know how many of the people who did not vote
were influenced by campaigns like Urban Outfitters' 2004 and
2008 efforts to convince Millennials that "voting is for old
people."[18] Perhaps potential voters who didn't turn out were

simply tired of having their expectations dashed. Either way, a widespread cultural turn away from disengagement and fake sincerity—and towards emotional investment in our shared civic future—seems a necessity for the American Left.

THE CULTURE QUESTION

Because when we talk about popular culture, we're talking about something with shifting meanings. Sometimes culture represents and reproduces the world as it is; in this guise, it normalizes the current political-economic climate. Pop culture can also be reflective—by presenting a glorious past that we're encouraged to replicate, or an inglorious one that we still haven't escaped. At other moments still, our culture can be aspirational, and contain a futurist impulse that inspires us to create or imagine something better than the present.

In a November 2016 piece for *The Establishment*, author Ijeoma Oluo has written that "we need to create a culture that won't vote for Trump."[19] But we're also charged with the task of creating one that can successfully oppose the politics he has unleashed, and the forces that led to his election. Our culture got us here. And if we're to endure, our culture will have to help get us out.

12B

From a pop culture perspective, Hillary Clinton's failed 2016 presidential bid was the greatest upset in American political history. This is not hyperbole.

The previous titleholder of this distinction was the Thomas Dewey versus Harry Truman contest in 1948. The image of a triumphant Truman grinning next to a mistaken *Chicago Daily Tribune* headline that pronounced "DEWEY DEFEATS TRUMAN" has been seared into our cultural subconscious as a symbol of premature political prognostication.

But in the days of Dewey versus Truman, there were no predictions on omnipresent social media websites; no ubiquitous websites like FiveThirtyEight to relay probabilities on a weekly basis; and no popular podcasts like *Keepin' it 1600* to provide liberals with a false sense of confidence. These media outlets set the expectations for a Clinton victory astronomically high.

As of September, Las Vegas odds-makers gave Clinton a 72% chance of winning.[20] Outside of *Current Affairs* editor Nathan Robinson's February 2016 article "Unless The Democrats Run Sanders, A Trump Nomination Means A Trump Presidency,"[21] few in mainstream media took the possibility that Clinton could lose seriously. As election results rolled in on the night of November 8th, 2016, pundits on major press outlets sat aghast, fondling maps of Pennsylvania, Michigan, and Ohio like weathermen withered by an unforeseen winter flurry.

THE POP CULTURE REACTION TO TRUMP

The shockwaves reverberated. In a Wednesday, November 9th, 2016 Instagram post of Kendrick Lamar's protest anthem "Alright," Cleveland Cavaliers forward LeBron James wrote, "As I woke up today looking and searching for answers on what has happened, this song hit it right on the head!"[22] Two days later in her e-mail newsletter *Lenny*, a distraught Lena Dunham proclaimed, "It's hard to feel it this week [but] the promise of Bernie Sanders' and Hillary Clinton's campaigns is only just beginning."[23] As disbelief turned to rage, Democrats and their critics searched blindly for a donkey to pin the blame on.

BLAME GAME

Despite the fact that Clinton was defeated primarily because of her inability to mobilize her own base in key swing states, some opined that polarization[24] was to blame for Trump's victory. An NPR feature from November 14th, 2016 urged audiences to "read across the lines we've drawn in our lives,"[25] and offered Arlie Hochschild's 2016 book *Strangers in Their Own Land* as an empathy-building toolkit to help liberals understand Trump supporters.

Elsewhere on a November 19th, 2016 episode of *Saturday Night Live*, comedian Colin Jost joked that: "Democrats lost the election"[26] because of their sensitivity to LGBTQ issues. The sentiment was echoed on November 18th, 2016 in *The New York Times* by writer Mark Lilla, who explained that a "post-identity"[27] liberalism was needed to unite Democrats who were too preoccupied with fringe minority issues.

DANCE WITH WHO BROUGHT YOU TO THE PARTY

These critiques were baseless. The Democratic Party has historically succeeded precisely because it is a repository for the preservation of voting rights, immigration reform, feminism, LGBTQ visibility, social programs, and hurdles facing the disadvantaged. Identity politics—along with the energy of young people—have never hurt the Left; they galvanize it, and make it a bulwark against the GOP's narrow and exclusionary vision for the country.

IN DEFENSE OF IDENTITY POLITICS

Should they ever choose to use it, the diversity of left-leaning people could be the Democrats' main source of political leverage. Yet American liberals like Arlie Hochschild have been seduced into believing empathy narratives that place the onus of inclusiveness, understanding, and open-mindedness on marginalized groups, instead of on conservative voters who castigate gays and lesbians and stigmatize minorities.

On America's political terrain, the burden of empathy always seems to run Left-to-Right, and never from Right-to-Left. In their rush to explain Hillary Clinton's defeat, many ignored and ostracized the very people on whom the Democratic Party depended. Predictably, it was only a matter of time before the blame-game targeted Millennials—the same generational cohort that delivered Barack Obama resounding victories in 2008 and 2012.

HOW THE LEFT LOST MILLENNIALS

A December 2nd, 2016 op-ed in *The Washington Post* titled "Yes, you can blame millennials for Hillary Clinton's loss"[28] detailed the following grim facts of Clinton's failure to convince Millennials to vote for her:

- National exit polls showed that Clinton received 55% of the 18–29 vote—down 5% from Obama's 60% in 2012.

- In Florida, Clinton suffered a whopping 16% decrease from Obama's numbers in 2012.

- In Pennsylvania, that figure was -17% for Clinton. In Wisconsin, it was a startling -20%.

Hillary Clinton made repeated attempts to ingratiate herself to Millennials. On September 19th, 2016, she wrote a post for *PolicyMic*—a Millennial-focused media company—titled "Here's What Millennials Have Taught Me."[29] In it, Clinton detailed a plan to offer college loan reform, a commitment to well-paying jobs, and a renewed social safety net for struggling Millennials. Pilfered e-mails released by WikiLeaks also revealed a comprehensive—if condescending—plan to secure the votes of Hispanic Millennials by appealing to their "brand loyalty"[30] for the Democratic Party. Despite these attempts, Clinton's Millennial support flagged.

Clinton's liberal-centrist candidacy was besieged by two factors: 1) relatively depressed turnout among progressive Millennials, and 2) high turnout among White Millennial conservatives. A similar dynamic was at work in Britain earlier in 2016: the majority of the country's Millennials wanted Britain to remain in the European Union, but turnout was highest among conservative Millennials who favored Brexit.[31] Millennials may be generally more progressive than their parents, but it meant nothing if Millennial progressives didn't turn out to support a candidate who they had severe misgivings about since the primaries.

Indeed, millions of Millennials were as excited by the prospect of opposing Hillary Clinton as they were by supporting Bernie Sanders. In his 2016 book *Our Revolution*, Bernie Sanders notes that his campaign "won large percentages of the vote from White, Black, Latino, Asian-American, and Native American youth."[32] An April 2016 report by *The Washington Post* opined that Sanders' ignition of "millennial liberalism" had the potential to create a "lasting numeric advantage for Democrats."[33]

Yet rather than place the onus on Clinton or the Democratic Party to feed the momentum of Sanders' message of Democratic Socialism, Millennials were instead blamed for not chauffeuring Clinton to the White House. Talk about entitlement!

DEMOCRATS EAT THEIR YOUNG

If White men largely deserted a GOP candidate in key swing states (as they did to John McCain and Mitt Romney in 2008 and 2012), they would not be blamed. Instead, the Republican Party was rewarded for doubling down on White male fury by offering up the most patently angry candidate—Trump—since Andrew Jackson. Unfortunately, the Democratic Party does not share the GOP's enthusiasm for catering to its own base.

Millennial people of color, feminists, and sexual minorities are being scapegoated; but the real problem is the Democratic Party's failure to offer compelling candidates who hold capitalism accountable for its considerable misdeeds If our support of Bernie Sanders was any indication, that's what Millennials *en masse* wanted. And we didn't get it.

MILLENNIALS KILL EVERYTHING

Pinning the blame on Millennials for killing Clinton's presidential bid feels familiar. Because Millennials have been accused of killing everything. An August 2016 article on Fusion.net[34] surveyed Internet media and found 47 different entities and industries that various writers have accused our generation of murdering: cereal, napkins, cinema, vacations, wine corks, the EU, suits, malls, the automobile industry, marriage, and homeownership (to name a few). Like fantasy football and parsing over Oscar snubs, blaming Millennials is a widely-practiced Internet pastime.

#CUZWEBROKE

What this exercise rarely considers are the financial straits facing Millennials—the ones that make taking a vacation or owning a house or car impossible, and that may make voting for a Wall Street crony objectionable. In an August 2016 article in *New Republic* titled "The Myth of the Millennial as Cultural Rebel,"[35] writer Laura Marsh explains what the Millennial blame-game misses:

> Business Insider's *story blaming millennials for a slump in the sales of paper napkins [...] contends that, like eating cereal, buying paper napkins is too much work for millennials. Similarly,* The Washington Post *has pointed out that young people have found ways to make the paper napkin's rival, the paper towel, look chic on social media. Neither article mentions that millennials are the first cohort in American history to enjoy lower living standards than their parents. Not buying napkins is a pretty painless way to save money.*[36]

On Twitter, the hashtag #CuzWeBroke is a testament to Millennial poverty. The Millennial interest group Association of Young Americans uses it to tag articles that express wonderment at why Millennials aren't buying luxury lamp fixtures and high-end turtleneck sweaters.

THE POLITICAL ECONOMY OF AMERICAN GENERATIONS

Here's the thing. Millennials aren't "supposed" to do anything—not get married, eat cereal, buy cars, use paper napkins, or get mortgages. We're a lot like any other age cohort: if we have disposable income and financial stability, we'll be more likely to spend money on consumer goods that have become less popular because we're economically depressed. And if 90% of our paycheck goes to paying rent, we'll probably be forced to delay marriage and make serious line-item cuts to our discretionary cereal budgets.

The insidious principle at work in flawed descriptions of Millennials is the notion that we're born with fixed, intrinsic traits that predetermine our political behavior, our habits of consumption, and our relationship goals. The "Millennials Are Killing X" articles don't take seriously enough the *material conditions* that influence our generation's behavior.

DIFFERENCE MAKERS

Make no mistake—there *are* characteristics that differentiate Millennials from other generations. But they don't have anything to do with napkins or wine corks. We're the most populous generation in American history, and the first to come of age fully under America's 35-year experiment with neoliberalism. We're the most ethnically and racially diverse generation in American history. We're the first (free-born) generation in American history to be poorer and have a lower standard of living than our parents. These concrete socioeconomic and political realities should be the basis of any conversation about Millennials. Because outside of them, Millennial identity has little meaning.

MILLENNIALS AND SOCIAL CONSTRUCTIVISM

It bears repeating that the category of "Millennials" was created explicitly for monetary purposes. In the mid-1980s, marketers

Neil Howe and William Strauss—who coined and popularized the term Millennials—founded a generational marketing firm called LifeCourse Associates. The self-proclaimed purpose of the firm is "to leverage quantitative data [to help] companies solve marketing problems and exploit strategic opportunities."[37] In other words, our current generational designations exist to help corporations divide the population into discreet age groupings that can be sold things. It isn't just that capitalism is a *part* of Millennial identity; it was the *cause*.

MILLENNIALS AND RACE

In retrospect, "Millennials" are to neoliberalism what "Blacks" were to colonial America: a new identity that was created in order to lubricate processes of capitalist accumulation and social domination. As with race, generations are *socially real*, but are practically nonexistent on the level of biology or genealogy. So efforts to define whom Millennials "are" are frequently part of a political or economic agenda. To say that we don't care about home ownership or that we "prefer to be praised instead of paid" is to provide a preemptive excuse for wage exploitation.

THE MOST DIVERSE (AND DISPRIVILEGED) GENERATION EVER

Inflammatory rhetoric about Millennials is reminiscent of America's history of racism and sexism, where ugly stereotypes do not jibe with reality:

African-Americans have been described as lazy despite providing 246-years of wage-free work during slavery. Asian-Americans have been described as cunning and untrustworthy despite serving admirably in wars when their populations were domestically interned and reviled. Women are cast as emotional, while their ability to manage the fragility of others forms the basis of many relationships.

Similarly, Millennials have been called entitled, even as our labor contributes disproportionately to Baby Boomers' enjoyment of Social Security—the biggest entitlement program ever. We were called fickle despite fighting and dying in Iraq and Afghanistan, and called lazy when our unpaid labor helped capitalism rebound during the Great Recession.

Millennials are the product of great movements of the past. The Civil Rights Movement and the push for immigration and nationalization reform in the 1960s; the sexual revolutions and the demise of organized labor in the 1970s; the rise of the female working class and the ascendancy of computer technology in the 1980s. In myriad ways, these upheavals are inseparable from Millennial identity. Our generation is the physical embodiment of sociological changes that more conservative Americans are still unable to come to grips with.

FUTURE SHOCK

In a November 2016 address given in Greece during the aftermath of the presidential election, President Obama noted that "in advanced economies, there are movements to put a stop to integration, to push back against technology, and to try to bring back jobs and industries that have been disappearing for decades."[38]

It isn't just that reactionary movements like Brexit and "Make America Great Again" recoil against technology, against ethnic groups, and against the western world's changing cultural terrain. People in these movements also actively project their own insecurities onto the populations that represent them. Millennials—in all our poor, colored, queer, marriage-delaying, ride-sharing, tech-savvy glory—are construed as America's problem children; the people from whom the country needs to be "taken back."

FUTURE SO BRIGHT, GOTTA WEAR SHADES

But the demographic momentum belongs to us. By 2043, the U.S.

Census Bureau predicts that America will become a "majority-minority"[39] nation, in which no one ethnic group will comprise more than 50% of the population. Our politics will enjoy all the progressivism that comes with this kind of diversity. The numbers are on our side. The only way we can lose is if we refuse to fight.

12C

I resolved to write this book in November of 2014. It was a landmark time in my life personally, and a momentous period for America politically. I had just turned 30 years old when the police officers who murdered Michael Brown and Eric Garner were acquitted without penalty. On Twitter and on the streets of Seattle, I watched as Millennial activists spurred the #BlackLivesMatter movement for criminal justice reform and the radical assertion of Black humanity. Meanwhile, the Republican Party drew first blood in the battle it would win with Trump's victory in 2016, gaining 13 seats in the House of Representatives, and another nine in the U.S. Senate.

Millennial turnout in the 2014 midterms was a paltry 21%. But we were clearly not disengaged or apathetic. When Vermont Senator Bernie Sanders began his run for the presidency, Millennial volunteers and canvassers turned out for him exuberantly. An April 2016 poll by Harvard showed that Millennial voters aged 18–29 had a 54% approval rating of Sanders (as opposed to 37% for Clinton, and 17% for Trump).[40] That kind of enthusiasm does not come out of nowhere. In spring of 2016, I caucused for Sanders while writing the early sections of this book.

EXCEPTIONS THAT PROVE THE RULE

It seemed to me that Millennials were on the right (or better yet, the Left) side of history. Great political dramas were coming together that were forcing us to be actors on the worldwide historical stage.

True, not all Millennials were here to save the United States from the ravages of racial inequality and galloping wealth inequalities: Darren Wilson, who shot and killed Michael Brown, is a Millennial. So is arch-capitalist Martin Shkreli. In 2015, GOP strategist Kristen Soltis Anderson even wrote a book called *The Selfie Vote: Where Millennials Are Leading America.* Perhaps this book helped the GOP figure out how to mobilize the White Millennials that turned out for Trump. Nonetheless, I see the rightward tendencies of Millennial conservatives as exceptions that prove a statistically verifiable truth: that Millennials are markedly more progressive.

According to Millennial researcher Sean McElwee[41] — a policy analyst at the progressive policy organization Demos — 43% of Millennials have a favorable view of socialism (compared to 23% of those over 65). 62% of us agree that we need a strong federal government to steward the economy (compared with 55% of those over 65).

IF WE VOTE

Compared with every other adult age cohort, Millennials are more likely to believe that government should protect the environment, reduce defense spending, and guarantee a higher standard of living. "Young people will likely shape the political landscape in the future," wrote McElwee in a March 2016 article in *The Washington Post*; "that is, if they vote."[42]

WHEN WE FIGHT, WE WIN

If I look to popular culture for anything in the fight to forge a better future, it's for symbols of resilience. Critic of capitalism though I am, I'm also infatuated by competition. I was born on November 8th, 1984 — two days after Ronald Reagan was elected to his second term. Of all the movies that have been released in my lifetime, Ryan Coogler's boxing pic *Creed* (2015) is my unequivocal favorite. Like Adonis (Johnson) Creed—running on Philadelphia's cold streets, shadowboxing in the gym, bobbing and weaving his way out of the burdens of the past—I see our battle against the neoliberal status quo as the ultimate character-defining contest.

If the Left in the United States simply played to its strengths— its historic support among people of color, young people, and class-conscious workers of all backgrounds—it would not have to obsess over small slivers of centrist swing voters. Rather than appealing to the center, Democrats in the United States should learn ride its left flank to victory. And a key to this strategy would be (further) unleashing Millennials as a political force. Because when we fight, we win.

MILLENNIALS ARE THE QUESTION AND THE ANSWER

70 years ago in her 1937 depression-era novel *Their Eyes Were Watching God*, author Zora Neale Hurston wrote "there are years that ask questions and years that answer." The same may be said of generations. When historians look back on us in 70 years, will they say we were up to the challenges we faced? That we took our depression-riddled upbringing personally, and ensured that other generations don't have to face adulthood behind the 8-ball? Or will it be written—as anti-Millennial diatribes and pundits would have us believe—that we shrank?

THE MILLENNIAL WHOOP

In 2016, music critics began to take note of a curious phenomenon in pop music. Since about 2010, copious amounts of songs contained a melodic snippet that alternated between the fifth and third notes of a major scale. Usually sung in "wa-oh-wa-oh-wa-oh"-type syllables, the cadence came to be called "The Millennial Whoop." It knows no genre. R&B crooner Frank Ocean has used it ("Ivy"), as have pop stars Katy Perry ("California Gurls") and

Taylor Swift ("Style"). You've heard it in commercials for beer and credit cards.

Music critic Patrick Metzger has written that the Millennial Whoop is a comforting formula meant to play on our sense of familiarity, our need for cultural predictability at a time of political dis-ease. "You know these notes, you've heard these before," writes Metzger in a comprehensive Millennial Whoop recap on *ThePatterning.com* from August of 2016: "In the age of climate change and economic injustice and racial violence, you can take a few moments to forget everything and shout with exuberance at the top of your lungs."[43]

But eventually the record stops. The lights come on, and it's time for everybody to decide how we'll be getting ho-wa-oh-wa-home. The conversation eventually has to turn to the arena where we make decisions about our collective fate. Politics.

THE MILLENNIAL AGENDA

So what are we to do? We started this book listening to "Billie Jean" and "The Message." I think we should end it with a different kind of playlist:

I'm providing a 10-point plan that I think should form the core of any Millennial politics moving forward. Too often, cultural critics and opponents of capitalism are prone to whine and moan without ever offering positive solutions. I don't want us to fall into that trap, and I think that the way out is to think constructively and creatively about the problems facing us.

These goals are attainable. Don't let anybody tell you different. If the GOP can rollback women's reproductive rights at the state-level in spite of the federal statute Roe v. Wade, the Left can introduce comprehensive legislation for student loan reduction and regulation. We just can.

These solutions are also nonpartisan. While they're informed by the proud tradition of American progressivism, the goalposts of that tradition have shifted over time:

Republican president Richard Nixon was a proponent of nationalized medicine and the founder of the Environmental Protection Agency. He would look a lot like a progressive in today's climate. Bill Clinton was a modern Democrat who rallied working-class Blacks and appealed to Gen-X rebels; but he expanded the prison-industrial complex in ways that a Republican like Dwight Eisenhower or even Ronald Reagan would not. So if you agree with any of these solutions but find them at odds with your current party affiliation, you should ask yourself why.

Drake is right: we need to start from the bottom. By addressing the straits of the least-advantaged American age cohort ever—Millennials—I think we can create a tide that raises all the other boats. So how else to articulate this policy platform than in a quintessentially Millennial format that so many have accused of killing our collective attention span?: The Listicle.

1. CHANGE THE MINIMUM AGE TO RUN FOR PRESIDENT FROM 35 TO 25

Nothing about age necessarily indicates maturity or experience. Donald Trump has overseen four bankruptcies, bragged about sexual assault on tape when he was 59, and is considerably less rich than he would've been had he simply invested his inheritance in conservative index funds. He was the oldest President-elect ever. Meanwhile, Millennial Mark Zuckerberg—who has been altogether free from personal scandal and was a self-made billionaire before he could legally rent a car—wouldn't even be eligible until 2019. Everything is wrong with this picture. Not making the office of the presidency accessible to Americans of a certain age enforces a sense of second-class citizenship—a feeling of being trapped in a world run by "adults." This needs to change for Millennials, and future generations as well.

2. FEDERAL ELECTION REFORM

In the 2016 presidential election, only 50% of the country's eligible 18-to-29 year-olds turned out to vote (as compared with 58% of the general population).[44] A huge part of the reason why voter turnout was so low in 2014 and 2016 was that America has allowed the Voting Rights Act to be systematically gutted. Closing polling stations coupled with restrictive voter ID laws and long lines have wreaked havoc on voting accessibility.

When even Taylor Swift—America's White feminist sweet-heart—posts an Instagram[45] of herself impatiently waiting in line to vote, you know you have a problem.

Election Day should be a legal holiday in all 50 states. No state should be allowed to require its citizens to register for a political party before voting. And federal legislation should mandate—and provide funds for—vote-by-mail infrastructure in all 50 states. Our duties at work and school shouldn't conflict with our civic duty to participate in electoral democracy. This is basic.

3. STUDENT LOAN DEBT & REGULATION

We accept that the Federal Reserve can literally *adjust the price of money* by setting interest rates that impact the citizenry's access to bank capital for major purchases like cars and homes. That being the case, the Department of Education should be able to abolish costly fees and penalties on student loans, or at least prevent them from being securitized by predatory private firms who profit from them. Additionally, student loan debts owed to private firms should become the subject of a preemptive bailout before they further entangle our financial system and put us at risk for a future recession.

If Ryan Gosling's character in *The Big Short* is clear about anything, it's that collatorized debt is a neoliberal tower of Jenga just waiting to come crashing down. I'm one of millions of Millennials who entered the job market in 2008, in a world beset by debt and economic downturn. We can prevent that from happening to our kids by not penalizing their decision to get an education.

4. JOB CLASSIFICATION REFORM

Interns. Freelancers. Temps. The Millennial debt burden has made many of us members of an undercaste of laborers who endure low-wage gigs that don't even pay benefits. Aware of our precarious situation, corporations and nonprofits in search of cheap labor prey on our desperation. They give us work, but refuse to classify us as employees.

The British think tank The Resolution Foundation discovered that several global firms were intentionally suppressing the pay of younger workers in order to pad the promised-pension packages of older employees. This is unacceptable and unfair.

In June 2015, the Supreme Court of California ruled that Uber drivers are to be treated as employees, not "contractors."[46] And in October 2016, New York became the first city in the country to protect freelance workers against client nonpayment.[47] Hopefully, the localized rumblings will treble into federal reform. An employee is an employee is an employee.

5. FEDERAL WAGE REFORM, AND
6. MANDATORY INCOME TAXES

When neoliberal economist Milton Friedman was a media darling whose radical ideas became increasingly normalized in the 1970s, his message was simple: starve the state of revenue so that it could not carry out any of its duties to protect and provide for vulnerable citizens. Friedman accomplished this by reducing the amount of taxable income available to the government: reduced tax rates on big businesses and the institution of widespread unemployment made it so that government was perennially cash-strapped.

With his doctrine of austerity dressed-up as a celebration of "freedom," Friedman was everywhere in the late 1970s and early

1980s. PBS aired his 10-part documentary *Free to Choose* in 1980. In a 1978 *Newsweek* article, he wrote "the only effective way to restrain government spending is by limiting government's tax revenue—just as a limited income is the only effective restraint on any individual's or family's spending."[48]

This is bonkers. It's the equivalent of saying that the only way to curb your spending is to quit your job, because then you won't have any money to spend.

But Friedman's ideas have persisted. Even many progressives and liberals detest taxes, despite the fact that the social programs they advocate would be impossible without them. We need a reversal of this philosophy, and a return to simple mathematics. With no tax revenue, government cannot pay for good schools, good roads, transit, or entitlement programs like Social Security.

The cities that Millennials live and work in are increasingly cash-strapped. Budgetary shortfalls happen when a city's tax base shrinks due to a) the disappearance of jobs and taxable income, and b) a reluctance to tax high-earners. As a result, many cities—and the people in them—take desperate measures on the path to financial solvency. Young people may look to the drug trade to supplant the income they get from poverty-wage jobs; and cash-strapped police departments lobby the federal government for grants and equipment that are tied to trumped-up crime rates and bogus arrest quotas.[49]

In the cities and states we live in, Millennials should fight regressive tax codes that place the government's financial burdens on sales taxes which disproportionately affect 99% of Americans. Washington State—where I reside—currently has the most regressive tax code in the nation; the state's poorest residents pay 17% of their family income in taxes, whereas the wealthiest 1% pay only 2.4%.[50] Nationwide, the poorest 20% of taxpayers pay more than double the tax rate paid by the richest 1%.

If America committed to growing its tax base with higher

wages, a more progressive tax structure, and a willingness to penalize businesses that stash taxable profits in overseas tax shelters, there would be less incentive for citizens to commit certain crimes, and less incentive for cities to manufacture crime rates. Millennial #BlackLivesMatter activists have forced us to talk about police brutality as a race issue; the point is seldom made that it is a socioeconomic one as well.

7. A FEDERAL TRANSPORTATION INITIATIVE, WITH
8. A FEDERAL JOBS PROGRAM, AND
9. A PATH TO CITIZENSHIP

For many Millennials, the mid-20th century days of automobile-centered lifestyles in homogenous suburbs are a pipe dream. And we should be glad. As the generation that saw the Exxon Oil Spill of 1989 repeated by British Petroleum in the Gulf of Mexico in 2010, the majority of Millennials support weaning America off of fossil fuel dependency.

There's no reason why a federal mandate—including dedicated financial subsidies—couldn't encourage companies like Ford or Boeing to reinvent themselves as pioneers of a countrywide rapid rail transit system.

Ever since Campbell Scott's excited rant about the "Super Train" in the 1992 film *Singles*, mass transit has been a symbol of what it means to live in a hip, youth-friendly urban environment. A coherent green jobs program to build this transit system could be coupled with a clear path to citizenship for immigrant Millennials, who could earn full political enfranchisement by getting a decent-paying job in infrastructural development for these transit projects.

10. A UNIVERSAL CAREGIVER MODEL

A major part of our generational situation as Millennials is that we're post-Boomers who will be entrusted with the task of caring for the previous generation while we work with limited resources to raise the next one. The stigma around so-called "pink collar" work is the result of deeply-rooted sexism—the lack of respect for work traditionally seen as feminine. This needs to end.

We are all vulnerable. We start off life in need of care, and we end it the same way. In between, we depend on the physical and emotional labor of countless service workers. The demise of the United States' industrial sector led to the creation of a service-oriented society.

But service does not have to be synonymous with low wages or poverty, except inasmuch as service work goes under-compensated. As writer and policy analyst Hanna Brooks Olsen has said, "the idea that we're going to create new manufacturing jobs is a distraction. We need to dignify the jobs we already have."[51]

In a 2016 issue of *Dissent Magazine*, Nancy Fraser describes how care work "is about the creation and maintenance of social bonds. One part of this has to do with ties between the generations—birthing and raising children, and caring for the elderly."[52] Fraser continued:

This sort of activity is absolutely essential to society. Simultaneously affective and material, it supplies the "social glue" that underpins social cooperation. Without it, there would be no social organization—no economy, no polity, no culture. The lion's share of the responsibility [for care work] has been assigned to women, although men have always performed some of it too.[53]

We need a policy of mandatory paid maternity/paternity leave, as well as accompanying stipends for childrearing and elder care. Several states already pay caregivers for the work they do to assist the aging, differently-abled, and mentally ill. If it weren't for this labor, many of our most vulnerable citizens would reside in state-run facilities, which cost exponentially more to maintain than paying an in-home caregiver. This model needs to be expanded to respect the labor that men and women put in to raise their families and care for their parents and grandparents.

DAWN AFTER DISINHERITANCE

Our age cohort inherited the label "Millennials" from demographers William Strauss and Neil Howe. But we also inherited something else: an ineffective political system, and an economy marred by inequality and insecurity. While some are content to go on decrying the status quo without ever attempting to build something better, I wonder what would happen if we lobbied for achievable reforms using the resources available to us.

As Millennials, speaking up clearly and in good faith in matters of love, life, and politics will allow us to identify and obliterate the obstacles that stand in the way of achieving a more perfect union.

—*Shaun Scott*
Seattle, Washington
February 20ᵗʰ, 2017.

Bibliographical Essay

As this book's author, the vast majority of time crafting *Millennials and the Moments That Made Us: A Cultural History of the U.S. from 1982–Present* from late 2014 to early 2017 was spent wading through source material. Writing was the icing on a very large and multilayered cake composed primarily of the fruits of other people's research.

The first phase of my research involved acquainting myself with the body of literature about neoliberalism that has emerged in the last decade. The high level summaries *The New Spirit of Capitalism* (2006), *The New Way of the World* (2014), *Never Let A Serious Crisis Go To Waste* (2013), *Pivotal Decade* (2010), *Age of Fracture* (2011), *Invisible Hands* (2010), and *The Neoliberal City* (2007) were formative.

From there, I sought other macro-histories that explained how the neoliberal turn in economics was reflected culturally. Without a doubt, the most impactful monographs in this regard were Mark Fisher's 2009 masterpiece *Capitalist Realism* and Andrew Hartman's 2015 study *A War For The Soul of America*. Lauren Berlant's *Cruel Optimism* (2011) and Franco Berardi's *Heroes* (2015) and Nicole Aschoff's *The New Prophets of Capital* (2015) contributed immensely as well.

With an overall historical framework of 1982 to the present established, I then sought after dedicated studies and sources from particular eras, which I broadly itemized into the 1980s, 1990s, 2000s, and 2010s for purposes of clarity and relatability. All throughout, I familiarized myself with Neil Howe and William Strauss' theory of generations:

A great creative challenge of this manuscript was borrowing the nomenclature, periodization, and symbolism of American generations that Howe and Strauss pioneered, while leaving behind some of the more trans-historical, speculative aspects of their framework. Here, the concrete writing that has been done about the Millennial socioeconomic situation proved indispensable: particularly Anya Kamenetz's *Generation Debt* (2006), Tamara Draut's *Strapped: Why America's 20- and 30-Somethings Can't Get Ahead* (2006).

Because neoliberalism has cast women in particular in the role of economic change agents, and anxieties about their changing role in society has informed so much of popular culture the last 30–40 years, I found it necessary to heavily incorporate the work of 3rd wave feminist scholars. I itemize most of these in the separate bibliographical essay for Chapter 3 ("American Mom"), but feel the need to stress the importance of Arlie Hochschild's 1983 text *The Managed Heart*: this book helped me to understand the cross sections of low-wage work, performative labor, and identity politics. Moving through that thicket of ideas provided something like the soul of my own manuscript's last three chapters.

From the start, I was also wary of having my book become a stand-in for a bland, normative, White Millennial experience. Because Millennials are defined by their diversity and their proximity to disprivilege, I thought it important to repeatedly tie Millennial identity to race, class, and gender. In this regard, I tried to emphasize cultural products produced by Millennials of color, and also relied on the work of Millennial POC thinkers such as Mychal Denzel Smith and Jenny Zhang to give my work dimensions it simply would not have had if I used "Millennial" as a synonym for "White 20-something." Engaging with diversity of experience was not a chore—as it seems to be for many—but a value-adding asset that made my book better.

I also relied on my own memory bank, as a Black Millennial, of particular pop culture spectacles that I thought would illustrate points I wanted to make about the cultural terrain of the previous 35 years. Because we currently live in the golden age of opinions, I was able to search the wide world of the Internet for essays and "thinkpieces" that provided useful commentary on pop culture artifacts like *The Simpsons*, Rihanna's music, or the television show *Broad City*. In a sense, one great "source" of ideas for this book was Twitter, where—through repeated interactions and engagements—my creative subconscious and authorial instincts were doubtlessly informed.

So you'll see that this book is a strange mélange of primary sources, secondary interpretive material, personal experience, and time spent in front of various screens. I often use these sources to set up my (admittedly) subjective reading of movies, music, and television shows. I feel I did not sacrifice scholarly rigor in so doing. I thought that by intellectualizing and articulating my own particular experience as a Millennial, I could capture something like a generational condition. As an old Talmud scripture says, "words that emanate from the heart enter the heart."

In the following pages you will find a complete bibliography that includes citations for all primary sources, secondary sources, interviews, and cultural artifacts referenced in my manuscript. For purposes of readability and ease of access, I processed links to all Internet links with the link shortener TinyURL.com, and then included the resulting URLs (which will never expire) along with a last-accessed date for every link in this bibliography.

Throughout this manuscript, I rely on excerpted material from thinkers who relay their expertise in various fields better than I could summarize with my own words. I sometimes edit these quotes for brevity; in most instances where this was the case, I include the original quotes in their full context in the endnotes.

Finally, I relied almost exclusively on digitized sources in my research: YouTube vids, Internet articles and thinkpieces, and especially e-books. When citing electronic books, I try to include page numbers when they were available to me, but often site the e-page ("Kindle Locations") instead.

Endnotes

Introduction

1. Pew Research Center. "Millennials overtake Baby Boomers as America's largest generation," April 25, 2016 (http://tinyurl.com/hapcwq3), last accessed December 27, 2016: "Millennials have surpassed Baby Boomers as the nation's largest living generation, according to population estimates released this month by the U.S. Census Bureau. Millennials, whom we define as those ages 18–34 in 2015, now number 75.4 million, surpassing the 74.9 million Baby Boomers (ages 51–69). And Generation X (ages 35–50 in 2015) is projected to pass the Boomers in population by 2028."

2. Pew Research Center. "The Generations Defined," May 8, 2015 (http://tinyurl.com/h7of9ro), last accessed December 27, 2016.

3. Taylor, Paul; Pew Research Center. *The Next America: Boomers, Millennials, and the Looming Generational Showdown* (New York: PublicAffairs, 2014), Kindle Location 740.

4. *City Arts Magazine.* "The Uphill Climb," October 26, 2016 (http://tinyurl.com/z8rvsrs), last accessed December 27, 2016.

5. Howe, Neil and Strauss, William. *Generations: The History of America's Future, 1584 to 2069* (New York: Quill, 1992).

6. This does produce difficulties. For instance, if I choose to say that Millennials were born between 1982–2004, it may change the complexion of data gleaned from Pew, which says the category corresponds to 1981–1997. For instance, that discrepancy in dates can impact statistics related to the size (in terms of population) of the Millennial generation. Nonetheless, there is little that can be said about the smaller Pew designation (for instance, that Millennials are the largest or most diverse or least prosperous generation) that can't also be said about the wider Howe-Strauss designation.

7. Mason, Paul. *Why It's Still Kicking Off Everywhere* (New York: Verso Books, 2012): See the sections in Mason's book about "The graduate with no future" (Kindle Location 978).

8. Zambreno, Kate. *Heroines* (New York: Harper Perennial, 2014), quoted from http://tinyurl.com/pmljogz [last accessed December 27, 2016].

9. And for the record, this so-called "golden age of capitalism" was actually terrible. For example, African-Americans and other racial minorities were excluded from the suburban dream by racially restrictive housing covenants. See the following lead for more info: Truth-out.org. "The 'Golden Age of Capitalism' Was an Era of Racism and Secret Coups," August 8, 2016 (http://tinyurl.com/jphj6hw), last accessed December 27, 2016.

10. Jameson first published an essay titled "Postmodernism, Or the Cultural Logic of Late Capitalism" in the July-August 1984 issue of *New Left Review*. That essay was later included in—and became the basis of—a 1991 book of the same name.

11. Keynesianism—as compared to neoliberalism—is an economic doctrine named for British economist John Maynard Keynes. As defined by Investopedia.com (http://tinyurl.com/27pvzvj), it is defined by "the concept that optimal economic performance could be achieved—and economic slumps prevented—by influencing aggregate demand through activist stabilization and economic intervention policies by the government." The notion of consensus in this case underscores that Keynesianism in the US during the period in question saw prosperity created by a coalition of strong labor unions, heavy regulation, high taxes, and a generous welfare state.

12. Fisher, Mark. *Capitalist Realism: Is There No Alternative?* (Winchester: Zero Books, 2009), p. 17.

13. *ibid*, p. 11.

14. Roosevelt said this on June 27, 1936, upon accepting the renomination from the Democratic Party for the office of the Presidency (http://tinyurl.com/ksqa3jq), last accessed December 27, 2016.

Part I Epigraph Citation

1. Baldwin, James. *Notes of a Native Son (Beacon Paperback)* (Boston: Beacon Paperback, 1984), p. 20.

Chapter 1

1. *Time Magazine.* "Millennials: The Me Me Me Generation," May 20, 2013 (http://tinyurl.com/q9dosty), last accessed January 2, 2017.
2. Fusion.net. "Here are all the things young people have been accused of killing," August 24, 2016 (http://tinyurl.com/hs3a449), last accessed January 2, 2017.
3. The *Wall Street Journal.* "'Snake People' Invade the Internet," August 15, 2015 (http://tinyurl.com/zlmksec), last accessed January 2, 2017.
4. QZ.com. "The myth of millennial entitlement was created to hide their parents' mistakes," June 30, 2016 (http://tinyurl.com/zfqr7j3), last accessed January 2, 2017.
5. Slate.com. "The Subjects of *New York Times* Millennial Trend Stories Aren't Actually Millennials," March 25, 2014 (http://tinyurl.com/lncnr2g), last accessed January 2, 2017.
6. I attended this event personally and recorded it using my iPhone. Fight me.
7. Yes, the naming-frenzy of the Generation "after" Millennials has already begun. Howe and Strauss have given this generation the name the "Homeland Generation" (not a reference to the hit television show). Because generations are products of history, it does seem somewhat silly to me to try to enforce generational boundaries so far in advance.
8. I first heard this formulation—"the world's oldest

millennial" —in a telephone interview with Millennial reproductive rights activist Amelia Bonow in October 2016. It has
stuck with me ever since.

9. Jay, Martin. *Adorno* (Cambridge: Harvard University Press,
    1984), p. 90.

10. You can read Reagan's speech about the War on Drugs at the
    following link (http://tinyurl.com/h4xod7m), last accessed
    February 15, 2017.

11. See the following YouTube vid of the debut of CNN2 (aka
    Headline News) at the following link (http://tinyurl.com/
    gkpe6z4), last accessed January 2, 2017.

12. Hackworth, Jason. *The Neoliberal City: Governance, Ideology,
    and Development in American Urbanism* (Ithaca: Cornell
    University Press, 2007), Kindle Location 672.

13. Cited from historian Kenneth T. Jackson's excellent analysis
    in episode 8 of the Ric Burns film *New York: A Documentary
    Film* ("Center of the World").

14. Friedman is quoted in *The Great Recession in Fiction, Film, and
    Television* (edited by Kirk Boyle and Daniel Mrozowski), p.
    27: "I have concluded that the only effective way to restrain
    government spending is by limiting government's explicit
    tax revenue—just as a limited income is the only effective
    restraint on any individual's or family's spending."

15. *New York Daily News.* "Ford to City: Drop Dead in 1975,"
    October 29, 2015, originally published October 30, 1975
    (http://tinyurl.com/jneb74p), last accessed January 2, 2017.

16. *ibid.*

17. The *New York Post.* "Why the Bronx burned," May 10, 2010
    (http://tinyurl.com/z7z6swg), last accessed January 2, 2017.

18. Rose, Tricia. *Black Noise: Rap Music and Black Culture in
    Contemporary America* (Hanover: Wesleyan University Press,
    1994), Kindle Locations 734–735.

19. Broadcaster Howard Cosell is often rumored to have said,
    "There it is, ladies and gentlemen, the Bronx is burning"

during this broadcast. But he didn't. I know, because I watched the whole game. You can too at this link (http://tinyurl.com/jbflqnk), last accessed January 2, 2017.

20. You can watch "The Message" at the following link (http://tinyurl.com/k82fwvm), last accessed January 2, 2017.

21. All lyrics reprinted from Genius.com.

22. The term "precariat" is a portmanteau derived from merging "precarious" with "proletariat." Author Guy Standing is widely credited with popularizing the term, and perhaps inventing it, although its origins are dubious.

23. Famous line from a monologue in Oliver Stone's 1987 film *Wall Street*.

24. NBCnews.com. "When Greed Was Good: Brokaw on the Go-Go 80s," September 5th, 2014 (http://tinyurl.com/js3mkrg), last accessed January 2, 2017.

25. Hackworth, *The Neoliberal City*, Kindle Location 687.

26. Shaviro, Steven. *Post Cinematic Affect* (Winchester: Zero Books, 2010), p. 6.

27. See Neil Howe's remarks at the 2010 "Portrait of the Millennials" at the Millennial Conference by Pew Research Center (http://tinyurl.com/hmbcthr), last accessed January 2, 2017.

28. The "back to basics" movement emerged in the late 1970s and was greatly expanded on the 1983 policy paper *A Nation at Risk*, which I cover more extensively in Chapter 2 ("American Dad").

29. Howe, Neil and William Strauss. *13th Gen: Abort, Retry, Ignore, Fail?* (New York: Vintage Books, 1993), pp. 14–15: "Around 1982, when 'Baby on Board' signs appeared on car windows, social trends started shifting away from neglect and negativism, toward protection and support. The abortion and divorce rates receded somewhat, teacher salaries gained ground, and a flurry of new books chastised parents for having treated kids so poorly in the 1970s. This

abrupt shift in societal attitudes marks the beginning of the Millennial Generation. Congress endorsed this trend by making all children born in poverty after September 30th, 1983 automatically eligible for Medicaid—but not those born before. As the babies of the early 1980s aged into school children, the newly positive adult attitudes began moving up the age ladder with them. *3 Men and a Baby* spawned a sequel, *3 Men and a Little Lady*. By the late 1980s, a new national priority had been declared: the task of smartening up and cleaning up the primary-grade kids destined to become the high school class of 2000."

30. This ad almost killed Michael Jackson, when a pyrotechnics display ignited his Jheri Curl, sending him to the hospital with 3rd degree burns that never completely healed. The pop star's ongoing addiction to painkiller drugs that culminated in his death in 2009 started with medications he took throughout the 1980s and 90s to cope with the burns suffered from the Pepsi ad.

31. Kitch, Carolyn. *Pages from the Past: History and Memory in American Magazines* (Chapel Hill: The University of North Carolina Press, 2005), Kindle Locations 2219–2220.

32. *Time Magazine.* "The Baby Boomers Turn 40," May 19, 1986 (http://tinyurl.com/jkbr6h3), last accessed January 2, 2017.

33. You can read this essay at this link (http://tinyurl.com/zym7gzl), last accessed January 2, 2017.

34. Sirota, David. *Back to Our Future: How the 1980s Explain the World We Live in Now—Our Culture, Our Politics, Our Everything* (New York: Ballantine Books, 2011).

35. The term "latchkey kids" refers to children who look after themselves at the conclusion of the school day until their parents get home. See the 1984 documentary *To Save Our Schools, to Save Our Children*.

36. *The New York Times.* "ARCHITECTURE REVIEW; 80's Design: Wallowing in Opulence and Luxury," November 13, 1988

(http://tinyurl.com/jj726zx), last accessed January 2, 2017.

Chapter 2

1. "Stagflated" is a word economists invented to describe the odd combination of economic stagnation and inflation that followed from the Vietnam War. For decades, Keynesian economists held that times of high unemployment and declining spending are offset by a low rate of inflation. That tenet turned out to be false, as the 1970s saw both a recession and a watered-down currency. It is often suggested that the country's massive military expenditures in this decade were to blame.

2. Hartman, Andrew. *A War for the Soul of America: A History of the Culture Wars* (Chicago: The University of Chicago Press, 2015), p. 186.

3. *ibid.*

4. Fisher, Mark. *Capitalist Realism: Is There No Alternative?* (Winchester: Zero Books, 2009).

5. "Law and order" entered political parlance in the 1960s as GOP politicians found that they could paint Civil Rights protestors and dissidents as lawbreakers who needed to be corralled. See Chapter 2 ("Law and Order: Civil Rights Laws and White Privilege") in George Lipsitz's *The Possessive Investment in Whiteness: How White People Profit from Identity Politics*.

6. You can read *A Nation at Risk* in its entirety at the following link (http://tinyurl.com/zvc97ga), last accessed January 2, 2017.

7. *ibid.*

8. *ibid.*

9. Mead, Corey. *War Play: Video Games and the Future of Armed Conflict* (New York: Houghton Mifflin Harcourt, 2013), Kindle Location 93.

10. *ibid*, Kindle Location 551.

11. *ibid*, Kindle Location 726.

12. Halter is quoted in Sirota, David. *Back to Our Future: How the 1980s Explain the World We Live in Now—Our Culture, Our Politics, Our Everything* (New York: Ballantine Books, 2011), p. 153.

13. "Remarks During a Visit to Walt Disney World's EPCOT Center Near Orlando, Florida," March 8, 1983 (http://tinyurl.com/zs93anc), last accessed January 2, 2017: "I don't want any of you young people to suffer what some of your parents are experiencing. I want you to have the training and the skills to meet the future. Even without knowing it, you're being prepared for a new age. Many of you already understand better than my generation ever will the possibilities of computers. In some of your homes, the computer is as available as the television set. And I recently learned something quite interesting about video games. Many young people have developed incredible hand, eye, and brain coordination in playing these games. The Air Force believes these kids will be outstanding pilots should they fly our jets. The computerized radar screen in the cockpit is not unlike the computerized video screen. Watch a 12-year-old take evasive action and score multiple hits while playing 'Space Invaders,' and you will appreciate the skills of tomorrow's pilot."

14. *ibid*.

15. Sirota, *Back to Our Future*, p. 158: "This gets to the deeper figurative truth of Reagan's prophecy about video games: While most of the gaming generation that came of age in the 1980s and beyond will never literally enlist and remote-control bomb Afghan villages, the games we've been playing for the last three decades have prepared us in the same way they've prepared those drone pilots."

16. ESPN.com. "Talk to me, Goose. Talk to me." (http://tinyurl.com/gmtvk89), last accessed January 2, 2017.

17. They really did this. FNS regulations allowed schools to apply garnishes like ketchup and relish to constitute as a vegetable so that less spending would go towards school lunches after the Omnibus Regulation Acts of 1980 and 1981 curtailed funding. The controversy was repeated in 2011 when a USDA bill allowed pizza with two tablespoons of tomato paste to qualify as a vegetable.

18. *The New York Times.* "WASHINGTON TALK; BRIEFING," September 28, 1981 (http://tinyurl.com/z5dpmvl), last accessed January 2, 2017.

19. Coontz, Stephanie. *The Way We Never Were: American Families and the Nostalgia Trap* (New York: Basic Books, 1992), Kindle Location 3232.

20. *ibid.*

21. See this McGruff ad at this link (http://tinyurl.com/h5gpjvm), last accessed January 2, 2017.

22. See the "walk home alone" ad at this link (http://tinyurl.com/gsqb8b3), last accessed January 2, 2017.

23. *ibid.*

24. Same citation as endnote #21 of this chapter.

25. Saval, Nikil. *Cubed: A Secret History of the Workplace* (New York: Doubleday, 2014), Kindle Location 2858.

26. *ibid,* Kindle Locations 2851–2856: "When CEOs like Thomas Watson Sr. referred to the 'IBM Family,' it was meant to suggest, warmly, that IBM hired not only an engineer but his wife and children as well.[53] But the phrase was not so facetious: wives—particularly executive wives—found themselves performing a multitude of tasks for their husbands employed in corporations. And the corporations knew it. They frequently screened the wives of potential employees, either by strongly suggesting that a wife attend an interview with her husband or by arranging an informal breakfast or dinner with the prospect and his wife."

27. *Deseret News.* "Alzado Says Steroids Caused His Cancer,"

June 28, 1991 (http://tinyurl.com/zn6vobm), last accessed January 2, 2017.

28. Fisher, Mark. *Capitalist Realism: Is There No Alternative?* (Winchester: Zero Books, 2009), p. 71.

29. Clarification: this song—which Gore was sickened that her daughter was able to listen to—led Gore to create the Parents Music Resource Center, which pioneered the creation of the "Parental Advisory" stickers.

30. Fisher, *Capitalist Realism*, p. 71.

Chapter 3

1. See the "Eye of the Tiger" music video at this link (http://tinyurl.com/a7jfjmf), last accessed January 2, 2017.

2. Dworkin, Andrea. *Intercourse (The Twentieth Anniversary Edition)* (New York: Basic Books, 2003), Kindle Location 173.

3. *ibid*, Kindle Location 161.

4. Steinem, Gloria. *Outrageous Acts and Everyday Rebellions* (New York: Open Road, 1983), p. 162.

5. *ibid*, p. 289.

6. *The New York Times*. "Your Mother Is in Your Bones," March 19, 1989 (http://tinyurl.com/jc5wnvd), last accessed January 2, 2017.

7. You often hear this term used to apply to the (often Millennial) children of immigrants—kids who immigrants had in order to be considered for certain naturalization benefits that they would not be eligible for if they had no American-born children.

8. Gilligan, Carol. *In a Different Voice: Psychological Theory and Women's Development* (Cambridge: Harvard University Press), p. ix.

9. *ibid*.

10. *The Atlantic*. "Women in the Work Force," September 1986 (http://tinyurl.com/on8k72m), last accessed January 2, 2017.

11. *ibid*.

12. *ibid.*
13. *ibid.*
14. Hochschild, Arlie. *The Second Shift: Working Parents and the Revolution at Home* (New York: Penguin Books, 1989), p. 243: "Women's move into the economy, as a new urban peasantry, is the basic social revolution of our time, and, on the whole, it has increased the power of women. But other realities also lower it. If women's work outside the home increases their need for male help inside it, two facts—that women earn less and that marriages have become less stable—inhibit many women from pressing men to help more."
15. NPR.org. "When Women Stopped Coding," October 21, 2014 (http://tinyurl.com/lf7ap97), last accessed January 2, 2017: "Modern computer science is dominated by men. But it hasn't always been this way. A lot of computing pioneers— the people who programmed the first digital computers— were women. And for decades, the number of women studying computer science was growing faster than the number of men. But in 1984, something changed. The percentage of women in computer science flattened, and then plunged, even as the share of women in other technical and professional fields kept rising. What happened? [...] This idea that computers are for boys became a narrative. It became the story we told ourselves about the computing revolution. It helped define who geeks were, and it created techie culture. Movies like *Weird Science*, *Revenge of the Nerds* and *WarGames* all came out in the '80s. And the plot summaries are almost interchangeable: awkward geek boy genius uses tech savvy to triumph over adversity and win the girl."
16. CFED.org. "Helping the Poor Is No Longer a Priority for Today's Nonprofits," August 9, 2013 (http://tinyurl.com/hf3nvfv), last accessed January 2, 2017: "In the last decade or so, nonprofits have stopped caring about the plight of the

poor. Back in the 1980s and 1990s, nonprofits joined together when cuts in social-safety-net programs were proposed. Organizations that represented mostly middle-class people, like the League of Women Voters, professional groups for social workers, and major nonprofit coalitions such as Independent Sector, joined their antipoverty and grass-roots colleagues to fight against threats to the poor.

A wide range of health and education institutions, women's groups, consumer and civic organizations, and charities that aided the elderly made fighting poverty one of their major program priorities. They worked in tandem with organizations that mobilized the poor to fight for their rights—most of them now gone—in effective partnerships that commanded the attention of political leaders and government agencies. The leaders of all those nonprofit organizations never lost sight of the enormous problems that poverty presented for civil society and democracy."

17. NPR.org. "The Look of Power: How Women Have Dressed for Success," October 20, 2014 (http://tinyurl.com/n8zovtl), last accessed January 2, 2017.

18. The *Wall Street Journal*. "The Phrase 'Glass Ceiling' Stretches Back Decades," April 3, 2015 (http://tinyurl.com/my5v4ey), last accessed January 2, 2017: "'Women have reached a certain point—I call it the glass ceiling,' Ms. Bryant told Adweek. 'They're in the top of middle management, and they're stopping and getting stuck.'"

19. You can watch the ad at this link (http://tinyurl.com/h8twclg), last accessed January 2, 2017.

20. Beck, Richard. *We Believe the Children: A Moral Panic in the 1980s* (New York: PublicAffairs, 2015), Kindle Location 87.

21. *ibid*, Kindle Location 5680.

22. *ibid*, Kindle Location 5682.

23. *ibid*, Kindle Location 163.

24. *ibid*, Kindle Location 245.

25. *ibid*, Kindle Location 2725–2728: "The media transmits and amplifies hysteria; it refines the stories told by paranoid fringe groups looking to frighten themselves. But hysteria doesn't take root in society until it can work its way into a community's most important institutions: the government, the justice system, the schools, medicine. In this respect it behaves just like any other issue around which people mobilize and around which social change takes place."

26. *ibid*, Kindle Location 355.

27. See Candice Bergen's appearance on SiriusXM Stars in a link titled "Why I Turned Down 60 Minutes" at the following link (http://tinyurl.com/zk6m7o6), last accessed January 2, 2017.

28. Read the full context of Dan Quayle's speech at the following link (http://tinyurl.com/hu7wbgq), last accessed January 2, 2017.

29. *Cracked*. "Why Every '80s Sitcom Decided to Kill Off the Mom," June 12, 2012 (http://tinyurl.com/7jrt8aa), last accessed January 2, 2017.

30. The pilot episode of *Full House* ("Our Very First Show") captures Uncle Jesse (played by John Stamos) as a reluctant and inept male role model.

31. See other quotes from *The Land Before Time* at the following links (http://tinyurl.com/h4j34pv), last accessed January 2, 2017.

32. See the famous "1984" ad at this link (http://tinyurl.com/pvfxjc2), last accessed January 2, 2017.

33. Carroll, Paul. *Big Blues: The Unmaking of IBM* (New York: Three Rivers Press, 1993), p. 87: "The fundamental insight that Jobs had first and that Gates had a bit later was that the situation should be reversed—that computer makers must go to the trouble of adapting their machines to the users. The way Jobs put it was that even IBM wasn't big enough to ship a mother with each personal computer it sold, so the trick was to figure out how to build motherhood into the

machine."

34. Hochschild, *The Second Shift*, p. 23.

35. The original "welfare queen" was a Chicago woman named Linda Taylor, who maintained 80 different aliases, 30 addresses, and 15 telephone numbers to dupe various government agencies into contributing to her tax-free cash flow of $150,000 a year in the late 1960s and early 1970s. As governor of California, Ronald Reagan was fond of casting Taylor as the leading role in his cautionary tale about welfare.

36. Slate.com. "The Welfare Queen," December 19, 2013 (http://tinyurl.com/owd9q84), last accessed January 2, 2017.

37. A Child Protective Services Agent in an episode from *The Simpsons* ("Home Sweet Home-Dum-Diddly Doodily," the third episode of the show's seventh season) sees that Maggie Simpson is wearing a sign that says, "I'm a stupid baby." He then proclaims, "Stupid babies need the most attention!"

38. Roberts, Dorothy. *Killing the Black Body: Race, Reproduction, and the Meaning of Liberty* (New York: Random House, 1997), p. 4: "State legislatures across the country are considering measures designed to keep women on welfare from having babies—a goal also advanced by Newt Gingrich's Contract With America and then incorporated in the newly enacted federal welfare law. The plans range from denying benefits to children born to welfare mothers to mandatory insertion of Norplant as a condition of receiving aid."

39. This episode is titled "What's behind the I.Q. test: are Whites really smarter than Blacks." See bibliographical information about it at this library link (http://tinyurl.com/z6w757s), last accessed January 2, 2017.

40. Read the full context of Obama's remarks about *The Bell Curve* at this link (http://tinyurl.com/zvbwpa8), last accessed January 2, 2017.

41. Don't get me wrong here: domesticity as it was socially

constructed was exploitative in the 1950s and 60s. But that meant it had tremendous value to structures of power that were largely male, and depended on. Coincidentally, men also came to resent the expectation that their salaries be shared with a mate—see Barbara Ehrenreich's book *The Hearts of Men*, where she explains that *Playboy* magazine was part of the mid-century male's backlash against... well, against the social order that was built to privilege them. #MaleTears.

42. *The New York Times.* "Hillary Clinton and the Return of the (Unbaked) Cookies," November 5, 2016 (http://tinyurl.com/hnlfhjn), last accessed January 2, 2017.
43. British MP Iain Macleod coined this term in a December 3, 1965 edition of *The Spectator*.
44. See Sarah Banet-Weiser's excellent book *Kids Rule!: Nickelodeon and Consumer Citizenship* (Durham: Duke University Press, 2007).
45. Fisher, Mark. *Capitalist Realism: Is There No Alternative?* (Winchester: Zero Books, 2009), p. 72.
46. *Jacobin.* "The Privatization of Childhood," September 3, 2015 (http://tinyurl.com/zysntfl), last accessed January 2, 2017.
47. See this episode of *Double Dare* at the following link (http://tinyurl.com/hc74omh), last accessed January 2, 2017.
48. Quoted from Brad Pike's awesome essay "The Passion of Marc Summers, Host of Nickelodeon's *Double Dare*" in the Thought Catalog compilation *We'll Always Have the 90s*.
49. *ibid*. See Ted Pillow's essay "90s Nickelodeon Plot Descriptions As Written By A Man In The Throes Of An Existential Crisis."

Part II

While I do not cite it directly in the course of this chapter, Chapter 4 owes a tremendous debt of gratitude to *Grunge, Nerds, and Gastropubs: A Mass Culture Odyssey* by Kevin Craft. The overall conception of Part II was enhanced greatly by historian Andrew Hartman's 2015 text *A War for the Soul of America: A History of the Culture Wars*.

Part II Epigraph Citation

1. *Mother Jones*. "Matt Groening." Accessed December 17th, 2016 (http://tinyurl.com/mzxxbv): "*The Simpsons* message over and over again is that your moral authorities don't always have your best interests in mind. Teachers, principals, clergymen, politicians—for the Simpsons, they're all goofballs, and I think that's a great message for kids. [Laughs.] I don't understand why William Bennett has such a problem with us."

Chapter 4

1. Benjamin Barber, "America as a Monumental Gamble," review of *The Cycles of American History*, by Arthur Schlesinger, *New York Times*, November 16, 1986 (http://tinyurl.com/h7nx7vz): "At some point, shortly before or after the year 1990, there should come a sharp change in the national mood and direction... the turn in the generational succession for the young men and women who came of political age in the Kennedy years. If public purpose holds enough problems at bay in the 1990s, this phase will continue until, perhaps toward the end of the first decade of the twenty-first century, the nation tires again of uplift and commitment and the young people who came of political age in the Reagan years have their turn in power. For, as Emerson pointed out, both conservatism and reform degenerate into excess... Yet in the American republic conservatism and reform... private interest and public purpose, join to define the political tradition. The two jostling strains in American thought agree more than they disagree [and are] indissoluble partners in the great adventure of democracy."

2. Francis Fukuyama, "The End of History?" *The National Interest* (Summer 1989), accessed December 17, 2016 (http://tinyurl.com/hwzsvsd). I cite this 1989 essay because it was the basis of what would become Fukuyama's 1992 book *The End of History and the Last Man*.

3. Cindy Drukier, "Gen X Turns 50—'We're doing well, thanks for asking,'" *Epoch Times*, December 30, 2015, accessed December 17, 2016 (http://tinyurl.com/hwek4vf): "In 1997, *Time* magazine ran a cover story: 'You called us slackers. You dismissed us as Generation X. Well, move over. We're not what you thought.'"

4. Fukuyama, "The End of History?": "If we admit for the moment that the fascist and communist challenges to liberalism are dead, are there any other ideological competitors left? Or put another way, are there contradictions in liberal society beyond that of class that are not resolvable?"

5. *ibid*: "This does not by any means imply the end of international conflict per se. This implies that terrorism and wars of national liberation will continue to be an important item on the international agenda. But large-scale conflict must involve large states still caught in the grip of history, and they are what appear to be passing from the scene."

6. *ibid*: "The end of history will be a very sad time. The struggle for recognition, the willingness to risk one's life for a purely abstract goal, the worldwide ideological struggle that called forth daring, courage, imagination, and idealism, will be replaced by economic calculation, the endless solving of technical problems, environmental concerns, and the satisfaction of sophisticated consumer demands. In the post-historical period there will be neither art nor philosophy, just the perpetual caretaking of the museum of human history."

7. This ad was available on a particularly garish YouTube clip of a 1993(?) Lisa Frank advertisement that was last accessed on December 17, 2016 (http://tinyurl.com/hkem6ea). In the

video a young girl goes on an extended monologue about Lisa Frank stationery that concludes with the following lines: "My friend says hey, we don't have to buy everything now — because Lisa Frank comes out with cool new stuff all the time. It's impossible to keep up with; but it's fun to try." A title card with the famous rainbow Lisa Frank logo then appears atop the words "You Gotta Have It!"

8. James Davison Hunter. *Culture Wars: The Struggle to Define America* (Basic Books, 1991), Kindle Locations 969–970: "The millennial and messianic promises of the Hebrew and Christian Scriptures provided the common symbols of hope for the future."

9. Anti-Defamation League. "Y2K and the 'Patriot' Movement." Accessed December 17, 2016 (http://archive.adl.org/y 2k/militias.html): "The approach of the third millennium and its related 'Y2K' computer problem has provided militia groups and other anti-government extremists—sometimes loosely referred to as the 'Patriot' movement—with a clarion call for their followers. Serving as a touchstone among the movement's conspiracy theories and symbolizing its worst fears of government repression and nationwide anarchy, the Y2K computer 'bug' represents for many of these far-right extremists a problem far beyond the capacity of the Federal Government to control."

10. This ad is available on a YouTube clip (http://tinyurl .com/a3j4u45) that was last accessed on December 17, 2016. In the commercial, a jogger is beset by social breakdown, rioting, panic, and the apparent incursion of martial law. Helicopters and scud missiles fly overhead, but the jogger is oblivious. At one point, a giraffe roams the streets inexplicably. A tragi-comic rendition of "Auld Lang Syne" plays in the background.

11. Kurt Cobain, quoted in *The Sex Revolts: Gender, Rebellion, and Rock 'n' Roll* (Cambridge: Harvard University Press, 1996).

12. *ibid.*
13. Wikipedia entry for *Nevermind* (https://en.wikipedia.org/wiki/Nevermind): *"Nevermind* became Nirvana's first number one album on January 11, 1992, replacing Michael Jackson at the top of the *Billboard* charts."
14. *U.S. News.* "For Diversity, Saturday Night Live Has a Viewership Problem." Accessed December 17, 2016 (http://tinyurl.com/h4sdmwj).
15. From the Genius.com annotation for "Territorial Pissings" (http://genius.com/836354), last accessed on December 18, 2016: "['Get Together'] was a 60's hippie anthem, spreading the word of peace and free love. Krist Novoselic's interpretation of it is the most important parts of the song. Novoselic distorts the song to make it sound like a piece of bullshit idealism—a hopeless dream, as hippie parents sold out and went corporate just like everyone before and after them. I think the band was saying the carefree times of the 60's are gone, and have left those growing up in the 90's in its wake. 'Maybe some baby boomers will hear that and wonder what happened to those ideals,' said Novoselic."
16. *The Hollywood Reporter.* "Kurt Cobain's 5 Most Unforgettable Moments," (http://tinyurl.com/4yfanoe), last accessed December 18, 2016: "For a 1992 cover story, photographers arrange to have the band wear Brooks Brothers suits to illustrate their sudden success. 'Kurt was very resistant,' celeb shutterbug Mark Seliger has said. 'He didn't want to be publicized. He didn't want anything but to be true to his fans and to the music.' To emphasize his discontent, Cobain shows up to the shoot in a T-shirt that reads: 'Corporate Magazines Still Suck.'"
17. This quote from Stoke Newington College's blog (http://tinyurl.com/jfkatm4) was last accessed on February 7, 2017, and requires a bit of editing, as it was written by elementary school students (but nonetheless contains a cogent bit of

analysis that, truth be told, gives me quite a bit of hope for the proverbial "next generation": "Kurt Cobain wanted to shock and surprise audiences by creating a memorable image which would challenge business values. The baby symbolises innocence and the dollar bill, grubby temptation. The image of an innocent baby swimming underwater greedily grasping after a one dollar bill on a fish-hook is difficult to reconcile. After all, it is an odd combination: a baby would not understand the concept of money—yet big business aims to 'hook' each and everyone of us from as early an age as possible. The dollar on a hook is a fishing image in which once the baby (and we) are hooked on the almighty dollar we can be reeled in and caught up in a world of money and greed and readily accept the values of capitalism. Only a few years before 'Greed is good!' was the motto of Gordon Gekko, the greedy capitalist from Oliver Stone's film, *Wall Street* from 1987."

18. Cross, Gary. *An All-Consuming Century: Why Commercialism Won in Modern America* (New York: Columbia University Press, 2000), p. 211: "In the 1980s and 1990s, commercial interests increasingly invaded another once sacred space of childhood, the classroom. With pressures on school budgets and demands for electronic aids in education, the traditional vaunted barrier between consumerism and the classroom was firmly breached."

19. GlobalIssues.org. "Children as Consumers" (http://tinyurl.com/czz8fn), last accessed December 18, 2016: "'In the 1960s, children aged 2 to 14 directly influenced about $5 billion in parental purchases,' McNeal [professor of marketing at Texas A&M University] wrote [in an April 1998 article in American Demographics]. 'In the mid-1970s, the figure was $20 billion, and it rose to $50 billion by 1984. By 1990, kids' direct influence had reached $132 billion, and in 1997, it may have peaked at around $188 billion. Estimates show that children's

262

aggregate spending roughly doubled during each decade of the 1960s, 1970s, and 1980s, and has tripled so far in the 1990s.'"

20. *Adweek*. "When Does Brand Loyalty Start?" (http://tinyurl. com/joyksrg), last accessed December 18, 2016: "'Kids are getting older younger,' says Carol Herman, a principal at strategic and creative consultancy The Acme Idea Company in Norwalk, Conn., and a 20-plus-year veteran of Grey, where she worked for clients including General Foods, Kraft and Playskool. 'We've always known that kids are impressionable and brand-conscious, but it's dribbled down.'"

21. Cross, *An All-Consuming Century: Why Commercialism Won in Modern America*, p. 210: "Childhood became locked in a vast interconnected industry that encompassed movies, TV shows, videos, and other media forms along with toys, clothing, and accessories, all in the business of selling fantasy."

22. *ibid*, p. 212: "Since the 1920s, American companies had used the allure of free educational materials to promote their brand names and products in American schools. But the effort to reach the young was redoubled in the 1980s and 1990s, and all subtlety was dropped. General Mills sent 8,000 teachers a science program entitled Gushers: Wonders of the Earth that taught children about volcanos by using Fruit Gushers candy as an illustration. The makers of Prozac passed out promotional material and provided speakers for 'depression awareness' programs in high schools."

23. *USA Today*. "Club team, Nike reap benefits of sponsorship" (http://tinyurl.com/gu5ncmr), last accessed December 18, 2016: "Sensing opportunity, Nike beefed up its youth basketball initiatives. In 1994, Benson was contacted by the company about forming a partnership. He drove to Asheville, N.C., where he met with a Nike rep at a Shoney's restaurant. 'I told (the rep) that Mr. Mercer and that group

were leaving, and that he probably wouldn't need me then, but he insisted that he wanted to do it,' Benson said. 'They said they'd been looking at our team for a couple years and liked how we ran it.' Initially, perks included just sneakers and uniforms, but that was a novelty then. Rines said that when they handed out gear at the first practices, 'it was like you'd won the lottery.'"

24. Cross, *An All-Consuming Century*, p. 212.
25. This commercial is available on a YouTube vid titled "Pepsi Commercial from the Home Alone VHS" (http://tinyurl.com/js2ufva), last accessed December 18, 2016.
26. Center for Science in the Public Interest. "Liquid Candy Report" (http://tinyurl.com/yz6rfrj), last accessed December 18, 2016: "Not surprisingly, the American Beverage Association defends the marketing of soft drinks in schools, saying: 'Beverage companies have helped narrow the education funding gap by providing grants, scholarships and employee volunteer programs to local schools. School partnerships with beverage companies also generate revenue from the sale of a wide variety of beverages that help schools pay for arts and theater programs, foreign language classes, computers and other technology, sports and physical education equipment... Each year, schools across America earn tens of millions of dollars from the sale of beverages at school. There are no strings attached to the money.'"
27. Meltzer, Marisa. *Girl Power: The Nineties Revolution in Music* (New York: Faber & Faber, 2010), p. 73: "The Spice Girls' beginnings were slightly inauspicious. In March 1994, hundreds of girls responded to an ad placed in Britain's *The Stage* newspaper asking: 'R U 18–23 with the ability to sing/dance? R U streetwise, ambitious, outgoing and determined?' The ad was placed by Chris and Bob Herbert, a father-son management duo who were looking to manufacture a girl group that could compete with Britain's

successful boy bands."

28. *ibid*, p. 73: "Their platform was a nebulous pro-female concept called girl power, which included slogans such as 'G-Force with a Zoom!' and 'Silence Is Golden but Shouting Is Fun.' Their lyrics and manifestas pushed sisterhood ('You stick with your mates and they stick with you') and equal rights ('I expect an equal relationship where he does as much washing up as I do'). So what exactly was the Spice Girls' definition of girl power? 'Girl Power is about being able to do things just as well as the boys—if not better—and being who you wannabe,' said Sporty."

29. I highly recommend VH1's *Behind the Music* about Salt-N-Pepa, available here (http://tinyurl.com/gwfloz9) in a link last accessed December 18, 2016.

30. Meltzer, *Girl Power*, p. 81: "As part of the 'Generation Next' campaign, a CD single was released exclusively through Pepsi. Customers could redeem twenty pull-tabs off their soft drinks for the single and a chance to see the group perform in Turkey. Six hundred thousand consumers redeemed the offer, equaling about 12 million cans sold. This kind of marketing was such a success at least in part because of how young the Spice Girls' fan base skewed. According to an American Psychological Association (APA) report from 2007 on the sexualization of girls, very young children are the most susceptible to marketing, and it's not until after eight years old that they can distinguish between regular TV programming and commercials designed to sell them something."

31. *New York Daily News*. "Girl Power the Spice Girls Hit New York to the Glee of Their Pre-Teen Fans" (http://tinyurl.com/z3hg566), last accessed December 18, 2016: "We've shown we do take our business seriously and we take our destinies into our own hands. We've always taken responsibility for everything we've done. It's obviously very unset-

tling for male-dominated newspapers to realize that five women in short skirts have got a brain."

32. *Animation World Network*. "Dr. Toon: When Reagan Met Optimus Prime," (http://tinyurl.com/zj4scmw) last accessed December 18, 2016: "Writing in issue three of Cereal Geek, a British magazine devoted to 1980s animation, Robert Lamb noted that: 'Shows based on toy lines like He-Man, She-Ra, G.I. Joe, My Little Pony, etc., also had the added joy of input and supervision from their respective toy companies. Different deals were struck that determined how much freedom the studios had to create and how much oversight the toy companies would wield... Hasbro maintained complete script control (over G.I. Joe) in order to showcase the toy line over the needs of the story... Hasbro mandated that all the cast be on the screen as much as possible. This played havoc with staging and drove up production costs.'"

33. From the Wikipedia entry about "Spice Girls dolls" (http://tinyurl.com/honthaf), last accessed December 18, 2016.

34. This episode ("The Bank Trick" [Season 2-Episode 14]) is available at this link (http://tinyurl.com/jsez4aa), last accessed December 18, 2016. Additional information can be found at this link (http://tinyurl.com/j7o2d9t), last accessed December 18, 2016.

35. *New York Times*. "TELEVISION; In 'Rugrats,' Babies Know Best," (http://tinyurl.com/gv2q45j) last accessed December 18, 2016: "Created to appeal across the board to young and old children as well as families, it is a quirkily drawn show that describes the world from a child's-eye-view, a vantage that is often uncomprehending but always slyly observant. Along the way, the show makes good-natured but biting fun of career-obsessed working moms, daydreaming dads, cranky grandparents and our media-driven consumer culture."

36. *ibid.*

37. "Circle of Life" is a song from *The Lion King* (1994) sound-track. It was written by Elton John, and it is insufferable.

38. This episode ("The Big Baby Scam" [Episode 9-Season 2]) is available at this link (http://tinyurl.com/ho988kh), last accessed December 18, 2016. Additional information can be found at this link (http://tinyurl.com/gnzv3vd), last accessed December 18, 2016.

39. Cindy Drukier, "Gen X Turns 50—'We're doing well, thanks for asking,'" *Epoch Times*, December 30, 2015, accessed December 17, 2016 (http://tinyurl.com/hwek4vf): "There was no Great Depression, major war, or a civil rights movement; terrorists were not yet brazen enough to attack the homeland. With nothing to galvanize them outward, Gen X turned inward."

40. *The Baltimore Sun*. "Beavis and Fire, Mass Media and Behavior" (http://tinyurl.com/jmjptw3), last accessed December 18, 2016.

41. More information is available about this episode ("Homer Defined" [Episode 5-Season 3]) of *The Simpsons* at this link (http://tinyurl.com/jh8444f), last accessed December 18, 2016.

42. HipHopDx.com. "RZA Says He Studied Under Quentin Tarantino To Prepare For *The Man with the Iron Fists*" (http://tinyurl.com/hf59oej), last accessed December 18, 2016.

43. Jameson, Fredric. *Postmodernism, or, The Cultural Logic of Late Capitalism* (Durham: Duke University Press, 1991).

44. Fukuyama, "The End of History?": "In the post-historical period there will be neither art nor philosophy, just the perpetual caretaking of the museum of human history. I can feel in myself, and see in others around me, a powerful nostalgia for the time when history existed. Such nostalgia, in fact, will continue to fuel competition and conflict even in the post-historical world for some time to come."

45. MentalFloss.com. "4 Simpsons Controversies That Didn't

End in Lawsuits" (http://tinyurl.com/z76e62z), last accessed December 18, 2016: "The real controversy began January 27th, 1992, when Bush declared to a meeting of the National Religious Broadcasters: 'We are going to keep on trying to strengthen the American family, to make American families a lot more like the Waltons and a lot less like the Simpsons.' *The Simpsons* quickly wrote and animated a new sequence for 'Stark Raving Dad,' which would be rerun three days later. Bart and his family watch the clip of Bush's speech and Bart replies, 'Hey, we're just like the Waltons. We're praying for an end of the depression, too.'"

46. *The Atlantic.* "Washington and the Contract With America" (http://tinyurl.com/ztuhumy), last accessed December 28, 2016: "The Contract, amazingly, contains not a single word about controlling medical costs, by far the fastest-rising category in federal and state spending. Its welfare reform package includes a limit on spending for today's main welfare programs. But these represent only about 1 percent of the entire federal budget, and the Contract's welfare package as a whole would probably increase welfare costs [...] Unlike the Contract's position on prison-building or term limits, the capital-gains proposal derives largely from the remnants of supply-side ideology [...] The result is that rich people with much of their income in capital gains pay a lower overall tax rate than even minimum-wage workers, all of whose income is subject to payroll taxes."

47. Fisher, Mark. *Capitalist Realism: Is There No Alternative?* (Winchester: Zero Books, 2009), p. 9.

Chapter 5

1. Economic Policy Institute. "The Productivity-Pay Gap" (http://tinyurl.com/zdeou5r), last accessed December 18, 2016: "Most Americans believe that a rising tide should lift all boats—that as the economy expands, everybody should

reap the rewards. And for two-and-a-half decades beginning in the late 1940s, this was how our economy worked. Over this period, the pay (wages and benefits) of typical workers rose in tandem with productivity (how much workers produce per hour). In other words, as the economy became more efficient and expanded, everyday Americans benefitted correspondingly through better pay. But in the 1970s, this started to change."

2. Animation World Network. "Animated Propaganda During the Cold War: Part Two" (http://tinyurl.com/mc7g9bf), last accessed December 18, 2016.

3. *Business Insider.* "Real Wages Decline Again—Literally No One Notices" (http://tinyurl.com/lfz87gb), last accessed December 18, 2016.

4. *The Washington Post.* "That Day is Finally Here—Reagan's Budget Cuts Begin" (http://preview.tinyurl.com/jchs5e8), last accessed on December 18, 2016.

5. *The Christian Science Monitor.* "Reagan cuts eat into school lunches" (http://tinyurl.com/h8hmtfr), last accessed December 18, 2016.

6. *Jacobin Magazine.* "How a Democrat Killed Welfare," by Premilla Nadasen (Winter 2016), p. 60.

7. Neil Howe and William Strauss. *13th Gen: Abort, Retry, Ignore, Fail?* (New York: Vintage Books, 1993).

8. *ibid*, p. 3.

9. This clip is available on YouTube in a video titled "2pac-T.H.U.G.L.I.F.E. (The Hate U Give Little Infants Fuck Everybody)" (http://tinyurl.com/z3g6px3), last accessed December 18, 2016.

10. This image can be viewed at this link (http://tinyurl.com/j3bgadv), and was last accessed on December 18, 2016.

11. This picture can be viewed at this link (http://tinyurl.com/zzwqw9x), and was last accessed on December 18, 2016.

12. This episode ("Patients, Patients," Season 4-Episode 25) can be viewed at this link (http://tinyurl.com/hnnnt9b), and was last accessed on December 18, 2016.

13. Kamenetz, Anya. *Generation Debt: How Our Future Was Sold Out for Student Loans, Credit Cards, Bad Jobs, No Benefits, and Tax Cuts for Rich Geezers—and How to Fight Back* (New York: Penguin Publishing Group, 2006), pp. 4–5: "In 2002, there were 68 million people in the United States aged eighteen to thirty-four. The social and economic upheaval of the past three decades, not to mention that of the past five years, affects us in complex ways. We have all come of age as part of Generation Debt. The Penn researchers use five milestones of maturity: leaving home, finishing school, becoming financially independent, getting married, and having a child."

14. *ibid*: "Miriam earns $28,000 a year and just manages the minimum payments on her loans. She is single. She hasn't passed the five milestones of adulthood; she is barely out of the driveway."

15. American screenwriting guru Sydney Field introduced the idea of the "plot point"—a series of motivating acts, confrontations and resolutions that define the life cycle of a character within a given film, and advance a movie's plot.

16. The moniker given to the generation that reached maturity during and just after World War I. The name is often reapplied to Generation X, as Gen-X is a comparatively small generation, wedged between the populous Baby Boomers and Millennials.

17. Coupland, Douglas. *Generation X: Tales for an Accelerated Culture* (New York: St. Martin's Press, 1991). The phrase "refugees from history" is one of several delicious verbal fragments in this book. Another personal favorite of mine is "Boomer Envy," which Coupland defines as "envy of material wealth and long-range material security accrued by older members of the baby boom generation by virtue of

fortunate births" (page 21).

18. The theme song of *Friends* is by The Rembrandts, and is titled "I'll Be There For You." Lyrics are available at the following link (http://tinyurl.com/kmxhlzq), last accessed December 18, 2016. It's a truly unfortunate listen.

19. The relevant clip from this episode ("The Fix Up," Season 3-Episode 16) can be viewed at this link (http://tinyurl.com/h2df9rk), which was last accessed on December 18, 2016.

20. *The San Francisco Gate.* "Why 'Seinfeld' lost a potential fan" (http://tinyurl.com/zmfrx7e), last accessed on December 18, 2016: "'On *Seinfeld*,' said Goodman, 'meanness is celebrated. Nobody is living an examined life. Getting yours is the goal. Anger and bitterness supplant happiness. Emotionless sex wins out over love, and the mundane is king.'"

21. *ibid.*

22. Lyrics to "Everyday Struggle" by The Notorious B.I.G. are available here (http://tinyurl.com/gvxxhhm), last accessed December 18, 2016.

23. *ibid.*

24. *Jacobin Magazine.* "Bill Clinton's Stone Mountain Moment" (http://tinyurl.com/z5eyukj), last accessed December 18, 2016: "The crime bill overflowed with new provisions and programs. It allocated nearly $10 billion for the construction of new prisons, expanded the number of death-penalty eligible federal crimes from two to fifty-eight, eliminated a statute that prohibited the execution of mentally incapacitated defendants, created special deportation courts for noncitizens accused of 'engaging in terrorist activity,' added new mechanisms for tracking sex offenders after they had served their sentences, introduced a 'three strikes' law that gave mandatory life sentences for third offenses, gave $10.8 billion dollars to local police departments to hire one hundred thousand new officers, introduced 'truth in

sentencing' requirements and allowed children as young as thirteen to be tried as adults."

25. Quote can be seen/heard in the 1994 film *Reality Bites* (directed by Ben Stiller), and also read at this website (http://tinyurl.com/zfwonxn), last accessed on December 18, 2016.

26. *New York Times.* "Graduates Whose Hero Could Be Peter Pan" (http://tinyurl.com/hsmw7l8), last accessed December 18, 2016: "Like baby birds with brand-new college diplomas, the four graduates in Noah Baumbach's *Kicking and Screaming* are having trouble leaving the nest. They prefer a pleasant limbo filled with witty asides, trivia contests and hair-splitting arguments about matters of no consequence. Girlfriends notice this aimlessness ('the characters in Grover's story spend time discussing the least important things,' says one young woman, criticizing the film's would-be writer), but they don't really mind. Audiences won't either, since *Kicking and Screaming* occupies its postage-stamp size terrain with confident comic style."

27. Coupland, Douglas. *Generation X: Tales for an Accelerated Culture* (New York: St. Martin's Press, 1991), p. 183: "Percentage of Americans 18–29 who agree that 'given the way things are, it will be much harder for people in my generation to live as comfortably as previous generations': 65. Who disagree: 33. Source is a telephone poll of Americans taken for Time/CNN in 1990, by Yankelovich Clancy Shulman."

28. *The New Yorker.* "Noah Baumbach, Kicking and Screaming Into Middle Age" (http://tinyurl.com/guggnp9), last accessed December 18, 2016: "When a boy selling cookies comes to the door, Max (Chris Eigeman) makes everybody hit the deck, to hide; later, when he breaks a glass, he puts a sign on the shards that says 'BROKEN GLASS.'"

29. *The New York Times.* "'Kids,' Then and Now" (http://

tinyurl.com/h87rsqm), last accessed December 18, 2016: "For cultural alarmists of the 1990s Clinton era, the film *Kids* represented a culmination of fears. Released 20 years ago this month, the film centers on a cabal of broken New York teenagers who spend 24 hours boozing, rolling blunts, fighting and indulging in unsafe, emotionally vacant sex. It is *Lord of the Flies* with skateboards, nitrous oxide and hip-hop."

30. *The New York Times*. "KIDS; Growing Up Troubled, In Terrifying Ways" (http://tinyurl.com/jorq5v3), last accessed December 18, 2016: "Mr. Clark offers neither analysis nor prognosis, but he stunningly captures a world beyond ordinary taboos. In this film's atmosphere, casual viciousness comes easily and fills all sorts of glaring gaps in the characters' lives. The very saddest of the lost characters in *Kids* are the little brothers, seen here sampling drugs, watching enviously at parties and trying to keep up with the tough talk. They've barely reached puberty and are already drifting into the older boys' decadent, irreversible extremes."

31. Gray, Jonathan. *Watching with The Simpsons: Television, Parody, and Intertextuality* (New York: Routledge Press, 2005), p. 59: "However, as became obvious when Bart was made a focus for a moral panic of sorts about youth rebellion for the American far right and grumbling parents alike, Bart's rebellion is several steps worse than the average sitcom mischief mastermind."

32. According to *The Simpsons'* user-generated Wikipedia page (http://tinyurl.com/gof7mor) last accessed December 18, 2016, Lisa Simpson has an IQ of 159. The page cites the episode "They Saved Lisa's Brain" (Episode 22-Season 10).

33. Gray, *Watching with The Simpsons*, p. 57: "... The hero will face and overcome the villainy due largely to the implicit or explicit help and advice of the parental donors/helpers, nearly always in a manner that moralizes the wisdom of the

advice or help, and that reaffirms the strength of the nuclear family unit in overcoming all obstacles."

34. More information about the episode "Girly Edition" (Episode 25-Season 9) can be found at the episode's Wikipedia page (http://tinyurl.com/zu27bpa), which was last accessed December 18, 2016.

35. Jameson, Fredric. *Signatures of the Visible* (New York: Routledge Classics, 1990), p. 228: "The negative or ideological moment of this new domestic realism will then become visible when we restore the situation itself, namely the reality of the great Depression, whose collective experience is surely the greatest punctual psychic trauma of U.S. history since the Civil War, in terms of which Hollywood's images of domesticity now suddenly come to be seen, not as 'realism,' but as compensatory wish-fulfillment and consolation. Conventional notions of mass culture as 'distraction' and 'entertainment' recover a certain force and content—but also become structurally restricted as to time and place—when they are historicized to include that from which public needs most urgently to be 'distracted.'"

36. Wilson, William Julius. *When Work Disappears: The World of the New Urban Poor* (New York: Random House Books, 1996).

37. *The Huffington Post.* "Astoria, Oregon: Where Everything Old is New Again" (http://tinyurl.com/m3al54n), last accessed December 18, 2016: "When the Bumble Bee factory closed in the 1980s, the town had to reinvent itself. Artists moved in and the town on a hill, speckled with Victorian mansions, became known as 'Little San Francisco.' Today, the town is equal parts industrial and artistic. A bartender at the funky, dimly lit VooDoo Room—adorned with everything from license plates and masks to bottle caps and a ouija board— told us about all of the young musicians moving to town, and all of the organic gardens popping up."

38. *Los Angeles Times.* "NEWS ANALYSIS: Will Disney Make

Anaheim Unhappiest Place on Earth?" (http://tinyurl .com/h2kbrn3), last accessed December 18, 2016: "Now Anaheim may become the third Southland city to lose the promise of a new Walt Disney Co. theme park and the enormous windfall of jobs and tax revenue it would bring. This possibility became evident Monday, when project director Kerry Hunnewell resigned before a Disney decision on whether to proceed with the proposed $3-billion Disneyland Resort and Westcot theme park, the largest proposed construction project in Southern California. The state and city are itching to win the project because of its promise to provide 28,000 jobs and add $2.4 billion to the moribund California economy, now in the worst downturn since the Great Depression. City economists say the expansion could generate $27 million a year in tax revenue for Anaheim alone."

39. *ibid.*
40. *ibid.*
41. Gay, Roxane. *Bad Feminist: Essays* (New York: Harper Perennial, 2014), p. 281: "Heroism can be a burden. We even see this in the trials and tribulations of comic book super-heroes. These heroes are often strong at the broken places. They suffer and suffer and suffer but still they rise. Still they serve the greater good. They sacrifice their bodies and hearts and minds because heroism, it would seem, means the complete denial of the self. Spider-Man agonizes over whether to be with the woman he loves and cannot forgive himself for the death of his uncle. Superman is reluctant to reveal his true identity to the woman he loves to keep her safe from danger. Every superhero has a sad story shaping his or her heroism."
42. *The Root.* "For the Record: 'Superpredators' is Absolutely a Racist Term" (http://tinyurl.com/zr4cebh), last accessed December 18, 2016: "As anyone who has even been half

paying attention to the 2016 election is aware, Clinton used the term [superpredator] while whipping up support for then-President Bill Clinton's 1994 crime bill. Yes, the same one that Sen. Bernie Sanders voted for and then-Sen. Joe Biden authored. Though Hillary Clinton didn't apologize for the remarks, she later acknowledged during a spin with Jonathan Capehart that she shouldn't have used the term and wouldn't use it today."

Chapter 6

1. Stanley Couch's commentary in Episode 8 ("The Adventure") of Ken Burns' 2001 film *Jazz* is on point here: "Miles Davis benefitted from the reaction that people were beginning to feel in the 1950s against the suburbanization of the United States. You had a lot of mass-packaging and the projection of a certain sublime mediocrity. So people wanted something that was elegant, but that had a bite to it."

2. The notion of the "post-war consensus," in truth, is a borrowed term from post-war British political history, but is nonetheless applicable to the American context, where the age of American prosperity running from 1945 until the mid-1970s was created with "strong labour unions, heavy regulation, high taxes, and a generous welfare state" (https://en.wikipedia.org/wiki/Post-war_consensus). For more information on the term in its original British context, consider David Dutton's *British Politics Since 1945: The Rise, Fall and Rebirth of Consensus*. For more on the American context, the oeuvre of economist John Kenneth Galbraith is indispensable.

3. Leland, John. *Hip: The History* (New York: Harper Perennial, 2005), p. 319: "Though jazz fans blame the commercial bigfooting of rock and roll or the overzealous flight into the avant-garde, jazz lost its hold on the American consciousness precisely when the patterns of American society to which it

gave meaning—the way we worked, produced, manufactured—went into decline, outshined by the more abstract economy of the brand. Jazz was about the means of production as the country began to see production as a drag. As Drucker said, 'The traditional factors of production—land, labor and capital—are becoming restraints rather than driving forces. Knowledge is becoming the one critical factor of production.'"

4. *The New York Times*. "'Can't Stop Won't Stop': A Nation of Millions" (review of Jeffrey Chang's *Can't Stop Won't Stop: A History of the Hip-Hop Generation*) (http://tinyurl.com/hyl5 8h2), last accessed December 19, 2016.

5. *The New York Times*. "Benign Neglect" (http://tinyurl .com/gkq8ee5), last accessed December 19, 2016: "In March 1970, Daniel Patrick Moynihan, then an adviser to President Richard Nixon, wrote a memo suggesting that the nation might benefit from a period of 'benign neglect' on the subject of race, a brief respite during which 'Negro progress continues and racial rhetoric fades.'"

6. *Time Magazine*. "Hip-Hop Nation" (http://tinyurl.com /ztm3rpb), last accessed December 19, 2016.

7. This vid is available to be viewed on YouTube on a clip titled "The Kids' Guide To The Internet" (http://tinyurl.com /mo7y8rj), last accessed December 19, 2016.

8. *Newsweek*. "Does the Parental Advisory Sticker Still Matter?" (http://tinyurl.com/hkjt9er), last accessed December 19, 2016: "The authoritative Black-and-White rectangle you probably recognize from your CD collection debuted in the summer of 1990. The label 'will appear on the lower right-hand corner at the discretion of record companies and individual artists,' a *USA Tonight* newscaster announced in May 1990. It has looked the same ever since, with a small tweak: 'Explicit Lyrics' was changed to 'Explicit Content' in 1996, after another round of congressional hearings."

9. See one of Tupac's corporate spots at this link (http://tinyurl.com/mgy8wze), last accessed February 20, 2017.
10. See the August 2015 *New York Times* story "Inside Amazon: Wrestling Big Ideas in a Bruising Workplace," available at the following link (http://tinyurl.com/hke9dl9), last accessed February 20, 2017.
11. *NPR.org.* "No Blank Space, Baby: Taylor Swift Is The Soul of Ryan Adams" (http://tinyurl.com/oru3tea), last accessed December 19, 2016: "Now, pop is critically cool, the mainstream music industry has flattened, and artists use whimsical covers as branding devices, not bold statements. It happens in every corner: country star Sam Hunt covers Mariah Carey to prove his '90s R&B bona fides; divo Sam Smith dares a little Whitney Houston to cement his reputation as a vocal powerhouse. A firmly indie artist like Empress Of turns to Katy Perry's oeuvre, not as a joke, but to show that today's biggest hits are on a continuum with her more experimental efforts. This is a natural progression for a culture whose ruling metaphor is the network, within which every connection is ostensibly equal. It's also reflective of a musical generation that grew up with hip-hop, which puts redeployment of others' music at the heart of the creative act, through sampling and verbal interpolations."
12. Sennett, Richard. *The Corrosion of Character: The Personal Consequences of Work in the New Capitalism* (New York: W.W. Norton & Company, 1998), Kindle Locations 713–719: "The ingredients necessary for flexible specialization are again familiar to us. Flexible specialization suits high technology; thanks to the computer, industrial machines are easy to reprogram and configure. The speed of modern communications has also favored flexible specialization, by making global market data instantly available to a company. Moreover, this form of production requires quick decision-making, and so suits the small work group; in a large bureau-

cratic pyramid, by contrast, decision-making can slow down as paper rises to the top for approval from headquarters. The most strongly flavored ingredient in this new productive process is the willingness to let the shifting demands of the outside world determine the inside structure of institutions. All these elements of responsiveness make for an acceptance of decisive, disruptive change."

13. *Los Angeles Times.* "The 'Batman' Who Took On Rap: Obscenity: Lawyer Jack Thompson put his practice on hold to concentrate on driving 2 Live Crew out of business. In Southern Florida he is loved and loathed" (http://tinyurl.com/zyy3owo), last accessed December 19, 2016: "'For me,' says Thompson, standing in the kitchen of his modest suburban home here, 'the appeal of the Batman lies in the fact that he was supposed to be a private citizen who was able to provide assistance to his government, a lone activist who helped authorities do a job that they seemed unable to accomplish on their own. To me, Luther Campbell isn't Luke Skyywalker (a stage name he adopted but has been enjoined from using by Lucasfilm), he's the Joker,' Thompson says. 'He's peddling obscenity to children and that is why I have to play Batman here—to assist, to cajole and to sometimes embarrass government into doing its job.'"

14. *ibid.*

15. See relevant sections of Jack Thompson's Wikipedia page (http://tinyurl.com/j8fbkff), last accessed on December 19, 2016: "Thompson filed a lawsuit on behalf of the parents of three children killed in the Heath High School shooting in 1997. Investigations showed that the perpetrator, 14-year-old Michael Carneal, had regularly played various computer games (including *Doom, Quake, Castle Wolfenstein, Redneck Rampage, Nightmare Creatures, MechWarrior,* and *Resident Evil*) and accessed some pornographic websites. Carneal had also owned a videotape of *The Basketball Diaries,* which includes a

high school student dreaming about shooting his teacher and some classmates."

16. *Los Angeles Times* [see Chapter 6, Endnote #13] (http://tinyurl.com/zyy3owo): "Unlike Batman alter-ego Bruce Wayne, Thompson is no millionaire philanthropist. He is a 'born-again' Christian and self-proclaimed 'radical conservative Republican' who put his legal practice on hold 6 months ago to concentrate on driving Miami rap entrepreneur Campbell and his 2 Live Crew out of business."

17. Dardot, Pierre and Laval, Christian. *The New Way of the World: On Neoliberal Society* (New York: Verso Books, 2014), Kindle Locations 5768–5784: "The theme of entrepreneurial government has not been without its sequel. Under Bill Clinton, the National Performance Review inspired by Osborne and Gaebler's book was launched. Following a 1993 report by Al Gore, whose programme was 'creating a government that works better and costs less' [...] The 'reinvention of government' is often depicted as a reinvention of left-wing politics. In truth, it is only the most striking example of the domination of the new neo-liberal rationality. In the late 1990s, reform of the instrument of public intervention became the basis of the agreement between Clinton and Blair and various other leaders of the European Left."

18. *The New York Times*. "POLITICS: THE TOBACCO ISSUE; Clinton Campaign to Use Anti-Smoking Pitch to Attack Dole" (http://tinyurl.com/jb7hkef), last accessed December 19, 2016: "The Clinton-Gore campaign plans to begin broadcasting on Monday its first commercial attacking Bob Dole on tobacco, seizing the issue to portray Mr. Clinton once again as protecting families and Mr. Dole as failing them. 'Bob Dole or Bill Clinton—who's really protecting our children?' the advertisement asks, after images of children smoking cigarettes are alternated with a quotation from Mr.

Dole questioning whether smoking is always addictive. The female narrator criticizes Mr. Dole for opposing an Administration plan to restrict tobacco advertising directed at young people."

19. The single best source on the topic of the "heroin chic" aesthetic remains Maureen Callahan's *Champagne Supernovas: Kate Moss, Marc Jacobs, Alexander McQueen, and the '90s Renegades Who Remade Fashion* (published in 2014). Of additional interest would be a May 22, 1997 article in *The New York Times* titled "Clinton Calls Fashion Ads' 'Heroin Chic' Deplorable," available at this link (http://tinyurl .com/j56c7pt), last accessed December 19, 2016. In this article, Clinton was quoted as saying, "American fashion has been an enormous source of creativity and economic prosperity for the United States. But the glorification of heroin is not creative, it's destructive. It's not beautiful; it's ugly."

20. One of Clinton's first uses of the phrase "bridge to the 21st century" came when he accepted the Democratic party's nomination ahead of the beginning of his second term in August 1996 (http://tinyurl.com/jbfa9pe). A ruthless article in the parody organ *The Onion* (http://tinyurl.com/gkpgbvg) joked that Clinton's words appeared to "come from my heart, when in fact they originated from my ass."

21. Indeed, many pharmaceuticals are simply chemical variants of drugs that are criminalized when purchased from street dealers. For instance, Heroin, Oxycontin, Methadone, and Morphine are all opiates—their impact on human physiology is practically identical. In a manner of interpretation, the main crime of street-dealers of heroin is not that they sell the drug—it's that they undercut the market share of billion-dollar pharmaceutical companies.

22. *The Milbank Quarterly.* "A History of Drug Advertising: The Evolving Roles of Consumers and Consumer Protection" (http://tinyurl.com/gl2gxoo), last accessed December 20,

2016: "Pharmaceutical industry spending on DTCA rose from $55 million in 1991 to $363 million in 1995, reflecting the industry's calculation that the profits earned from pitching products directly to patients outweighed any loss of goodwill from a profession that for decades it had relied on to promote its products."

23. Stats about childhood TV viewing rate are available from ChildTrends.org's article "Watching Television," available at this link (http://tinyurl.com/j69mekd), last accessed December 20, 2016. The estimate of 24 hours per week is a conservative estimate based on a graph contained in this study.

24. See citation from endnote #22: "The pharmaceutical industry quickly seized on the policy change, more than doubling its spending on television advertising from $310 million to $664 million between 1997 and 1998, with the total spending on DTCA advertising rising from $1.3 billion in 1998 to $3.3 billion in 2005."

25. *The New York Times.* "Abroad at Home; Black and White" (http://tinyurl.com/jca9jfj), last accessed December 20, 2016: "[Clinton] quoted part of the *Post* interview and a statement [Sistah Souljah] had made on a music video: 'If there are any good White people, I haven't met them.' 'Her comments before and after Los Angeles,' Mr. Clinton said, 'were filled with a kind of hatred that you [the Rainbow Coalition] do not honor.' The criticism infuriated Mr. Jackson. He said afterward that Sister Souljah 'represents the feelings and hopes of a whole generation of people,' and that she said she had been misquoted in *The Post.* In fact the interview was tape-recorded."

26. *Los Angeles Times.* "Federal and State Prison Populations Soared Under Clinton, Report Finds" (http://tinyurl.com /q5ozqsn), last accessed December 20, 2016: "The federal and state prison populations rose more under former President

Bill Clinton than under any other president, according to a report from a criminal justice institute to be released today. In fact, the analysis of U.S. Justice Department statistics by the left-leaning Justice Policy Institute, a project of a San Francisco-based justice center, found that more federal inmates were added to prisons under Clinton than under presidents George Bush and Ronald Reagan combined."

27. *Bloomberg*. "Bill Clinton: 'We Cast Too Wide a Net' With Three-Strike Law" (http://tinyurl.com/jg9hnul), last accessed December 20, 2016: "Former President Bill Clinton said Wednesday that a 1994 crime bill he signed contributed to the rates of incarceration that his wife has criticized in her run for the Democratic presidential nomination. 'The problem is the way it was written and implemented is we cast too wide a net and we had too many people in prison,' the former president said of the law, which established mandatory life sentences for those convicted of a third violent felony, in an interview with CNN."

28. From Bill Clinton's 1996 State of the Union Address (http://tinyurl.com/jevpdcl), last accessed December 20, 1996: "I call on Congress to pass the requirement for a V-chip in TV sets so that parents can screen out programs they believe are inappropriate for their children. When parents control what their young children see, that is not censorship; that is enabling parents to assume more personal responsibility for their children's upbringing. And I urge them to do it. To make the V-chip work, I challenge the broadcast industry to do what movies have done, to identify your program in ways that help parents to protect their children."

29. Economic Policy Institute's "Wage Stagnation in Nine Charts" (http://tinyurl.com/kqhsc3c), last accessed December 20, 2016: "Clinton thus supported a two-step rise in the minimum wage in 1996-97, from $4.25 to $5.15 an hour, the rate at which it remained for the rest of Clinton's presidency.

But this modest increment did little to reverse the precipitous fall in the real value of the minimum wage. At $5.15
when Clinton left office, the minimum wage was still 35
percent below its real value in 1968 even though the
economy had become 81 percent more productive between
1968 and 2000."

30. *ibid.*

31. Alan Greenspan, quoted on politifact.com (http://tinyurl
.com/nnq59yj), last accessed December 20, 2016: "The performance of the U.S. economy over the past year has been quite
favorable… Continued low levels of inflation and inflation
expectations have been a key support for healthy economic
performance… Atypical restraint on compensation increases
has been evident for a few years now, and appears to be
mainly the consequence of greater worker insecurity. The
willingness of workers in recent years to trade off smaller
increases in wages for greater job security seems to be
reasonably well documented. The unanswered question is
why this insecurity persisted even as the labor market, by all
objective measures, tightened considerably."

32. The best summary of Clinton's saga is W. Joseph Campbell's
1995: The Year the Future Began (Berkeley: University of
California Press, 2015).

33. This clip is available at a YouTube vid called "1998—Top Ten
Monica Lewinsky" (http://tinyurl.com/zongjfk), last accessed
on December 20, 2016.

34. A couple of clips of this Conan O'Brien skit can be seen at
these links (http://tinyurl.com/j852yhj) and (http://tinyurl
.com/zbh4wj2), both of which were last accessed on
December 20, 2016.

35. This outrageous song can be found at the YouTube link "Bill
Clinton"—Mo Booty Mo Problems (http://tinyurl.com/
zc4um89), last accessed December 20, 2016.

36. The full transcript of this speech is available online thanks to

the Miller Center (http://tinyurl.com/ohaj7oh), last accessed December 20, 2016.

37. *ibid.*

38. *ibid.*

39. *ibid*: "Now, let me say, in addition to all the positive benefits, I think it's important to point out that the hours between 3 and 7 at night are the most vulnerable hours for young people to get in trouble, for juvenile crime. There is this sort of assumption that everybody that gets in trouble when they're young has just already been abandoned. That's not true. Most of the kids that get in trouble get in trouble after school closes and before their parents get home from work. So in the adolescent years, in the later years, it is profoundly important to try to give kids something to say yes to and something positive to do."

40. Jack Thompson said this in a 2005 interview with Lou Dobbs (of CNN), in 2005. The full transcript of the interview can be viewed at (http://tinyurl.com/zuhtj2k), last accessed December 20, 2016.

41. Lewis, Sydney. *A Totally Alien Life-Form: Teenagers* (New York: New Press, 1997).

42. The lyrics to Pearl Jam's "Jeremy" can be found at this link (http://tinyurl.com/haxo5sj), last accessed December 20, 2016.

43. *ibid.*

44. Neil Howe and William Strauss. *13th Gen: Abort, Retry, Ignore, Fail?* (New York: Vintage Books, 1993), p. 22: "Confused about their nation's direction in a 'New World Order,' older Americans are using a profoundly negative image of 13ers to rekindle a sense of national community—and urgency. Some of the same resource once directed against an external 'Evil Empire' are now being used against the new generation coming of age. Military bases are being retooled into prisons. Naval ships are patrolling for drugs. And in what (Boomer)

Attorney General William Barr has called a 'peace dividend' from the ending of the Cold War, 300 FBI agents who once tracked foreign spies are now sleuthing around inner-city neighborhoods."

45. Hersch, Patricia. *A Tribe Apart: A Journey into the Heart of American Adolescence* (New York: Ballantine Books, 1998), p. 13: "Over the years, the tone of discourse on adolescents has become shrill and frightened. Increasingly desperate attempts to understand and know them fragment them into pieces of behavior that are 'good' or 'bad.' They are labeled and classified like so many phyla in the animal kingdom, by how they look and how they act. Theories abound on how to manage them, fix them, and improve them, as if they were products off an assembly line: just tinker with the educational system, manipulate the drug messages, impose citywide curfews, make more rules, write contracts, build more detention centers, be tough. Maybe if we just tell adolescents to say no, no, no to everything we disapprove of, maybe then they will be okay. But the piecemeal attempts to mend, motivate, or rescue them obscure the larger reality: We don't know them."

46. The pilot episode of *Daria* ("Esteemsters" [Episode 1-Season 1]) aired on March 3rd, 1997. You can read more information about the episode at this link (http://preview.tinyurl .com/zpp437l), last accessed December 20, 2016.

47. Moore narrated the 2002 film *Bowling for Columbine*.

48. *BuzzFeed*. "Why 'Seinfeld' Is The Most Villainous Sitcom In Human History," available at this link (http://preview.tinyurl.com/gpjkv2m), last accessed on December 20, 2016: "The successful social satirist must show a) how the average liberal is latently selfish and hypocritical, or b) how the average conservative fails to comprehend how trapped he is by the same system he supports. A world-class satirist knows the truth about his audience and does not care

how exposing that truth will make audiences feel."

49. This quote is so frequently attributed to Jameson, who cited this quote in a 2003 article titled "Future City," which appeared in *New Left Review* (http://tinyurl.com/h5gjhch). Jameson cites it apocryphally, with no attribution. It has also often been attributed to Slavoj Žižek.
50. Busta Rhymes' *E.L.E. (Extinction Level Event): The Final World Front* was released on December 15, 1998.

Part III

In sculpting Part III of *Millennials and the Moments That Made Us*, I relied heavily on the framework of Naomi Klein's 2007 book *The Shock Doctrine: The Rise of Disaster Capitalism*. Her description of the ways neoliberalism relies upon disasters and catastrophes to implement its pro-market reforms was indispensable. Robin James' 2010 book *Resilience & Melancholy: Pop Music, Feminism, Neoliberalism* was also a tremendously valuable resource that helped me imagine all the ways in which popular culture simulates the ebbs and flows of 21st century capitalism. In describing the significance of Millennial celebrities Mark Zuckerberg and LeBron James in Chapters 8 and 9, I borrowed from Deleuze and Guattari's notion of "reterritorialization," where beleaguered populations inhabit threadbare terrain, and then go about the work of rebuilding it using the surrounding wreckage.

Chapter 7

1. *National Public Radio.* "Goodbye, Music Tuesday: Starting Today, Albums Come Out On Friday" (http://tinyurl.com/gqw3qn7), last accessed December 23rd, 2016.
2. Quoted in the documentary *Downloaded* (2013), directed by Alex Winter.
3. *ibid.*
4. *ibid.*

5.   The figure of 60 million users was cited in the documentary *Downloaded*. The statistic about the decline in CD sales is cited from *ABC News'* "RIAA: New Data Show Napster Hurt Sales" (http://tinyurl.com/jkfplel), last accessed December 23, 2016.

6.   Quoted in the documentary *Downloaded* (2013), directed by Alex Winter.

7.   *ibid.*

8.   *The Washington Post.* "Many millennials are about to lose their most-trusted news source: Jon Stewart" (http://tinyurl.com/jex83wr), last accessed December 23, 2016.

9.   Shiller, Robert J. *Irrational Exuberance (Second Edition)* (Princeton: Princeton University Press, 2009), p. 3: Greenspan's "irrational exuberance" speech in 1996 came near the beginning of what may be called the biggest historical example to date of a speculative upsurge in the stock market. The Dow Jones Industrial Average (from here on, the Dow for short) stood at around 3,600 in early 1994. By March 1999, it passed 10,000 for the first time. The Dow peaked at 11,722.98 in January 14, 2000, just two weeks after the start of the new millennium. The market had tripled in five years.

10. *ibid*, p. 129.

11. *ibid*, p. 52: "The growth of online trading, as well as the associated Internet-based information and communication services, may well encourage minute-by-minute attention to the market. After-hours trading on the exchanges also has the potential to increase the level of attention paid to the market, as investors can track changing prices in their living rooms during their leisure time."

12. James, Robin. *Resilience & Melancholy: Pop Music, Feminism, Neoliberalism* (Winchester: Zero Books, 2015), Kindle Locations 159–168: "Resilience discourse is what ties contemporary pop music aesthetics to neoliberal capitalism and

racism/sexism [...] Instead of expending resources to avoid damage, resilience discourse recycles damage into more resources. Resilience discourse thus follows a very specific logic: first, damage is incited and made manifest; second, that damage is spectacularly overcome, and that overcoming is broadcast and/or shared, so that; third, the person who has overcome is rewarded with increased human capital, status, and other forms of recognition and recompense, because: finally, and most importantly, this individual's own resilience boosts society's resilience."

13. Lyrics to Jay Z's "Never Change" are available at the following link (http://genius.com/Jay-z-never-change-lyrics), last accessed December 23, 2016.

14. Lyrics to Jay Z's "Girls, Girls, Girls" are available at the following link (https://genius.com/Jay-z-girls-girls-girls-lyrics), last accessed December 23, 2016.

15. Williams, Raymond. *Television: Technology and Cultural Form* (New York: Routledge Books, 2004 republication of 1974 text), Kindle Location 144: "In the contemporary debate about the general relations between technology, social institutions and culture, television is obviously an outstanding case. Indeed its present importance, as an element in each of these areas, and as a point of interaction between them, is in effect unparalleled."

16. Banet-Weiser, Sarah. *Kids Rule!: Nickelodeon and Consumer Citizenship* (Durham: Duke University Press, 2007), Kindle Locations 4517–4520: "This is one way to adjust Williams' notion of flow—Williams was remarking upon the ways in which the seemingly disparate elements of programming, advertising, and channel promotional spots all flowed together seamlessly, as a way to capture a viewer's attention and encourage capitalist consumption without the viewer being aware of it. Flow, for Williams, was a form of ideology."

17. Williams, *Television: Technology and Cultural Form*, p. 92.
18. I watched the television coverage of the morning of 9/11 from 7:00AM Eastern Standard Time until just after the South Tower of the World Trade Center fell at approximately 10:30AM. I owe media scholar Deborah Jaramillo for this research tactic. Jaramillo watched and time-coded television coverage of the first days of the Iraq War in March 2003. She spoke at the opening of the Prelinger Archives' September 11 Television Archive (https://archive.org/details/911), and her remarks inspired me to re-watch NBC's 9/11/2001 pre-attack footage, as well as the network's coverage of the attacks themselves. In so doing, I utilized YouTube vids of that morning's coverage, which were taken from the Washington DC NBC affiliate (WRC). All quoted material, time markers, and analysis in the following sections are based on the following YouTube links of the coverage (http://tinyurl.com/grbojkz) and (http://tinyurl.com/jkx3hln), both of which were last accessed on December 23, 2016.
19. Quoted from Episode 8 ("The Center of the World") of the film *New York: A Documentary Film*.
20. The trajectory of General Electric's stock (stock symbol: GE) is available on Yahoo Finance's website. The stock hit a low of $1.14 on September 11th, 1981 and ascended to $59.88 in September of 2000.
21. Research taken from Sarah Keeling's article "Advising the Millennial Generation," published in NACADA Journal in Spring 2003, and available at the following link (http://tinyurl.com/j9flt28), last accessed December 23, 2016. Keeling cites Neil Howe and William Strauss' 2000 book *Millennials Rising*, in which the authors report that 70% of students worry about finding a job. Keeling also references an article titled "Student stress is rising, especially among women," published in *The Chronicle of Higher Education* and written by L. Reisberg. In her article, Keeling ties these

incidences of stress to a rising culture of alcohol abuse among young Millennials in the early 2000s on college campuses.

22. CNN.com. "Study: U.S. employees put in most hours" (http://tinyurl.com/zvfjjje), published on August 31, 2001, and last accessed December 23, 2016: "In hard numbers, what Johnson is saying is that his ILO statistics show that last year the average American worked 1,978 hours—up from 1,942 hours in 1990. That represents an increase of almost a week of work. And it registers Americans as working longer hours than Canadians, Germans, Japanese and other workers. 'But if we're working ourselves to death in the United States,' he asks, 'why are we increasing the hours? Almost every year we increase the hours of work. American workers put in long hours to make up the gains' in efficiency seen in France and Belgium.'"

23. Aschoff, Nicole. *The New Prophets of Capital* (New York: Verso Books, 2015), Kindle Locations 55–59: "Indeed, capital's ability to periodically present a new set of legitimating principles that facilitate the willing participation of society accounts for its remarkable longevity despite periodic bouts of deep crisis."

24. Quoted from Episode 8 ("The Center of the World") of the film *New York: A Documentary Film*.

25. *The New York Times*. "Does This Town Still Know How to Give a Victory Parade?" (http://tinyurl.com/zx6vvmr), last accessed December 23, 2016.

26. *ibid.*

27. *Advertising Age*. "United Airlines Expands TV Campaign" (http://tinyurl.com/ja58omf), last accessed December 23, 2016. Also, see "American Get-together Breaks" (http://tinyurl.com/h75ybwu) [last accessed December 23, 2016] for information about American Airlines' 9/11 World Series ads.

28. Fox's intro to Game One of the World Series is available at this YouTube link (http://tinyurl.com/zww5dy2), last accessed December 23, 2001. The entire game is available to be viewed here on YouTube (http://tinyurl.com/zlxqumz), last accessed December 23, 2001.

29. *ibid.*

30. This speech is available on YouTube at the following link (http://tinyurl.com/zsxc5gs), last accessed December 23, 2016. Clips of it can also be seen in ESPN's stellar "30 for 30" documentary *First Pitch* (2015).

31. The Game Three World Series intro is available on YouTube at this link (http://tinyurl.com/jmez9lw), last accessed December 23, 2016.

32. *USA Today*. "Curt Schilling's letter to America" (http://tinyurl.com/grjfepj), last accessed December 23, 2016.

33. Fox's broadcast of Super Bowl XXXVI was formerly available at this YouTube link (http://tinyurl.com/ze5mk6z), but the broadcast has since been removed by the NFL due to copyright infringement. Kinda sucks, because the game was great and the propaganda was even better.

34. Jaramillo, Deborah L. *Ugly War, Pretty Package: How CNN and Fox News Made the Invasion of Iraq High Concept* (Indianapolis: Indiana University Press, 2009), Kindle Locations 2771, 2774: "Although it came as no great surprise, a *New York Times* article in April 2008 revealed that the Pentagon, under orders from the Bush administration, used military analysts as 'a kind of media Trojan horse' to feed news programs predetermined talking points about the invasion (Barstow 2008). A former aide to Victoria Clarke said that the decision to use analysts as public relations tools was made in the year before the invasion. The Pentagon's roster included over seventy-five officers, most of whom worked for Fox News Channel."

35. This entire report is available at this link (http://tiny url.com/j3vcuyb)[last accessed December 23, 2016]. And it is

absolutely worth reading the whole thing, so you can see how your favorite team is a tool of the federal defense establishment.

36. This speech—which I can scarcely stand to watch, because I'm a Seahawks fan—is available at the following YouTube link (http://tinyurl.com/zkz6orm), last accessed December 23, 2016.

37. Jaramillo, *Ugly War, Pretty Package*, Kindle Locations 2650–2652: "Older toys still in circulation also received a boost from the buildup to the war. Sales of Hasbro's GI Joe line increased before and during the 2003 invasion. Noting that Hasbro had expected the increase, one retail spokesman remarked, 'People get rather patriotic, and they go out and buy their GI Joes. It happened before the [1991] Persian Gulf War.'"

38. *MTV News*. "On Veterans Day, A Sobering Look at the Iraq War's Toll" (http://tinyurl.com/ztp4oob), last accessed Friday, December 23, 2016.

39. Statistics in this paragraph are from a table titled "Operation Iraqi Freedom Military Deaths" provided by the U.S. Department of Defense. Table is available at this link (http://tinyurl.com/hcf2o2v), last accessed December 23, 2016.

40. This podcast is available at this link (http://tinyurl.com/z9avcvo), last accessed December 23, 2016.

41. Mead, Corey. *War Play: Video Games and the Future of Armed Conflict* (Boston: Houghton Mifflin Harcourt, 2013), Kindle Locations 193–194: "Advanced computing systems, computer graphics, the Internet, multiplayer networked systems, the 3-D navigation of virtual environments—all these were funded by the Department of Defense."

42. Sirota, David. *Back to Our Future: How the 1980s Explain the World We Live in Now—Our Culture, Our Politics, Our Everything* (New York: Ballantine Books, 2011), p. 156: "As

the 1980s video-game craze exploded in the 1990s and beyond, the Pentagon 'realized we had to get the flow of information about life in the army into pop culture,' said Colonel Casey Wardynski."

43. Žižek, Slavoj. *Welcome to the Desert of the Real: Five Essays on September 11 and Related Dates* (New York: Verso Books, 2002), p. 62: "In short, America should learn humbly to accept its own vulnerability as part of this world, enacting the punishment of those responsible as a sad duty, not as an exhilarating retaliation—what we are getting instead is the forceful reassertion of the exceptional role of the USA as a global policeman, as if what causes resentment against the USA is not its excess of power, but its lack of it."

44. *ibid.*

45. More information about this is available at the Rambo Wikipedia page (http://tinyurl.com/hu6vu8d), last accessed December 23, 2016.

46. For more about the unintended consequences of Reagan's dalliances in the Middle East, see Chalmers Johnson's 2000 book *Blowback: The Costs and Consequences of American Empire* (Holt Paperbacks).

47. Kanye West later sampled Daft Punk's "Harder, Better, Faster, Stronger" in his hit 2007 single "Stronger."

Chapter 8

While I do not cite it directly, Chapter 8 ("People You May Know") owes much to Benjamin Nugent's monograph *American Nerd: The Story of My People* (New York: Scribner, 2008).

1. TechCrunch.com. "The Chan-Zuckerberg Initiative May Be More Important Than Facebook" (http://tinyurl.com/h2l72pt), last accessed December 23, 2016.

2. *ibid.*

3. *The Atlantic.* "Facebook = Google + Yahoo + Microsoft + Wikipedia…" (http://tinyurl.com/zv3ah3l), last accessed

December 23, 2016.

4. Kirkpatrick, David. *The Facebook Effect: The Inside Story of the Company That Is Connecting the World* (New York: Simon & Schuster, 2010), pp. 154–155: "You didn't need to hit a little 'next' button. They were attempting to encourage that 'Facebook trance' that kept people clicking through pages on the service."

5. George Carlin popularized the phrase "the pussification of the American male" in the 1999 stand-up comedy special *You Are All Diseased*. A *Slate* article titled "How Did America Get So 'Pussified'?" summarized this current in masculinity (http://tinyurl.com/pp4vpvo), last accessed December 23, 2016.

6. Seriously. Just type "men are getting soft" or "there are no more men" into Google and carouse the results. Millennial conservative Tammy Lahren was the latest to add to the dogpile in a 2016 YouTube rant titled "Where are the men?" (http://tinyurl.com/jcez9ey), last accessed February 7, 2017.

7. The *Independent*. "Why Mark Zuckerberg wears the same clothes to work everyday" (http://tinyurl.com/havdvs5), last accessed December 23, 2016.

8. *The Merchants of Cool* first aired February 27, 2001. It was directed by Barak Goodman for PBS *Frontline*.

9. From a Boston.com article by film reviewer extraordinaire *Wesley Morris* (http://tinyurl.com/j24gfsj), last accessed December 23, 2016: "Hannah is a Chicago comedy writer with a romantic's ADD. She falls in love not as sport but as a condition of the heart. It's too tempting to roll your eyes at the film's blissful navel-gazing, but Joe Swanberg has an uncanny talent for making the randomness of downtime feel as alive as it seems generationally true."

10. *The New York Times*. "A Generation Finds Its Mumble" (http://tinyurl.com/jpkuoc5), last accessed December 23, 2016: "Recent rumblings—perhaps one should say

mumblings—indicate an emerging movement in American independent film. Specimens of the genre share a low-key naturalism, low-fi production values and a stream of low-volume chatter often perceived as ineloquence. Hence the name: mumblecore. But what these films understand all too well is that the tentative drift of the in-between years masks quietly seismic shifts that are apparent only in hindsight. Mumblecore narratives hinge less on plot points than on the tipping points in interpersonal relationships. A favorite setting is the party that goes subtly but disastrously astray. Events are often set in motion by an impulsive, ill-judged act of intimacy."

11. See this Urban Dictionary definition at this link (http://tinyurl.com/omsbb), last accessed December 23, 2016.

12. *Business Insider*. "How The Cupcake Blew Up and Became a Major Craze" (http://tinyurl.com/js4apnq), last accessed December 23, 2016.

13. Read Paul Graham's essay "Economic Inequality" (http://tinyurl.com/h7mhjxj), last accessed December 23, 2016. Contrast it with former Seattle Seahawks offensive lineman Russell Okung's rebuttal (http://tinyurl.com /z24sfyh), last accessed December 23, 2016.

14. Dean, Jodi. *Blog Theory: Feedback and Capture in the Circuits of Drive* (Cambridge: Polity, 2010), Kindle Locations 546–547: "Geek norms emerge, claim neutrality and appropriateness, and then retreat, leaving in their wake a pro-capitalist, entrepreneurial, and individualistic discourse of evaluation well suited for the extension and amplification of neoliberal governmentality."

15. *American High School* is a 2009 direct-to-DVD coming-of-age romantic comedy film directed by Sean Patrick Cannon.

16. *The New York Times*. "Lunch Period Poli Sci" (http://tinyurl.com/gq9uxmx), last accessed December 23, 2016.

17 Frank, Thomas. *What's the Matter with Kansas?: How*

Conservatives Won the Heart of America (New York: Henry Holt, 2004), pp. 17–18: "The red-state/blue-state idea appeared to many in the media to be a scientific validation of this familiar stereotype, and before long it was a standard element of the media's popsociology repertoire. The 'two Americas' idea became a hook for all manner of local think pieces (blue Minnesota is only separated by one thin street from red Minnesota, but my, how different those two Minnesotas are); it provided an easy tool for contextualizing the small stories (red Americans love a certain stage show in Vegas, but blue Americans don't) or for spinning the big stories (John Walker Lindh, the American who fought for the Taliban, was from California and therefore a reflection of blue-state values); and it justified countless *USA Today*-style contemplations of who we Americans really are, meaning mainly investigations of the burning usual—what we Americans like to listen to, watch on TV, or buy at the supermarket."

18. There are a number of excellent monographs that reference the Business Roundtable specifically, and that sketch out the right-ward turn in American media generally. I recommend *Pivotal Decade* (2010) by Judith Stein, *Invisible Hands: The Businessmen's Crusade Against the New Deal* by Kim Phillips-Fein (2010), and Jason Stahl's *Right Moves: The Conservative Think Tank in American Political Culture since 1945* (2016).

19. Phillips-Fein, Kim. *Invisible Hands: The Businessmen's Crusade Against the New Deal* (New York: W.W. Norton & Company, 2010), Kindle Locations 138–144: "The political economy of the postwar period was sustained by the Keynesian belief that consumption is the key determinant of economic growth, and that therefore public policies should primarily seek to stimulate consumption while encouraging some income redistribution. This vision of the economy no longer enjoys wide support in either political part."

20. Kimmel, Michael. *Angry White Men: American Masculinity at the End of an Era* (New York: Nation Books, 2013), pp. 37–38: "So, if I were to try to channel Rush Limbaugh or Mike Savage, my task would be to redirect that anger onto others, those even less fortunate than you. Perhaps the reason you are so unhappy is because of all those immigrants who are streaming into America, driving the costs of labor lower and threatening 'American' jobs. Or perhaps it's because women—even, perhaps, your own wife—want to enter the labor force, and that's what is driving down labor costs, as corporations no longer need to pay men a 'family' wage, since they no longer support a family. Your grievances are not with the corporations, but with those just below you."

21. NPR.org. "Blogger Jailed for Refusing to Turn Over Video," October 25, 2006 (http://tinyurl.com/j8ynvyk), last accessed December 23, 2016.

22. *Time Magazine.* "You—Yes, You—Are TIME'S Person of the Year," December 25, 2006 (http://tinyurl.com/mnzk8hw), last accessed December 23, 2016.

23. Hardt, Michael and Negri, Antonio. *Multitude: War and Democracy in the Age of Empire* (New York: Penguin Publishing Group, 2004), p. 2.

24. You can see the "Mosh" music video at this link (http://tinyurl.com/gpv5yoy), last accessed December 23, 2016.

25. *Bomb Magazine.* "Chuck D" (http://tinyurl.com/hrep82a), last accessed December 23, 2016.

26. Psychologist Sherry Turkle uses this term to describe Millennials in her 2011 book *Alone Together: Why We Expect More From Technology and Less from Each Other.*

27. *BuzzFeed.* "Why 'Seinfeld' Is The Most Villainous Sitcom In Human History," July 11, 2014 (http://tinyurl.com/gov75f5), last accessed December 23, 2016.

28. This episode of *The Daily Show* can be viewed at this link

(http://tinyurl.com/gqnzuh5), last accessed December 23, 2016.

29. *Satire TV: Politics and Comedy in the Post-Network Era,* edited by Gray, Jonathan; Jones, Jeffrey P.; Thompson, Ethan (New York: NYU Press, 2008), p. 4: "In October 2004, Jon Stewart of Comedy Central's *The Daily Show with Jon Stewart* created a similar stir when he appeared as a guest on CNN's *Crossfire* and lambasted the hosts for a 'dog and pony show' debate format that, he charged, hurt the state of U.S. politics more than it could possibly help it (figure 1.1). In that presidential election year, Stewart was the go-to public figure for political commentary, as *The Daily Show* regularly featured heavily in discussions of politics."
30. *The Stewart/Colbert Effect: Essays on the Real Impacts of Fake News,* edited by Amarnath Amarasingam (Jefferson: McFarland & Company, Inc., 2011), Kindle Locations 1102–1104: "The news-opinion program *Crossfire* invited Jon Stewart on their show (and surely came to regret it), and there was the wide-spread coverage of his thrashing of MSNBC's Jim Kramer over the coverage the real news was providing of the economic collapse."
31. *ibid,* Kindle Location 929.
32. *ibid,* Kindle Location 944.
33. *Satire TV: Politics and Comedy in the Post-Network Era,* edited by Gray, Jones, Thompson, p. 100.
34. ibid, pg. 126.
35. *The Stewart/Colbert Effect: Essays on the Real Impacts of Fake News,* edited by Amarasingam, Kindle Location 582.
36. *ibid,* Kindle Location 1789.
37. Colbert's routine can be watched in its entirety on YouTube at this link (http://tinyurl.com/ox2heyc), last accessed December 23, 2016.
38. *ibid.*
39. Butler, Judith. *Frames of War: When Is Life Grievable?* (New

York: Verso Books, 2009), Kindle Location 1364.

40. *Satire TV: Politics and Comedy in the Post-Network Era*, edited by Gray, Jones, Thompson, p. 172.

41. A 2006 article in BBC News (http://tinyurl.com/8u7l9), last accessed December 23, 2016, indicated that teenagers between 12 and 17 "made up a disproportionately large group of iTunes users," and were "twice as likely to visit the music store than any other population group." Nielsen data from 2006 (http://tinyurl.com/hq2mcxc), last accessed December 23, 2006, also indicates that users aged under 18–34 made up 38% of YouTube's viewership, despite being a much smaller population bloc than their 35–55 year-old counterparts. All of these statistics indicate that the iTunes and YouTube viewership in the 2000s skewed younger.

42. *Satire TV: Politics and Comedy in the Post-Network Era*, edited by Gray, Jones, Thompson, p. 19.

43. *The Stewart/Colbert Effect: Essays on the Real Impacts of Fake News*, edited by Amarasingam, Kindle Location 1065.

44. Dean, Jodi. *Blog Theory: Feedback and Capture in the Circuits of Drive* (Cambridge: Polity, 2010), Kindle Locations 145–152: "I take the position that contemporary communications media capture their users in intensive and extensive networks of enjoyment, production, and surveillance. My term for this formation is communicative capitalism. Just as industrial capitalism relied on the exploitation of labor, so does communicative capitalism rely on the exploitation of communication. As Michael Hardt and Antonio Negri argue, 'communication is the form of capitalist production in which capital has succeeded in submitting society entirely and globally to its regime, suppressing all alternative paths.'[6] A critical theory of communicative capitalism requires occupying (rather than disavowing) the trap in which it enthralls and configures contemporary subjects. I argue that this trap takes the form that modern European philosophy

heralded as the form of freedom: reflexivity. Communicative capitalism is that economic-ideological form wherein reflexivity captures creativity and resistance so as to enrich the few as it placates and diverts the many."

45. Fraser, quoted in *Satire TV: Politics and Comedy in the Post-Network Era*, edited by Gray, Jones, Thompson, p. 65.

46. The episode of *The Daily Show* that Obama appeared on can be viewed at this link (http://tinyurl.com/jfndhxg), last accessed December 23, 2016.

Chapter 9

1. U.S. Census Bureau. "Millennials Outnumber Baby Boomers and Are Far More Diverse" (http://tinyurl.com/p4c24lt), last accessed December 24, 2016.

2. The origins of the term "post-racial" stretch all the way back to an October 5, 1971 article in *The New York Times* titled "Compact Set Up for Post-Racial South." However, the term definitely became employed most popularly in the aftermath of Barack Obama's election in 2008. The term refers to the (obviously false) notion that the United States had transcended "historical" racial barriers and inequities.

3. *Satire TV: Politics and Comedy in the Post-Network Era*, edited by Gray, Jonathan; Jones, Jeffrey P.; Thompson, Ethan (New York: NYU Press, 2008), p. 234.

4. *ibid*: "Chappelle's comic voice—in his standup and his series—reflects the dynamic, complex, and conflicted nature of sociopolitical comedic discourse in the post-civil rights moment. *Chappelle's Show*'s consistent engagement with the politics of racial representation was the element that cast the series as both anomaly and model within the niched and narrowcasted televisual milieu of the post-network era. The series, like the comic, enjoys dual credibility through ties to the Afrocentricism of the Black hip-hop intelligentsia, as well as the skater/slacker/stoner ethos of suburban life. This cred

allows Chappelle to speak for and to Gen X and Gen Y subcultures in both the Black and White communities."

5. *The Los Angeles Times.* "Comedian Dave Chappelle resurfaces and speculation begins anew," March 13, 2013 (http://tinyurl.com/hclaqpo), last accessed December 24, 2016: "Individual *Chappelle's Show* sketches have amassed hundreds of thousands of views on Comedy Central's website, while the DVD boxed set of the show's three seasons has shattered sales records. The show's Season 1 sales in 2004 surpassed *The Simpsons* to become the overall bestselling television show on DVD at the time, according to Videoscan."

6. *PBS NewsHour.* "White Millennials are products of a failed lesson in colorblindness," March 26, 2015 (http://tinyurl .com/pslvjm4), last accessed December 24, 2016.

7. *The Nation.* "Exclusive: Lee Atwater's Infamous 1981 Interview on the Southern Strategy," November 13, 2012 (http://tinyurl.com/htga5br), last accessed December 24, 2016.

8. *Invisible Man, Got the Whole World Watching: A Young Black Man's Education* (New York: Nation Books, 2016), p. 40: "Hurricane Katrina was the first instance, in my lifetime, where our national conversation on race had to concern itself with questions of inequality, poverty, and government neglect."

9. *New York Post.* "Steph Shows a Side Rarely Seen," September 7, 2005 (http://tinyurl.com/grtt7yq), last accessed December 24, 2016.

10. This lucid Kobe Bryant essay is available at the following Reddit link (http://tinyurl.com/jaxwe2q), last accessed December 24, 2016: "Recently I have come to visualize my place as a Black athlete within our society. I've always been aware of our history, from Jackie Robinson to Sweetwater Clifton. But I never felt like I deserved to be a part of our

tradition because I grew up overseas, in Italy [...] When I went to visit the victims of Hurricane Katrina and saw how their faces lit up when they saw me, how they embraced me, and how my presence lifted their spirits, I realized how wrong I'd been about everything. I've wasted all these years wanting to do things for our people but thinking I wasn't the one to do them, that I wouldn't be welcomed. But now I see that isn't true."

11. This clip of Fox News' Hurricane Katrina coverage can be viewed at this link (http://tinyurl.com/jqz33nb), last accessed December 24, 2016.

12. *The Guardian*. "Exiles from a city and from a nation," September 10, 2005 (http://tinyurl.com/z2mrmmm), last accessed December 24, 2016: "What we saw unfold in the days after the hurricane was the most naked manifestation of conservative social policy towards the poor, where the message for decades has been: 'You are on your own.' Well, they really were on their own for five days in that Superdome, and it was Darwinism in action—the survival of the fittest. People said: 'It looks like something out of the Third World.' Well, New Orleans was Third World long before the hurricane."

13. Kanye West's defiant rant can be viewed at this YouTube link (http://tinyurl.com/hhjj5o2), last accessed December 24, 2016.

14. *ibid*. This was effing great.

15. Klein, Naomi. *The Shock Doctrine: The Rise of Disaster Capitalism* (New York: Henry Holt and Co., 2007), p. 4.

16. *ibid*, p. 519: "Within weeks, the Gulf Coast became a domestic laboratory for the same kind of government-run-by-contractors that had been pioneered in Iraq. The companies that snatched up the biggest contracts were the familiar Baghdad gang: Halliburton's KBR unit had a $60 million gig to reconstruct military bases along the coast. Blackwater was hired to protect FEMA employees from looters. Parsons,

infamous for its sloppy Iraq work, was brought in for a major bridge construction project in Mississippi. Fluor, Shaw, Bechtel, CH2M Hill—all top contractors in Iraq—were hired by the government to provide mobile homes to evacuees just ten days after the levees broke. Their contracts ended up totaling $3.4 billion, no open bidding required."

17. The *Wall Street Journal*. "The Promise of Vouchers," December 5, 2005 (http://tinyurl.com/hyrzp3c), last accessed December 24, 2016.
18. ESPN. "Steve Gleason statue unveiled," July 27, 2012 (http://tinyurl.com/h8yy7y4), last accessed December 24, 2016: "The blocked punt that etched Steve Gleason into Saints lore and became symbolic of New Orleans' resilience in the face of disaster is now immortalized in a nine-foot statue outside the Superdome."
19. Obama's full speech "Remarks by the President on the Ten Year Anniversary of Hurricane Katrina" can be read at the following link (http://tinyurl.com/jq4nq5x), last accessed December 24, 2016.
20. *ibid.*
21. Pew Research Center. "Obama's Favorite Theologian? A Short Course on Reinhold Niebuhr" (http://tinyurl.com /h29wzaf), last accessed December 24, 2016.
22. The YouTube vid where Obama expresses admiration for Reagan's institution of neoliberalism can be seen at the following link (http://tinyurl.com/zfflrpe), last accessed December 24, 2016.
23. CBS News. "Obama's Youth Movement," February 15, 2008 (http://tinyurl.com/j86ufoy), last accessed December 24, 2016: "The key to Obama's appeal to young voters may be that he resembles them. In a *New York Times* essay contest on the state of American college students, Nicholas Handler labeled his generation 'Post-Everything': 'post-Cold War, post-industrial, post-baby boom, post-9/11.' Obama himself

is a collage of 'posts.' *Time* magazine recently observed that, like Tiger Woods and Angelina Jolie, Obama has 'one of those faces that seem beamed from a postracial future.'"

24. ABC News. "Young Black Turnout a Record in 2008 Election," July 21, 2009 (http://tinyurl.com/hb8lx77), last accessed December 24, 2016.

25. The statistics from Pew Research (http://tinyurl.com/n3mzmuq), last accessed December 24, 2016, are telling: "In the last three general elections—2004, 2006, and 2008—young voters have given the Democratic Party a majority of their votes, and for all three cycles they have been the party's most supportive age group. This year, 66% of those under age 30 voted for Barack Obama making the disparity between young voters and other age groups larger than in any presidential election since exit polling began in 1972."

26. This speech can be read in its entirety at the following link (http://tinyurl.com/67yqbb), last accessed December 24, 2016: "Four years ago, I stood before you and told you my story of the brief union between a young man from Kenya and a young woman from Kansas who weren't well-off or well-known, but shared a belief that in America, their son could achieve whatever he put his mind to. It is that promise that's always set this country apart—that through hard work and sacrifice each of us can pursue our individual dreams but still come together as one American family, to ensure that the next generation can pursue their dreams as well."

27. This speech can be read in its entirety at the following link (http://tinyurl.com/hcm9542), last accessed December 24, 2016.

28. This speech can be read in its entirety at the following link (http://tinyurl.com/jqfx52k), last accessed February 7, 2017.

29. Obama's 2016 State of the Union address can be read in its entirety at the following link (http://tinyurl.com/zaw6f6e), last accessed December 24, 2016.

30. Obama's eager receipt of Rock's advice was recounted vividly in Michael Eric Dyson's 2016 book *The Black Presidency: Barack Obama and the Politics of Race in America* (p. 119): "'My dad used to say, "You can't beat White people at anything,"' Rock said as Obama and I listened intently, intrigued by his proposition. "'Never. But you can knock 'em out." Like if you have six and the White guy has five, he wins. If you're Black, you can't let it go to the judges' decision 'cause you're gonna lose. No matter how bad you beat this man up.' By then Obama and I were nodding our heads in agreement. We knew the odds were often stacked against Blacks in the competition to get a decent shot at a job or a seat in school. 'Larry Holmes and Gerry Cooney are the perfect example of life,' Rock stated. 'Larry Holmes beats the shit out of this guy—for eleven rounds. He knocks him out in the eleventh round. They had to stop the fight. The man is bloody. He's been beaten the whole fight. They go to the judges' scorecards. Larry Holmes is losing the fight. If he didn't knock him out, he would have lost the title. That is essentially the Black experience.'"

31. *The New Republic.* "Obama's Choke Revisited," May 28, 2013 (http://tinyurl.com/z4vqq3r), last accessed December 24, 2016.

32. *The New Way of the World: On Neoliberal Society* (New York: Verso Books, 2013), Kindle Locations 6745–6747: "The new subject is the man of competition and performance. The self-entrepreneur is a being made to 'succeed', to 'win'. Much more so than the idealized figures of heads of enterprises, competitive sport is the great social theatre that displays the modern gods, demi-gods."

33. Klein, *The Shock Doctrine*, p. 73.

34. The short-lived "You Didn't Build That!" meme was one of the great moments of Obama's campaign against Mitt Romney. It has its own Wikipedia page with the full text of

the (totally worth it) rant: (http://tinyurl.com/hp5nsdo), last accessed December 24, 2016.

35. *The Stranger*. "Potty-Mouthed President Obama Expertly Dissects Ayn Rand's Novels," October 25, 2012 (http://tinyurl.com/jft3fac), last accessed December 24, 2016: "Ayn Rand is one of those things that a lot of us, when we were 17 or 18 and feeling misunderstood, we'd pick up. Then, as we get older, we realize that a world in which we're only thinking about ourselves and not thinking about anybody else, in which we're considering the entire project of developing ourselves as more important than our relationships to other people and making sure that everybody else has opportunity—that that's a pretty narrow vision. It's not one that, I think, describes what's best in America. Unfortunately, it does seem as if sometimes that vision of a 'you're on your own' society has consumed a big chunk of the Republican Party."

36. *The Guardian*. "Beware the Chicago boys," June 13, 2008 (http://tinyurl.com/h6bolvp), last accessed December 24, 2016.

37. Spence, Lester. *Knocking the Hustle: Against the Neoliberal Turn in Black Politics* (New York: Punctum Books, 2015), p. 100: "Obama consistently used poor and working-class Black men to make claims about Black irresponsibility."

38. Complex.com. "Remember the Time When Barack Said Low-Income Kids Shouldn't Buy Air Jordans," January 22, 2015 (http://tinyurl.com/hodff5e), last accessed December 24, 2016.

39. The whole "FIX IT!" routine can be seen at this YouTube link (http://tinyurl.com/jrdjexy), last accessed December 24, 2016.

40. Slate.com. "The Visit That Never Ends," December 21, 2010 (http://tinyurl.com/hen9abj), last accessed December 24, 2016.

41. See the Congressional Budget Office's February 2012

summary of the American Recovery and Reinvestment Act (http://tinyurl.com/atjo5c8), last accessed December 24, 2016.

42. See The House's statement on "Investing in Pell Grants to Make College Affordable" (http://tinyurl.com/z883c7v), last accessed February 7, 2017.

43. Dyson, *The Black Presidency*, p. 160: "'The point is that we are able then to make strides on issues that can close the achievement gap, or close the gap on insurance, without calling them targeted programs,' Obama argued. 'They are programs that help people who need the help the most. And we do that not only because it's good for those individuals; it's good for the economy as a whole. It's good for everybody. I've been trying to get out of this zero sum approach that says either you're helping Black people or Hispanics, or you've got these broad generalized programs that ignore the particular problems,' Obama told me."

44. CQ Researcher. "The Gig Economy," March 18, 2016 (http://tinyurl.com/gnffce8), last accessed December 24, 2016.

45. Investing.com. "Nearly 95% of all new jobs during Obama era were part-time, or contract," December 21, 2016 (http://tinyurl.com/gm8e47x), last accessed December 24, 2016.

46. Kamenetz, Anya. *Generation Debt: How Our Future Was Sold Out for Student Loans, Credit Cards, Bad Jobs, No Benefits, and Tax Cuts for Rich Geezers—and How to Fight Back* (New York: Penguin Publishing Group, 2006), p. 83: "It's an American rite of passage to wait tables or bartend, babysit or work construction during your formative years."

47. The full transcript and context of Sunkara's remarks—which came during a 2014 appearance on *The Tavis Smiley Show*—can be seen at this link (http://tinyurl.com/jhwlvsj), last accessed December 24, 2016.

48. This Pew Research report is available at the following link (http://tinyurl.com/7s8pmgx), last accessed December 24,

2016.

49. *Sports Illustrated*. "Ahead of His Class" (http://tinyurl.com /j4uo8c6), last accessed December 24, 2016.

50. Klosterman, Chuck. *But What If We're Wrong?: Thinking About the Present As If It Were the Past* (New York: Penguin Publishing Group, 2016), p. 196.

51. *The Great Recession in Fiction, Film, and Television: Twenty-First-Century Bust Culture* (Lanham: Lexington Books, 2013). Edited by Boyle, Kirk and Mrozowski, Daniel.

52. Boltanski, Luc and Chiapello, Eva. *The New Spirit of Capitalism* (New York: Verso Books, 2006), p. 218: "This makes it possible to transfer the burden of market uncertainty onto wage-earners, but also subcontractors and other service providers. It breaks down into internal flexibility, based upon a profound transformation in the organization of work and the techniques employed (multitasking, self-control, development of autonomy, etc.), and external flexibility. The latter presupposes a so-called network organization of work, wherein 'lean' firms seek the resources they lack from among a profusion of subcontractors, as well as a labour force that is malleable in terms of employment (casual jobs, temping, self-employed workers), working hours, or the duration of work (part-timers, variable hours)."

53. *ibid*, p. 364: "In a network world, everyone thus lives in a state of permanent anxiety about being disconnected, rejected, abandoned on the spot by those who move around. This is why today local roots, loyalty, and stability paradoxically constitute factors of job insecurity and are, moreover, increasingly experienced as such, as is indicated by the reluctance of young people in marginal positions—for example, doing jobs or living in regions in decline—to settle down in life, to borrow to buy accommodation (rather than renting), to marry (rather than cohabit), to have children (rather than an abortion in the hopes of keeping one's job), and so on.

Thus, disaffiliation can be initiated by self-defensive behaviour in a situation of job insecurity, the paradoxical result of which is to increase the insecurity."

54. You can read this article in *Millennial Magazine* at the following link (http://tinyurl.com/z4x88ju), last accessed February 20, 2017.

55. Gilbert's excoriation of James can be read at this link (http://tinyurl.com/z4kwqt6), last accessed December 24, 2016.

56. Whitson and Macintosh, quoted in Jules Boykoff's *Power Games: A Political History of the Olympics* (New York: Verso Books, 2016), Kindle Locations 2826–2829.

57. *The Ringer.* "Pat Riley Gets What He Wants," June 28, 2016 (http://tinyurl.com/zqplujs), last accessed December 24, 2016.

58. *Time Magazine.* "Millennials: The Me Me Me Generation," May 20, 2013 (http://tinyurl.com/q9dosty), last accessed December 24, 2016.

59. Raab, Scott. *The Whore of Akron: One Man's Search for the Soul of LeBron James* (New York: HarperCollins Publishers, 2011), p. 99.

60. *ibid.*

61. *ibid*, pp. 21–22: "In the end, what truly matters is this: Cleveland fans love the city, cherish the teams more deeply, and pull for them with far more passion than fans anywhere else. Other Rust Belt cities have been stripped of a middle class over the past fifty years by the same socioeconomic Katrina, but only Cleveland became the armpit of a nation."

62. James' outfit in this Instagram post was pretty fly tho, to be fair (http://tinyurl.com/jjpu43j).

63. Pink, Daniel H. *Free Agent Nation: How America's New Independent Workers Are Transforming the Way We Live* (New York: Hachette Book Group, 2001).

64. Line taken from the Bible's famous messianic verses, where children assume a leadership role in the Christian

millenarian fantasy of world peace. Isaiah 11:4–11:6: "The earth will shake at the force of his word, and one breath from his mouth will destroy the wicked. He will wear right-eousness like a belt and faithfulness the sash around his waist. The wolf will live with the lamb, the leopard will lie down with the goat, the calf and the lion and the yearling together; and a little child shall lead them all."

Part IV

The Summer 2016 edition of *Bitch Magazine* arrived at a fortuitous time, just as I was piecing together Chapter 10 ("Millennial Man") and Chapter 11 ("Millennial Woman") of this book. That issue contained several essays—which I cite extensively in Part IV— that dealt with notions of heroism and emotional labor. These themes are central to my understanding of Millennial gender norms and the culture that co-signs them.

I would also like to reiterate my reliance on the theoretical work of Arlie Hochschild—both in affirming her work, and in disagreeing with it vehemently. Hochschild's 1983 book *The Managed Heart* pioneered the concept of emotional labor. It refers to the emotional stress placed on some populations to placate the people who patronize them, and also—by extension—to the façade that predators and abusers construct to appear sensitive and nonthreatening.

The concept of emotional labor is a powerful interpretive tool for understanding the artistry of recalcitrant Millennial women such as Rihanna and Jenny Zhang (Chapter 11), and also for seeing through the feigned sincerity of many Millennial male performers (Chapter 10). Hence, Hochschild's stunning reversal in her 2016 book *Strangers in Their Own Land* came as a surprise to me:

In *Strangers in Their Own Land*, Hochschild places the burden of "empathizing" with conservatives on the very people who stand to be most disenfranchised by their policies. Forgetting that politics is war by other means, Hochschild seems to think that America's gulfing divides of race, class, and gender can be solved by putting "understanding" those who seek to widen those divides further. Tellingly, the emotional burden to practice empathy never seems to be placed on those who disagree with #BlackLivesMatter or #ShoutYourAbortion. So in Chapter 12 ("The Millennial Agenda"), I explain that the Left in America will have to learn to attend to its own social base of disaffected workers, people of color, and Millennials if it is to triumph in future federal and local elections.

While I do not cite them directly in Part IV of this book, the following two texts helped to craft the central thesis of Chapters 10, 11, and 12, which is that our focus on popular culture will have to become explicitly political if we, as Millennials, are serious about transforming the status quo we inherited: Sarah Jaffe's 2016 book *Necessary Trouble: Americans in Revolt*, and *The Future We Want: Radical Ideas for the New Century* (2016), by Sarah Leonard and Bhaskar Sunkara.

Part IV Epigraph Citation

1. Drake said this in a post to his blog (http://tinyurl .com/842k9c9, last accessed December 25, 2016) on November 7, 2011. While he may intend it in the following sense, to me it sort of illustrates that pop culture simulacrum — of which social media is definitely a form — is a necessary but not sufficient form of political engagement.

Chapter 10

1. The *Wall Street Journal*. "The 'Trophy Kids' Go To Work," October 21, 2008 (http://tinyurl.com/gqlnx7a), last accessed December 25, 2016.

2. Alsop, Ron. *The Trophy Kids Grow Up: How the Millennial Generation is Shaking Up the Workplace* (San Francisco: Jossey-Bass, 2008).

3. *ibid*, Kindle Location 104: "In my research, I found the millennials frequently written off as narcissistic, arrogant, and fickle. Although there is certainly some truth in such negative perceptions, the millennials also can be quite impressive in their ambitions and achievements. They are a generation of conflicting characteristics—self-absorbed but also civic minded, for instance. Keep in mind, however, that the traits ascribed to the millennials certainly don't apply to every member of that generation. They are common but not universal attributes."

4. *ibid*, p. 4. "A strong sense of entitlement is one of the most striking characteristics of the millennial generation. Young people have extremely high expectations about their jobs—everything from a desire for frequent performance feedback and fast promotions to a need for work-life balance and opportunities to perform community service."

5. Hess' 2011 TEDx Talk can be seen at this link (http://tinyurl.com/mo5tz9v), last accessed December 25, 2016. And yes, I am sitting here on Christmas morning, working on the obscure crevices of my book's endnotes. Don't say I didn't go the extra mile for my generation.

6. Klosterman, Chuck. *But What If We're Wrong?: Thinking About the Present As If It Were the Past* (New York: Penguin Publishing Group, 2016), p. 45: "What that constitutes in our present culture is debatable, but here's a partial, plausible list [...] The prolonging of adolescence and the avoidance of adulthood."

7. As much as we talk about technology defining Millennials, I think the rate of technological change seen in the years spanning 1890–1920 surpasses that of any other 30-year span in American history. I mean, imagine being 15 years old in 1890—by the time you turn 45 in 1920, you've lived through the invention of the automobile, indoor plumbing, domestic/civic electricity, motion pictures, and much more. I

think the world of 1890 would be FAR less recognizable to someone born in 1920 than the world of 1980 would be to someone born in 2010. I promise that makes sense.

8. From an April 10th, 1899 speech by Roosevelt titled "The Strenuous Life" (http://tinyurl.com/ydrqfv6 [last accessed December 25, 2016]): "Above all, let us shrink from no strife, moral or physical, within or without the nation, provided we are certain that the strife is justified, for it is only through strife, through hard and dangerous endeavor, that we shall ultimately win the goal of true national greatness."

9. In chapter 2 of his awesome 2008 book *A People's History of Sports in the United States*, Dave Zirin talks a ton about this formative period for American sports.

10. See Oldstone-Moore's Fall 2011 paper "Mustaches and Masculine Codes in Early Twentieth-Century America" at this link (http://tinyurl.com/zsqxkpz), last accessed December 25, 2016.

11. *The Atlantic.* "The Next New Deal," April 1992 (http://tinyurl.com/hmbrs73), last accessed December 25, 2016: "The Social Security Administration keeps no direct records of how much each person contributes. It just keeps records of each person's wage history, to which a politically determined benefit formula is applied when that person retires. Today's retirees, as it happens, receive benefits north two to ten times what they would have earned had they invested all their lifetime Social Security taxes (both their own and their employer's) in Treasury bonds. Meanwhile, largely because of the very steep increases in Social Security taxes in recent years, most economists agree that under current law Social Security will not offer large categories of younger partici-pants anything approaching a fair market return on what they paid into the system."

12. "The Silver Tsunami" (sometimes "The Gray Tsunami") is a metaphor used to describe an aging population.

13. Howe, Neil and Peterson, Peter G. *On Borrowed Time: How the Growth in Entitlement Spending Threatens America's Future* (Piscataway: Transaction Publishers, 2004).

14. Cited from *The Man in the Arena: Selected Speeches, Letters & Essays by Theodore Roosevelt* at this link (http://tinyurl .com/hsj79sr), last accessed December 25, 2016.

15. *The Guardian.* "Are comic book movies actually fascist?" July 14th, 2016 (http://tinyurl.com/h3wzl6z), last accessed December 25, 2016: "'Captain America,' McTiernan says, presumably spitting out the syllables like a sour grape. 'The cult of American hyper-masculinity is one of the worst things that has happened in the world during the last 50 years. Hundreds of thousands of people died because of this stupid illusion. So how is it possible to watch a movie called *Captain America?*'"

16. *The Guardian.* "Man of Steel: does Hollywood need saving from superheroes?" June 12, 2013 (http://tinyurl.com /j66fzup), last accessed December 25, 2016: "'Being a superhero is a way of working out your personal problems,' my 26-year-old son told me when I asked him about the popularity of the genre among his age group and younger. 'You're an ordinary person with no special skills—and suddenly you wake up one day and you're awesome. So if you're asking me if the superhero genre is going to fade away soon, the answer is no.' You wake up awesome. Not because you did something special like beat Hitler or cure polio. All you did was wake up. And suddenly you were awesome. It is the dream of the fame-hungry X Factor generation."

17. The lyrics (http://tinyurl.com/hzgnfug [last accessed December 25, 2016]): "I just don't wanna go/ Out in the streets no more,/ I just don't wanna go [...] Because these people they give me the creeps [...] I just can't pay the price of shopping around no more... I just can't pay the price,

because there's just nothing that's worth the cost."

18. The *Blossom* opening sequence/theme song "My Opinionation" can be seen in its entirety at this link (http://tinyurl.com/hkbcrhv), last accessed December 25, 2016.

19. Kotsko, Adam. *Why We Love Sociopaths: A Guide To Late Capitalist Television* (Winchester: Zero Books, 2012), p. 4: "My hypothesis is that the sociopaths we watch on TV allow us to indulge in a kind of thought experiment, based on the question: 'What if I really and truly did not give a fuck about anyone?' And the answer they provide? 'Then I would be powerful and free.'"

20. "Hot Ticket" was Episode 3 of Season 1 of *Master of None*, and was released on November 6, 2015.

21 "Parents" was Episode 2 of Season 1 of *Master of None*, and was released on November 6, 2015.

22. Ansari, Aziz. *Modern Romance* (New York: Penguin Press, 2015), p. 15: "That's the thing about the Internet: It doesn't simply help us find the best thing out there; it has helped to produce the idea that there is a best thing and, if we search hard enough, we can find it. And in turn there are a whole bunch of inferior things that we'd be foolish to choose."

23. See the citation for the epigraph of Part IV.

24. "From Time" and "Too Much" really do represent Drake at his sincerest best.

25. For what it's worth, "6PM in New York" is statistically my "Most Played" song in iTunes. By a mile.

26. Drake once coauthored "The 10 Snipe Commandments"—a how-to Bro Code for fornicating that, like Ansari, also referred to women as "things" (http://tinyurl.com/gswmpwc [last accessed December 25, 2016]).

27. From the scattered references Drake has made to this period of his life in the songs "Star 67" and "0 to 100/The Catch Up," it's hard to know how successful his career as a scammer

was; on the former, he rapped that he "couldn't do it, had to leave that shit alone."

28. ElectronicBeats.net. "The Man Who Has Everything: Mark Fisher on Drake's *Nothing Was the Same*," September 24, 2013 (http://tinyurl.com/jczhkhx), last accessed December 25, 2016.

29. *Rolling Stone*. "Drake: High Times at the YOLO Estate" (http://tinyurl.com/mozrgs5), December 25, 2016: "I'm not after pussy like I was three years ago, when I was trying to make up for all the years when no girl would talk to me [...] I haven't met somebody that makes everybody else not matter."

30. Timberg, Scott. *Culture Crash: The Killing of the Creative Class* (New Haven: Yale University Press, 2015), p. 96: "As *New York* magazine documented in one of the few clear-eyed looks at this momentous change, in a single pre-Internet year—1986—thirty-one number-one songs came from twenty-nine different artists. By the Internet era, things were very different. Between 2008 and September 2012, a period of almost five years, there were only sixty-six number-one songs, and nearly half of them were turned out by just six artists—Katy Perry, Rihanna, Flo Rida, the Black Eyed Peas, Adele, and Lady Gaga."

31. This Tweet—from December of 2012—can be read here (http://tinyurl.com/hpume8j), last accessed December 25, 2016.

32. Ansari appears on the single version of "All Me," and not the album version which was released on Drake's 2013 album *Nothing Was the Same*.

33. According to *Fortune* Magazine (http://tinyurl.com/hqr2kxb), Drake signed a $19 million deal with Apple in 2015.

34. *Sports Illustrated*. "LeBron: I'm coming back to Cleveland" (http://tinyurl.com/leddnff), December 25, 2016.

35. Pew Research Center. "For First Time in Modern Era, Living

With Parents Edges Out Other Living Arrangements for 18-to-34-Year-Olds," May 24, 2016 (http://tinyurl.com/zr8z mpd), last accessed December 25, 2016.

36. *ibid.*
37. Highsnobiety.com. "Study Says Drake Is Worth $3 Billion to Toronto," June 27, 2016 (http://tinyurl.com/z76m98y), last accessed December 25, 2016.
38. Fox Sports. "LeBron's foundation to spend $41M to send kids to college," August 13, 2015 (http://tinyurl.com/pdtfhug), last accessed December 25, 2016.
39. See citation from endnote #34.
40. *Jacobin Magazine*. "Breaking Cleveland's Curse," June 13, 2016 (http://tinyurl.com/gw6pxuq), last accessed December 25, 2016.
41. The Ringer. "No Country for Old LeBron," March 13, 2016 (http://tinyurl.com/zrvqnll), last accessed December 25, 2016.
42. ESPN.com. "Hero ball," August 13, 2012 (http://tinyurl.com /h5f74bc), last accessed December 25, 2016.
43. There are whole YouTube vids dedicated to compiling the criticism James and Kevin Durant have absorbed from NBA greats. One such vid is available at this link (http://tinyurl.com/hr6vgv7), last accessed December 25, 2016.
44. Smith said this in an ESPN.com vid that is viewable at this link (http://tinyurl.com/j56bfwf), last accessed December 25, 2016.
45. See Eric Anderson's paper "Theorizing Masculinities For A New Generation" at this link (http://tinyurl.com/z4bkeu6), last accessed December 25, 2016.
46. James said this at the Cavaliers' 2016 championship parade, no less (http://tinyurl.com/zm5xqxw [last accessed December 25, 2016]).
47. Golden State Warriors head coach Steve Kerr has forged a friendship with Seahawks head coach Pete Carroll. Kerr visited Seahawks' training camp in 2014, and was seen

wearing a Seahawks T-shirt the morning after the Warriors clinched their 2015 NBA Championship (http://tinyurl.com /zg9k233 [last accessed December 25, 2016]).

48. NBC Sports. "Trust issues linger for Kam Chancellor with Seahawks," September 27, 2015 (http://tinyurl.com/zp45zmb [last accessed December 25, 2016]).

49. "Golden State Warriors use tech to their on-court advantage," June 3, 2016 (http://tinyurl.com/h2q6wnt), last accessed December 25, 2016.

50. *The New York Times*. "Inside Amazon: Wrestling Big Ideas in a Bruising Workplace," August 15, 2015 (http://tinyurl.com /o2vdvtf), last accessed December 25, 2016.

51. CNN.com. "3 Times Trump defended his 'locker room' talk," October 9, 2016 (http://tinyurl.com/zmnyhy9), last accessed December 25, 2016.

52. *The Guardian*. "Richard Sherman: castration tweet no surprise in 'country built off slavery'," November 10, 2016 (http://tinyurl.com/ze8r9c3), last accessed December 25, 2016.

53. *GQ*. "Richard Sherman Gets Ready To Do Battle with the NFL," September 8, 2016 (http://tinyurl.com/jypjlnv), last accessed December 25, 2016.

54. *The News Tribune*. "Is state law too protective of police in shootings? Seahawks' Doug Baldwin thinks so," November 21, 2016 (http://tinyurl.com/h5ggsqr), last accessed December 25, 2016.

55. *The Guardian*. "Seahawks' Doug Baldwin: US is being destroyed by classism in age of Trump" (http:// tinyurl.com/zvgeggo), last accessed December 25, 2016.

56. To expand on this: James has not affiliated himself with #BlackLivesMatter officially. That said, he did appear before an NBA game wearing an "I CAN'T BREATHE" T-shirt to mourn Eric Garner in late 2014, and posted a picture of him and his Miami Heat teammates in Black hoodies after the

murder of Trayvon Martin. He also delivered an impassioned speech about police brutality with Chris Paul, Dwyane Wade and Carmelo Anthony at the 2016 ESPY Awards in July 2016.

57. *The Atlantic.* "Opinion Flashback: Klosterman's 2004 Takedown of Soccer," June 19, 2010 (http://tinyurl.com /gsvbk67), last accessed December 25, 2016. Klosterman is clearly seeking attention in his remarks on soccer, but he needs to be held accountable for them: "It's not xenophobic to hate soccer; it's socially reprehensible to support it. To say you love soccer is to say you believe in enforced equality more than you believe in the value of competition and the capacity of the human spirit. It should surprise no one that Benito Mussolini loved being photographed with Italian soccer stars during the 1930s; they were undoubtedly kindred spirits."

58. See endnote #45 of this chapter.

59. *ibid*: "In times of homohysteria, men must adhere to extremely rigid body language and must present themselves as heterosexual even as ages as young as eight. [...] In my research, I show that softer and more inclusive masculinities are proliferating among White teenage and undergraduate boys (both within and outside of formal education). Almost all of the youth that I study are distancing themselves from conservative forms of muscularity, hyperheterosexuality and masculinity. Data from my studies of heterosexual men, in both feminized and masculinized spaces, support this. These findings have led to a new way of theorizing masculinities. My theory argues that with decreasing stigma against homosexuality, there no longer exists a hierarchical stratification of masculinities. Instead, decreasing cultural homophobia permits various forms of masculinities to exist without hegemonic dominance of any one type."

60. *The New York Times.* "Michael B. Jordan Gives Millennials

Their 'Rocky' With 'Creed,'" October 28, 2015 (http://tinyurl.com/p924148), last accessed December 25, 2016.

61. *The Atlantic.* "The Work That Makes Work Possible," March 23, 2016 (http://tinyurl.com/hy7wf4y), last accessed December 25, 2016. See also CNN.com, "America's fastest growing job pays poorly," March 11, 2013 (http://tinyurl.com/zr2fnc6), last accessed December 25, 2016.

Chapter 11

1. *Bitch Magazine.* "Damage Control: Where comic books meet disaster economics," Summer 2016 edition.
2. *ibid.*
3. *Bitch Magazine.* "SUPERPOWER PLAY: A new generation of children's cartoons struggles to smash gender norms," Fall 2016 edition.
4. Pozner, Jennifer L. *Reality Bites Back: The Troubling Truth about Guilty Pleasure TV* (Berkeley: Seal Press, 2010), Kindle Locations 2054–2061: "In ABC's post-9/11 reality docu-series *Profiles from the Front Line*, Jerry Bruckheimer's cameras followed members of the U.S. military in Afghanistan. The male heroes they chose to bring into our living rooms were brave soldiers, surgeons, and weapons inspectors. In contrast, the women they profiled were a blonde, ponytailed medic who bragged that military work keeps women thin, some grieving White war wives, widows, and moms who kept the home fires burning, and Sergeant First Class Danette Jones, an African-American cook whose 'job is to supervise the kitchen, ensure everything is getting done properly, and that the soldiers are happy and fed.'"
5. See Arlie Russell Hochschild's 1989 book *The Second Shift: Working Parents and the Revolution at Home.*
6. Susan B. Anthony passage quoted in Rebecca Traister's *All the Single Ladies: Unmarried Women and the Rise of an Independent Nation* (New York: Simon & Schuster, 2016),

Kindle Locations 221–233.

7. Hochschild, Arlie Russell. *The Managed Heart: Commercialization of Human Feeling* (Berkeley: University of California Press, 1983), pp. 6–7: "The flight attendant does physical labor when she pushes heavy meal carts through the aisles, and she does mental work when she prepares for and actually organizes emergency landings and evacuations. But in the course of doing this physical and mental labor, she is also doing something more, something I define as emotional labor. This labor requires one to induce or suppress feeling in order to sustain the outward countenance that produces the proper state of mind in others—in this case, the sense of being cared for in a convivial and safe place. This kind of labor calls for a coordination of mind and feeling, and it sometimes draws on a source of self that we honor as deep and integral to our individuality. Beneath the difference between physical and emotional labor there lies a similarity in the possible cost of doing the work: the worker can become estranged or alienated from an aspect of self—either the body or the margins of the soul—that is used to do the work."

8. Penny, Laurie. *Unspeakable Things: Sex, Lies, and Revolution* (New York: Bloomsbury, 2014), p. 51.

9. *ibid.*

10. Weigel, Moira. *Labor of Love: The Invention of Dating* (New York: Farrar, Straus and Giroux, 2016), p. 10.

11. Traister, *All The Single Ladies*, Kindle Location 205.

12. Power, Nina. *One Dimensional Woman* (Winchester: Zero Books, 2009), p. 39: "The so-called 'Bechdel Test', first described in Alison Bechdel's comic strip *Dykes to Watch Out For*, consists of the following rules, to be applied to films, but could easily be extended to literature: Does it have at least two women in it, Who [at some point] talk to each other, About something besides a man."

13. Episode 1 of Season 1 of *Broad City* ("What a Wonderful World") aired January 22, 2014.

14. Dunham's character Hanna said this in episode 1 of Season 1 of *Girls* ("Pilot"), which aired on April 15, 2012.

15. Zeisler, Andi. *We Were Feminists Once: From Riot Grrrl to Covergirl, the Buying and Selling of a Political Movement* (New York: PublicAffairs, 2016), Kindle Locations 44–50.

16. *ibid*, Kindle Locations 105–107.

17. *ibid*, Kindle Locations 130–140.

18. Jezebel.com. "Don't Go Calling Taylor Swift a Feminist, Says Taylor Swift," October 22, 2012 (http://tinyurl.com/j5zrodt), last accessed December 25, 2016.

19. Quartz.com. "Taylor Swift and Kanye West are having a public argument about men taking credit for women's success," July 18, 2016 (http://tinyurl.com/zas4ucy), last accessed December 25, 2016.

20. Observer.com. "'I Thought I Was Being Called Out': TSwift Just Apologized to Nicki Minaj," July 23, 2015 (http://tinyurl.com/jukpklw), last accessed December 25, 2016.

21. Ali Wong's comedy special *Ali Wong: Baby Cobra* was released on May 5, 2016.

22. Levy, Ariel. *Female Chauvinist Pigs: Women and the Rise of Raunch Culture* (New York: Free Press, 2005), pp. 87–88.

23. Episode 1, season 1 of *Ugly Betty* ("Pilot") aired on September 28, 2006.

24. Power, *One Dimensional Woman*, p. 6.

25. The video clip in which Hillary Clinton brags about voting for a border to keep out illegal immigrants can be seen at this link (http://tinyurl.com/q2lbgev) last accessed December 25, 2016.

26. *The Los Angeles Times*. "Lena Dunham, America Ferrera: We're female millennials, and we choose Hillary Clinton," March 21, 2016 (http://tinyurl.com/zewsjl3), last accessed

December 25, 2016.

27. Pozner, *Reality Bites Back*, Kindle Location 3929.

28. *The New York Times*. "The Bitch America Needs," September 10, 2016 (http://tinyurl.com/hrqog4p), last accessed December 25, 2016.

29. *ibid.*

30. Shaviro, Steve. *Post Cinematic Affect* (Winchester: Zero Books, 2010), p. 8.

31. See endnote #7 of this chapter.

32. The (famously difficult to understand) lyrics of Rihanna's "Work" can be read at this link (http://tinyurl.com/zkkk3yr), last accessed December 25, 2016.

33. Beyoncé sampled this audio from a TEDx Talk given by Adichie in 2013, which can be viewed here (http://tinyurl.com/qbkvhwb), last accessed December 25, 2016.

34. Harris, Tamara Winfrey and Samudzi, Zoé. "BEING AND RECLAIMING OURSELVES: A conversation on sexuality, respectability, and the pressures of Black girlhood," *Bitch Magazine*, Summer 2016 edition.

35. I'm not 100% sure who first devised this formulation of the phrase "I don't give a fuck," but they deserve credit.

36. James, Robin. *Resilience & Melancholy: Pop Music, Feminism, Neoliberalism* (Winchester: Zero Books, 2015), Kindle Locations 2371–2375: "The album's lead single, 'Diamonds,' in both its music and its video, evokes directionless drift and melancholic 'meh.' In a way, the song is structured like Ravel's *Bolero*: it's one long crescendo over a rhythmic ostinato. Bolero, however, goes somewhere—it has a goal, a direction (namely, the climax). 'Diamonds,' however, doesn't go anywhere; it's more an unending loop of soft peaks and valleys."

37. "How It Feels" was originally published by Poetry Magazine in their July/August 2015 issue. It is also available in the 2015

collection *The Selected Jenny Zhang.*

38. Zeisler, *We Were Feminists Once*, Kindle Location 140.

39. *n+1.* "The Woman's Party," Fall 2016 (http://tinyurl.com /h7w6ebg), last accessed December 25, 2016: "Fraser's answer is to propose what she calls a 'universal caregiver' model based on the assumption that all workers are also caregivers and all caregivers are also workers. Conceiving a new welfare state based on this model would mean rethinking the length of the workday, socializing child care, decoupling Social Security and health insurance from employment, and returning to the welfare rights movement's call for a guaranteed minimum income. Above all, it would mean placing feminist insights and concerns at the center, rather than the periphery, of any left politics."

Chapter 12

1. *Orlando Sentinel.* "Athletes of color paved way for Barack Obama's run," November 5, 2008 (http://tinyurl.com /zyjq5t5), last accessed December 26th, 2016.

2. Politico.com. "How Trump Did It," February 1, 2016 (http://tinyurl.com/zwq9w7p), last accessed December 26th, 2016.

3. I interviewed Amelia Bonow on October 3, 2016 for a *City Arts Magazine* feature I wrote about Millennials titled "The Uphill Climb" (http://tinyurl.com/z8rvsrs), last accessed December 26th, 2016.

4. This pencil drawing can be viewed at this link (http:// tinyurl.com/j82dudz), last accessed December 26, 2016.

5. Episode 17, season 11 of *The Simpsons* ("Bart to the Future") first aired on March 19th, 2000.

6. Lyrics to Rihanna's "Needed Me" are sourced from Genius.com.

7. Draut, Tamara. *Strapped: Why America's 20- and 30-Somethings Can't Get Ahead* (New York: Knopf Doubleday, 2006), Kindle

Locations 2490–2495: "More than previous postwar generations, today's young adults were taught from an early age to
look to themselves for their own security and success. We
grew up in the political era of 'personal responsibility,' and at
home we learned to be self-sufficient as latchkey kids as our
Baby Boomer mothers entered the workforce. And now, as
we struggle to buy homes and start families, we tend to
question our ability to be completely self-reliant rather than
ask if our nation's priorities are in the right place. The last
place we'd look for help is the government. And that's
exactly what Reagan conservatives and their successors
hoped to achieve."

8. Bloomberg.com. "What This Election Taught Us About
Millennial Voters," November 9th, 2016 (http://tinyurl.com
/hhu6rmg), last accessed December 26, 2016.

9. *The New York Times.* "White Women Voted Trump. Now
What?" November 10, 2016 (http://tinyurl.com/glynlct), last
accessed December 26, 2016.

10. *The Washington Post.* "Trump recorded having extremely
lewd conversation about women in 2005," October 7, 2016
(http://tinyurl.com/hhhs4mz), last accessed December 26,
2016.

11. Pozner, Jennifer L. *Reality Bites Back: The Troubling Truth about
Guilty Pleasure TV* (Berkeley: Seal Press, 2010), Kindle
Location 1642.

12. *The Nation.* "Donald Trump Won on White-Male
Resentment—but Don't Confuse That With the Working
Class," November 10, 2016 (http://tinyurl.com/go4ztpj), last
accessed December 26, 2016.

13. Mike Davis' "Not a Revolution—Yet" is probably the single
best broad-brush diagnosis of the 2016 American presidential election I've seen in my reading on the subject,
because it also points the way forward for the Democratic
Party. You can read it at this link (http://tinyurl.com/j3jf9dd),

last accessed December 26, 2016.

14. *ibid.*
15. BloombergPolitics.com. "David Plouffe: Hillary Clinton's Millennial Problem Is Huge," September 27, 2016 (http://tinyurl.com/j798t7o), last accessed December 26, 2016.
16. CNN.com. "Colin Kaepernick: 'It would be hypocritical of me to vote,'" November 15, 2016 (http://tinyurl.com/jdmj ffw), last accessed December 26, 2016.
17. *The New York Times.* "As ID Laws Fall, Voters See New Barriers Rise," October 25, 2016 (http://tinyurl.com /gt3woe5), last accessed December 26, 2016.
18. Urban Outfitters ran these shirts in 2004 and recalled them shortly thereafter, only to sell them again in 2008. As it turns out, a chairman of Urban Outfitters is a staunch conservative, who was accused by Punkvoter.com of "[intentionally] selling voter suppression" (http://tinyurl.com/hpzqmcf), last accessed December 26, 2016.
19. TheEstablishment.com. "We Have To Create A Culture That Won't Vote For Trump," November 11, 2016 (http://tinyurl .com/j9otd27), last accessed December 26, 2016.
20. Fortune.com. "Las Vegas Gamblers Bet Hillary Clinton Will Win the Presidency," September 23, 2016 (http://tinyurl .com/jyyw2jt), last accessed December 26, 2016.
21. *Current Affairs.* "Unless The Democrats Run Sanders, A Trump Nomination Means A Trump Presidency," February 23, 2016 (http://tinyurl.com/hbo6tuw), last accessed December 26, 2016.
22. James' post is viewable at this link (http://tinyurl.com /hgz97bp), last accessed December 26, 2016.
23. LennyLetter.com. "Don't Agonize, Organize," November 11, 2016 (http://tinyurl.com/jkdqsxh), last accessed December 26, 2016.
24. It's 100% wrong to blame political divides on "polarization." This is a total tautology. It's like blaming rain on "weather."

Politics is a contest. Trump became President because he won that contest. The way to prevent future GOP presidents is to win future contests—not to pretend that the contest does not exist.

25. NPR.org. "One Way To Bridge The Political Divide: Read The Book That's Not For You," November 14, 2016 (http://tinyurl.com/hjxjypa), last accessed December 26, 2016.

26. IJR.com. "SNL Flips the Script with Very Un-PC Joke on 'Why Democrats Lost the Election.' It Didn't Go Over Well," November 21, 2016 (http://tinyurl.com/gqqfdy6), last accessed December 26, 2016.

27. *The New York Times*. "The End of Identity Liberalism," November 18, 2016 (http://tinyurl.com/z9x2qzz), last accessed December 26, 2016.

28. *The Washington Post*. "Yes, you can blame millennials for Hillary Clinton's loss" (http://tinyurl.com/zrul3oc), last accessed December 26, 2016.

29. *PolicyMic*. "Here's What Millennials Have Taught Me" (http://tinyurl.com/j684q35), last accessed December 26, 2016.

30. Fusion.net. "DNC email uses cringeworthy language about Latino voters," July 24, 2016 (http://tinyurl.com/z87p8vz), last accessed December 26, 2016.

31. "The Brexit Crisis: A Verso Report" (New York: Verso Books, 2016), Kindle Locations 1107–1111: "In any case, the figures contrasting young people's Europhilia with their elders' Europhobia have to be mitigated by taking into account two variables: the first is that the turnout among the 18 to 24 set was significantly lower than the average. As a result, while the young Remainers were the most motivated to express their views, their weight was relatively limited within their entire cohort."

32. Sanders, Bernie. *Our Revolution: A Future to Believe In* (New York: St. Martin's Press, 2016), Kindle Location 46.

33. *The Washington Post.* "Bernie Sanders is profoundly changing how millennials think about politics, poll shows," April 25, 2016 (http://tinyurl.com/zbbsh62), last accessed December 26, 2016.

34. "Here are all the things young people have been accused of killing," August 24, 2016 (http://tinyurl.com/hs3a449), last accessed December 26, 2016.

35. *New Republic.* "The Myth of the Millennial as Cultural Rebel" (http://tinyurl.com/zcd25vq).

36. *ibid.*

37. See LifeCourse Associates' website (http://tinyurl.com/z mxeots).

38. WhiteHouse.gov. "Remarks by President Obama at Stavros Niarchos Foundation Cultural Center in Athens, Greece," November 16, 2016 (http://tinyurl.com/z8ut3fk), last accessed December 26, 2016.

39. PRI.org. "America will become majority-minority in 2043," October 3, 2014 (http://tinyurl.com/gpxv5ec), last accessed December 26, 2016.

40. NPR.org. "Harvard Poll: Millennials Yearn For Bernie, but Prefer Clinton To Trump," April 25, 2016 (http://tinyurl.com /ztccf3e), last accessed December 26, 2016: "Perhaps not a surprise given his ability to draw large, predominantly young crowds to rallies, Sanders is by far the most popular of the five presidential candidates included in the Harvard poll. In fact, with 54 percent viewing him favorably and just 31 percent unfavorably, he's the only candidate in the survey who has a positive net favorable number."

41. *The Washington Post.* "Millennials are significantly more progressive than their parents," March 24, 2016 (http://tinyurl.com/jkz83md), last accessed December 26, 2016.

42. *ibid.*

43. See Metzger's essay at this link (http://tinyurl.com/hot wmvg), last accessed February 20th, 2017.

44. KQED.org. "How Millennials Voted in the 2016 Presidential Election," November 15, 2016 (http://tinyurl.com/h8opwo5), last accessed December 26, 2016.

45. Swift's Instagram post is available at this link (http://tinyurl.com/zd2f65c), last accessed December 26, 2016.

46. US News.com. "Employee or Contractor? Uber Ruling Could Affect Other Companies," June 18, 2015 (http://tinyurl.com /ojkwjsg), last accessed December 26, 2016.

47. See the Freelancer's Union's blog for more information (http://tinyurl.com/zxtafjx), last accessed December 26, 2016.

48. Friedman quoted from DailyKos.com, "Translating Code: Starve the Beast," July 26, 2010 (http://tinyurl.com/gp admpo), last accessed December 26, 2016.

49. Hackworth, Jason. *The Neoliberal City: Governance, Ideology, and Development in American Urbanism* (Ithaca: Cornell University Press, 2007), Kindle Locations 548–556: "Compounding the desire to circumvent state law and the decrease in federal outlays to cities, there has been a very specific increase in federal mandates to deal with social problems. Policies to encourage the construction of prisons and the employment of more police officers have been among the most significant (Gilmore 1998; Schlosser 1998). Schlosser (1998) points out that of the 1.8 million people currently in prison in the United States, 600,000 are housed in local jails; with increased pressure to impose mandatory-minimum sentences and to relieve overcrowding, the imperative to build more prisons only figures to increase. Moreover, the highly publicized increase in federal funding for new police officers in the mid-1990s came with a less publicized caveat that after a specific span of time (usually two years), localities were required to finance police officer salaries, thus increasing pressure on their budget. The net effect of these changes is that local governments are increasingly forced to respond to unfunded federal decrees—partic-

ularly social control mandates—by incurring debt. Bond market gatekeepers, as a consequence, become more influential."

50. *The Seattle Times.* "Washington suffers most regressive tax system in U.S." March 3, 2015 (http://tinyurl.com/nw6zpyd), last accessed December 26, 2016.

51. I interviewed Hanna Brooks Olsen on September 30, 2016 for a *City Arts Magazine* feature I wrote about Millennials titled "The Uphill Climb," (http://tinyurl.com/z8rvsrs), last accessed December 26, 2016.

52. *Dissent Magazine.* "Capitalism's Crisis of Care," Fall 2016 (http://tinyurl.com/hjkty7u), last accessed December 26, 2016.

53. *ibid.*

Acknowledgements

Love and respect to my parents, Barry and Megan, for putting me in a position to succeed, think, and reflect as a youth. This book is the outgrowth of their efforts, and could not have happened without them. Whether in my father's household in Seattle or my mother's home in New York, I was always surrounded with books, documentaries, and other fodder that helped me look at society critically from an early age. Ever since my dad surprised me after school with a copy of Michael Jackson's album *Dangerous* in November of 1991, I've been on this ride as a student of popular culture.

When I was just starting to embark on a career as a professional writer at age 30 in winter of 2014, my community support system in Seattle helped me cultivate my skills. My friends and comrades Jake Uitti and Caleb Thompson of *The Monarch Review* were the first editors to publish my essays, and editor Leah Baltus of *City Arts Magazine* gave me a job as a columnist that helped me build my voice as a writer. Working with these editors gave me literary insights that I employed at every opportunity in this manuscript.

Artist Trust is a Seattle-area nonprofit that provided me with a research grant, which helped me pay for the glut of source material—magazine subscriptions, books, iTunes rentals, and more—that I needed to complete this manuscript. In an era of neoliberal disinvestment from the arts and education, Artist Trust is a vital organization. I hope this book reflects well on their mission. It could not have been made without them.

I would also like to thank my book's two workshop readers and research assistants: Graciela Nuñez Pargas and Lily Shay are two energetic and civically engaged Millennials who provided stellar feedback about this book's early chapter drafts. By seeing my book in light of their criticism, I was able to make crucial changes to my approach—as a writer, and not just a dispenser of facts—that greatly enhanced the quality of the overall manuscript. Because I saw firsthand the chances that Graciela and Lily take in their private lives and their commitment to their political ideals, I approached this book with more verve and personality than I would have on my own. I hope this book provides them a fraction of the inspiration that they have provided me. I'm glad that they are my friends, and I'm damn proud to be part of any generation that would have them as members.

In these reader sessions—and especially outside of them—my partner Natasha Varner (a PhD in History from the University of Arizona) also provided indispensable professional consultation and asked challenging questions about my methodology that helped me improve my book's clarity and competitive standing. Additionally, the emotional support she provided when this book was very far from being a reality led directly to this book's completion. I will never forget angrily leaving the film The Lobster with her in the summer of 2016, fuming that my book did not yet have a publisher, and feeling emboldened by her support of my decision to court Zero Books immediately. Within a month this book was placed at Zero Books, so that the conception of this manuscript and the realization of my connection with Natasha will always be linked in love. I am thankful.

Lastly, thank you to Marissa Jenae Johnson for agreeing to write the foreword to my book, and to photographer Leon Fishman for allowing me to use—as this book's cover—a photo of his that captures what I wanted this text to convey. The raised fists, tools of digital empowerment, and pensive expressions of the photo subjects in Leon's cover image should give us all inspiration for the future. Meanwhile, I have followed Marissa's career ever since she staged a fierce interruption of Bernie Sanders when the Vermont senator swung through Seattle in 2015 on a campaign stop during his presidential bid. I have come to realize that her unflinching articulation of her social standing as a Black woman and Millennial is literally the future of American politics.

To the extent that we are able to answer the concerns that the most vulnerable bring to the table, this experiment called democracy will succeed. To the extent that we do not, we will fail in it together.

Zero Books
CULTURE, SOCIETY & POLITICS

Contemporary culture has eliminated the concept and public figure of the intellectual. A cretinous anti-intellectualism presides, cheer-led by hacks in the pay of multinational corporations who reassure their bored readers that there is no need to rouse themselves from their stupor. Zer0 Books knows that another kind of discourse - intellectual without being academic, popular without being populist - is not only possible: it is already flourishing. Zer0 is convinced that in the unthinking, blandly consensual culture in which we live, critical and engaged theoretical reflection is more important than ever before.

If you have enjoyed this book, why not tell other readers by posting a review on your preferred book site. Recent bestsellers from Zero Books are:

In the Dust of This Planet
Horror of Philosophy vol. 1
Eugene Thacker
In the first of a series of three books on the Horror of Philosophy, *In the Dust of This Planet* offers the genre of horror as a way of thinking about the unthinkable.
Paperback: 978-1-84694-676-9 ebook: 978-1-78099-010-1

Capitalist Realism
Is there no alternative?
Mark Fisher
An analysis of the ways in which capitalism has presented itself as the only realistic political-economic system.
Paperback: 978-1-84694-317-1 ebook: 978-1-78099-734-6

Rebel Rebel
Chris O'Leary
David Bowie: every single song. Everything you want to know, everything you didn't know.
Paperback: 978-1-78099-244-0 ebook: 978-1-78099-713-1

Cartographies of the Absolute
Alberto Toscano, Jeff Kinkle
An aesthetics of the economy for the twenty-first century.
Paperback: 978-1-78099-275-4 ebook: 978-1-78279-973-3

Malign Velocities
Accelerationism and Capitalism
Benjamin Noys
Longlisted for the Bread and Roses Prize 2015, *Malign Velocities* argues against the need for speed, tracking acceleration as the symptom of the ongoing crises of capitalism.
Paperback: 978-1-78279-300-7 ebook: 978-1-78279-299-4

Poor but Sexy
Culture Clashes in Europe East and West
Agata Pyzik
How the East stayed East and the West stayed West.
Paperback: 978-1-78099-394-2 ebook: 978-1-78099-395-9

Readers of ebooks can buy or view any of these bestsellers by clicking on the live link in the title. Most titles are published in paperback and as an ebook. Paperbacks are available in traditional bookshops. Both print and ebook formats are available online.

Find more titles and sign up to our readers' newsletter at
http://www.johnhuntpublishing.com/culture-and-politics
Follow us on Facebook at https://www.facebook.com/ZeroBooks
and Twitter at https://twitter.com/Zer0Books